Machine Learning and AI For Absolute Beginners

2 books in 1

AI for Absolute Beginners

Machine Learning for Absolute Beginners 3rd Edn.

Oliver Theobald

Find me at

www.scatterplotpress.com

For introductory video courses on machine learning

Email: oliver.theobald@scatterplotpress.com

TABLE OF CONTENTS

BOOK 1: AI FOR ABSOLUTE BEGINNERS

PROLOGUE

Japan clings to a reputation for high-speed trains, robots, and futuristic cities, but that's not quite the impression you get walking past one of Japan's many DVD stores or watching someone at the office fiddling with the fax machine.

The pace of technological change in Japan may appear slow, but when change does occur, it is meticulously choreographed and premeditated. There are several examples in Japan's rich history, but nothing compares with the country's swift transition to an industrialized powerhouse.

You might have thought the fax machine was overstaying its utility by several decades, but only 160 years ago, Japan was governed by a feudal system left over from medieval times. The drawing of the curtain on Japan's feudal era and the dismantling of the ruling samurai class in the 1860s was highly organized and efficient. Over the space of a decade, top-knot hairstyles, killing swords, and wages paid in units of rice were phased out and replaced with the steel and metal of a modern industrialized nation.

The transformation has intrigued me ever since I moved to Japan, especially as we look ahead to the future of artificial intelligence and knowledge work. The samurai class, similar to accountants, lawyers, and other knowledge workers today, were well-educated and respected members of society. Trained in combat and schooled in calligraphy, history, mathematics, and science, they enjoyed a secure and elevated social standing in Japan's social hierarchy.

Before steam-powered ships arrived on Japan's coastlines, technological advancement was minimal, and the samurai's main threat was rivalry with neighboring clans. The arrival of the ships soon marked the advent of the Meiji Restoration, a period of rapid industrialization and westernization in Japan. Foreign powers, particularly the United States and several European countries, forced Japan to open its borders to international trade. This exposure to Western technology and ideas spurred a revolution in Japan's economic, political, and social systems.

The samurai, previously the military and administrative elite, found their social and economic status removed from underneath them. The feudal system, which had provided them a guaranteed income and status in society, was dismantled. A modern conscript army based on the Western model also replaced the samurai as the nation's defenders. Moreover, the rise of industry and commerce created new wealth and opportunities, leading to the emergence of a new class of rich merchants and industrialists.

These changes didn't happen overnight, but the transition was significant and swift in the grand scope of Japan's history. The samurai, who had enjoyed a secure position at the top of the social order for centuries, had to adapt to a new environment that no longer valued their traditional skills or recognized their social privileges.

Similar to the changes brought by modern machinery and weaponry in the 19th Century, AI poses a threat to a large and highly skilled segment of today's workforce. Despite increased globalization, knowledge workers have always found reassurance in their local knowledge, language abilities, and unique domestic expertise. However, the unfolding revolution of AI is poised to dramatically reshape the boundaries of work.

The experience of Japan offers some rare insights as well as valuable lessons about resilience and transformation in the face of technological change. Faced with upheaval, the samurai reacted in two ways. The first was rebellion and resistance. This natural course of action materialized in violent but futile clashes with the Emperor's modern-equipped army.

The second and more productive course of action was to embrace change and adapt to new technology. For the samurai who took this path, education played a key part. Exposure to foreign languages gave former samurai living in the port city of Nagasaki a head-start in an economy open to foreign trade and keen to learn from Western powers. The Charter Oath issued by the Emperor in 1868 stated that "knowledge shall be sought throughout the world" and those with a tongue for foreign languages were among the first to be dispatched overseas. Others stayed in Japan and became teachers, bureaucrats, and artists in the new nation.

For members of the new Japan, education and retraining were vital to their future fortunes. While the samurai had enjoyed privileged access to education (compared to merchants, farmers, and the lowest class of Japanese society), their pre-Meiji education was relegated to foundational knowledge in an evolving economy. Their classical education, though comprehensive for the time, didn't fully prepare them for the significant shift brought about by rapid modernization and westernization. Beyond literacy and basic arithmetic, many elements of samurai training were undesirable or obsolete, especially in warfare and philosophy. Battles would now be fought with modern weaponry, and, like ancient Greek and Latin, knowledge of the Chinese analects offered marginal utility in a modern era where Western ideas on free markets, industrialization, and capitalism ran supreme. The Meiji Government chose to overhaul Japan's education system and replaced it with standard practices from the West. In this way, the samurai weren't prepared to prosper in the new Japan based on their education alone. Instead, they had to recalibrate and adapt to new practices and employment pathways.

The parallels to today are striking, as professional writers, lawyers, artists, and web developers find themselves needing to acquire new skills such as text prompt writing and data literacy in response to the rise of generative AI technology. The speed at which AI is seeping into all aspects of modern work—from marketing to contract writing—underscores AI and data literacy as key skill sets for the modern workforce. Just as the Meiji Restoration in Japan introduced new job titles, there will be new opportunities in what the authors of *Human + Machine: Reimagining Work in the Age of AI* call the "missing middle", the nexus or fertile space where humans and machines collaborate to exploit what each side does best.

According to the missing middle theory, the most effective and cost-efficient path is to merge automated tools with the flexibility of human workers to achieve optimum results. This is similar to how chefs and waitstaff work alongside automatic cashier machines inside Japanese restaurants today.

Virtually every sector has the potential to maximize productivity and innovation by finding the right balance between human creativity, judgment, and empathy, and AI's speed, scalability, and quantitative capabilities. In the ongoing era of AI and with new tools such as ChatGPT, we aren't just bystanders but active participants. As knowledge workers, we can embrace AI as a partner in our daily tasks, optimizing our abilities and complementing our skills. As leaders, we can champion AI to foster a culture of innovation, driving transformation and competitive advantage inside our organizations.

These transformations won't just impact individual tasks, but entire workflows, industries, and even societies. As a result, we need to recognize and address the challenges that AI presents, including ethical considerations, job displacement concerns, and the need for re-skilling. By proactively confronting these issues, we can ensure that the rise of AI benefits more people and not only a select few.

Admittedly, this is a narrow path to walk, and this book does not hold the wisdom and solutions to a fair and symbiotic future for humans and machines. Instead, I hope to hold your hand through understanding the fundamentals of artificial intelligence and prepare you for important discussions and decisions regarding the use of AI in your organization or daily life. This includes a series of practical thought experiments included in multiple chapters.

Lastly, please keep in mind that this book is aimed at non-technical readers, including marketers, product managers, entrepreneurs, and students, seeking to build or expand their understanding of artificial intelligence. While the following chapters provide a solid foundation of core AI techniques, the book does not delve into highly technical aspects or run through coding examples for building AI programs. For a more in-depth exploration of algorithms and coding prediction models using Python, you may like to read my other titles *Machine Learning for Absolute Beginners* or *Machine Learning With Python*. These books offer a more technical and detailed treatment of machine learning algorithms and will help to complement your understanding of AI gained from reading this book.

## 1

INTRODUCTION

Machine intelligence represents a significant milestone in human innovation and after decades of research and two AI winters, artificial intelligence now dominates mainstream attention and is promising revolutionary changes in the way we work, create, and live our lives.

While the inception of AI as a field of study can be traced back to the 1950s, it's only in recent years that this technology has formed a significant component in our daily lives. Today, it manifests in various forms, from digital assistants like Siri and Alexa to recommendation engines on TikTok, Netflix, and Amazon, as well as new content generation tools like ChatGPT and DALL-E.

Despite its growing ubiquity, AI is still often misunderstood and confused with data science, which is an intersecting field based on extracting insight from data and with its own set of use cases. To elaborate, a company might use the principles of data science to uncover new insights by analyzing customer interactions and website support tickets. This process involves aggregating and examining the data to identify common customer issues, peak times for customer support queries, or correlations between support ticket volume and specific product features. Following data science methodology, the overall goal is to be as precise as possible at identifying patterns and trends that might help to inform the company's decision-making.

Artificial intelligence, on the other hand, performs a different role that relies less on detective work and more on general intelligence. AI, for example, can be used by a company to power customer service chatbots on their website that mimic human interactions, answer simple customer questions, and refer more complex queries to human representatives. By applying artificial intelligence, the company's overall goal is to automate key parts of the customer service process, enhance efficiency, and enable 24/7 customer support without relying solely on human capital.

As highlighted in these two examples, data science focuses on extracting insights and knowledge from raw data, whereas artificial intelligence aims to simulate and embed human intelligence into machines. However, in many cases, AI will leverage insight derived from data science to enable machines to learn and make intelligent decisions. It's important, therefore, to acknowledge the overlap between data science and AI, while also understanding that AI and data science remain two different approaches to solving complex problems.

In addition to data science, AI encompasses a variety of subfields and techniques including machine learning, deep learning, generative AI, natural language processing, cybernetics, and computer vision, among a number of others. Regardless of the methods used, artificial intelligence, at its core, comes back to the overarching mission of creating systems capable of performing tasks that would otherwise require human intelligence. Such tasks include understanding human language, recognizing patterns, learning from experience, making informed decisions, and even displaying emotional intelligence.

Learning from experience and making informed decisions falls into the subfield of machine learning, which is covered in more depth in Chapter 5. In short, machine learning entails the use of statistical methods to create prediction models that improve their performance on a specific task through experience and exposure to data. An example of this can be seen in email spam filters, which learn to distinguish spam from regular emails more accurately over time.

Pattern recognition, meanwhile, forms the basis of many AI applications, from biometric identification systems that recognize fingerprints or retina patterns to recommendation systems that analyze our online shopping patterns to suggest products we are likely to buy.

Emotional intelligence in AI, while still in its nascent stage, aims to enable machines to recognize and respond to human emotions. It has potential applications in areas such as mental health and customer service, where it's possible for AI to assist in providing assistance, empathy, and emotional support to humans.

Understanding these different use cases and the breadth of AI helps underline the fact that AI is not one monolithic technology or technique but rather a collection of technologies and approaches that strive to emulate human intelligence. Acknowledging this diversity is crucial for appreciating the full spectrum of AI technology and recognizing the multitude of use cases.

Another essential insight for those keen on understanding AI further is the realization that AI is still only in its first stage of evolution. This first stage is known as *narrow AI* or *weak AI*, which describes systems designed to perform a narrow task, such as voice recognition or recommending relevant products. These systems excel at the specific tasks they were designed to undertake but lack the understanding or consciousness to freely apply their capabilities to other use cases.

At the same time, we are edging closer to the next stage of AI development, known as *artificial general intelligence (AGI)* or *strong AI*. AGI refers to a version of AI that possesses the ability to understand, learn, adapt, and implement its knowledge across a broad range of tasks at a comparable or superior level to that of a human being. To help grasp the concept of general AI, it's useful to think of science fiction portrayals where AI entities, like Data from Star Trek or Ava from the movie Ex Machina, mingle with humans and exhibit cognitive abilities that are indistinguishable from ours. These AI entities are often shown to possess self-awareness, emotions, creativity, and the ability to understand and exhibit human-like behaviors, which are all hallmarks of general AI.

However, as with any powerful new technology, AGI provokes a selection of ethical and societal concerns that we must navigate with care, and we will examine these concerns in later chapters. We will also look further at the three stages of AI development and discuss the potential ramifications of the final stage known as superintelligent AI. Beyond that, we will explore the major subfields of AI including machine learning, natural language processing, computer vision, generative AI, and deep learning. The final chapter will lay down a series of tips and insights for adopting AI in your job or organization.

For now, understand that your journey into AI has many potential paths and the field will continue to evolve as we edge closer to the next stage of machine intelligence.

## 2

A BRIEF HISTORY

From its humble beginnings as a scientific curiosity to the powerful technology we know today, the journey and rise of AI has seen alternating periods of scarcity and abundance, doubt and optimism, and up-and-down levels of support, culminating in a sprint toward exponential growth. To understand where we are now as well as the future prospects of AI, we first need to look back at its past.

While the roots of artificial intelligence can be traced back to the period of classical philosophers who attempted to describe human thinking as a symbolic system (which was the original focus of AI research), the modern field of study and AI terminology have emerged relatively recently. The term *artificial intelligence* was introduced and formally established as a distinct field of research at the Dartmouth Conference held in 1956.

The idea of designing intelligent machines fascinated scientists, mathematicians, and technology researchers in the years before the conference, including prominent British mathematician and logician Alan Turing. Considered as the father of modern computing, Turing made significant contributions to computation and machine intelligence in the 1940s and 1950s. This included the Turing Test, which was designed to assess a machine's ability to exhibit intelligent behavior indistinguishable from that of a human. According to the Turing Test, a machine can be considered intelligent when it can engage in a task without being detected as a machine, such as chatting with a human.

Inspired by Turing and other research developments, the Dartmouth Conference was held at Dartmouth College in Hanover, New Hampshire, in the summer of 1956. The conference was organized by John McCarthy, Marvin Minsky, Nathaniel Rochester, and Claude Shannon, four leading figures in the fields of mathematics, cognitive science, and computer engineering. Their official proposal for the conference expressed an optimistic view regarding the trajectory of AI-related technology and outlined a research project that would explore the possibilities of machines imitating human intelligence. Invitations were sent to researchers known to be active and interested in the field of machine-based intelligence. The final list of participants included the four organizing members as well as notable figures such as Allen Newell and Herbert A. Simon, who contributed significantly to AI's development over their lifetimes.

Lacking the on-stage theatrics, sponsored booths, and free swag common at events today, the attendees were shown their rooms and quickly put to work. Mirroring an eight-week-long hackathon, the conference's attendees spent their days attempting to build computer programs capable of imitating human intelligence. This included working on problems still considered core to the field of AI today, such as natural language processing, problem-solving, learning and adaptation, and perception.

However, perhaps the most lasting outcome of the conference was the agreement on terminology and the establishment of AI as its own distinct field of study. Steered by John McCarthy, the term *artificial intelligence* replaced previous and now forgotten descriptors including *automata studies* and *complex information processing*. This change in terminology had the effect of focusing attention on the simulation and impersonation of human intelligence.

Equally important, the conference nurtured a community of researchers who helped to establish AI as a legitimate field of study and who would go on to become leaders in AI research for several decades. In addition, the conference played a crucial role in securing financial backing for AI research, which was aided by the conference's optimistic outlook and the Cold War's emphasis on automation and computational technologies. This resulted in significant funding from government organizations and helped lay the groundwork for the rapid expansion of AI research.

The years following the Dartmouth Conference formed the first golden era of AI research and projected unbound optimism regarding AI's future. Swept up in the excitement, researchers started making ambitious forecasts, predicting machines would be capable of achieving complex human tasks in a matter of years.

Funding was abundant during this time and AI research centers sprung up at prestigious universities across the United States including Stanford University, MIT, and Carnegie Mellon. The crux of AI research centered on rule-based systems as researchers attempted to encode human knowledge and intelligence into machines as a set of logical rules, which later gave birth to the development of expert systems in the 1970s and early 1980s.

In practice, expert systems operate under a collection of predefined rules that generate a recommendation such as a medical diagnosis through a sequence of decisions. Commonly structured as "if-then" statements, fixed rules are set such as "if the patient has a fever above 38°C, then they may have an infection" and "if the patient has a rash and has been exposed to poison ivy, then they may have contact dermatitis". By stacking a series of if-then statements, expert systems are designed to analyze a patient's medical history and symptoms in order to provide a potential diagnosis or propose additional tests and treatments.

While these systems are capable of performing well at narrow and well-defined tasks, they are largely flawed as an effective long-term solution. Firstly, they rely on the expertise and manual input of human professionals to contribute knowledge to the system. Translating this knowledge into a structured format of rules demands significant time and effort, which means that expert systems lack the ability to autonomously learn and update their knowledge base. Moreover, as knowledge and expertise evolve over time, these systems depend on regular updates in order to stay current and accurate. The net result is a system that is expensive and resource-intensive to build and maintain. What's more, failure to keep the system up-to-date carries the risk of an outdated or incorrect recommendation.

The next problem is the domain specificity of these systems. Their design and rule base are tailored to solving specific problems, making it difficult to transfer them across tasks. Deploying expert systems across different contexts requires substantial modifications or, in many cases, the development of entirely new systems. Even when deployed within a specific context, the contextual understanding of expert systems is severely limited. Operating within the constraints of predefined rules, expert systems struggle to grasp the broader context or interpret information outside their explicit rule library. This lack of adaptability and flexibility poses challenges when facing complex, ambiguous, or special scenarios that require nuanced judgment.

Over time, these challenges became increasingly apparent, along with the obvious failure of artificial intelligence to deliver on the ambitious promises made by AI researchers. By the mid-1970s, many of the expected breakthroughs turned out to be more difficult than originally anticipated. Rule-based systems, which had been the primary approach to AI research up to this point, were proving expensive and time-consuming to run, and failing to replicate the nuanced and complex nature of human intelligence.

The overall lack of progress resulted in growing skepticism, which spread to policymakers—leading to significant funding cuts. In the United States, the government, especially the Defense Advanced Research Projects Agency (DARPA), reduced and eventually cut most of its AI research funding. In the United Kingdom, the infamous *Lighthill Report*, published in 1973, critically assessed the lack of progress made by AI research, which also resulted in cuts in government support for AI research at many British institutions.

Broad funding cuts prompted the beginning of the end for many AI projects and interest in the field dwindled throughout the AI research community. This period of deflated funding and interest, starting in the mid-1970s and extending into the early 1980s, became known as "AI winter". Used to describe a period of disillusionment and fall-off in AI funding, the term is a takeoff on the idea of a "nuclear winter", a dark period marred by coldness and barrenness.

Despite challenging circumstances, a group of AI researchers persisted and continued their work throughout this period, with their efforts eventually leading to a resurgence in interest over the subsequent decade. The evolution of machine learning in the 1980s marked a pivotal transformation in the landscape of AI research. Instead of attempting to encode knowledge as a set of predefined rules, machine learning proposed the notion that computers could learn from data, identify patterns, and make decisions with minimal human involvement. While the theoretical foundations of machine learning had been established in earlier decades, research funding and general interest had, until this point, been channeled into expert systems.

This breathed new life into the AI research community. The pivot, however, was not instant but rather a gradual process driven by a series of breakthroughs and milestones. One of the critical milestones during this period was the application of an algorithm technique called backpropagation. Short for "backward propagation of errors", backpropagation significantly improves the efficiency of multi-layer neural networks. It enables the model to adjust its internal parameters in response to the difference between its actual output and the desired output, thereby improving the model's accuracy through a series of iterations. While multi-layer neural networks and the concept of backpropagation existed prior to the 1980s, their applicability was limited due to computational constraints. The increasing power of computers in the 1980s made it feasible to train larger neural networks, opening up new possibilities for machine learning.

The growing availability of digital data during this period also benefited machine learning. As computers became more prevalent in business, academia, and government, large volumes of data started to accumulate. With large datasets needed to learn patterns effectively, demand for machine learning began to rise. This combination of computational power, algorithmic innovation, and data availability set the stage for the application of machine learning across a broad range of research projects, from speech recognition and computer vision to medical diagnosis. By the end of the 1980s, machine learning had firmly established itself as the leading approach in AI research, but this return to optimism would again prove harmful. Just as volcanic lava can shoot high into the air before it starts to fall or an athlete's career can reach its peak before it starts to decline, there's often a point in AI development where doom presents itself as a triumph in disguise.

Repeating patterns of the past, the next downturn was caused by a variety of new and familiar factors, spanning inflated expectations, technical challenges, and economic pressures. Despite various technological advancements, machine learning models were still costly and painfully slow to run. What's more, the hype surrounding AI once again led to inflated expectations that the present technology failed to live up to. When these expectations weren't met, both investors and the public started to pull back their support, leading to a decrease in funding and interest, similar to the outbreak of the first AI winter.

The economic conditions of the time played a role too. The conclusion of the Cold War in 1991 led to large cuts in defense spending, which impacted funding for AI research, and a recession in the early 1990s tightened budgets both in industry and academia, further reducing resources available for AI research. Still, research into AI and machine learning persisted throughout this period, albeit at a slower pace than years prior. The experience of a second AI winter led researchers to adopt a more measured approach to their work, with a focus on specific and solvable problems as well as making more realistic claims about AI's capabilities.

As the 1990s rolled on, the rise of the Internet set the stage for the next wave of development as vast amounts of digital data became available. Interest and funding in AI started to rebound by the late 1990s and early 2000s, thanks in part to some technical advances and the growing importance of digital data. The success of AI systems across a variety of tasks, ranging from chess competitions to speech recognition, also helped improve AI's brand image and rebuild confidence in the field. This included IBM Deep Blue's win over Garry Kasparov to become the first AI system to defeat a reigning world chess champion.

By the turn of the millennium, AI was on a path of steady growth and development. The emergence of new algorithms in the early

2000s for solving classification problems and a series of practical demonstrations helped to reinforce AI's credibility and illustrate the real-world applicability of AI systems. This included a defining moment in the field of AI robotics after Stanford's autonomous car, Stanley, won the 2005 DARPA Grand Challenge by driving 131 miles across the desert without direct human intervention.

However, the real revolution was still brewing and one that would push the boundaries of AI capabilities closer to reality. The late 2000s, more than anything else, marked a leap forward in deep learning, a subfield of machine learning and another example of AI theory well ahead of its time. The concepts and principles of deep learning have their roots in the 1980s but remained unrealized for several decades. Once again, this wasn't necessarily a theoretical shortcoming but rather a limitation of the technology available.

Deep learning, named so for its use of "deep" networks with many layers of decision-making, describes a different way of learning from complex data. In deep learning, multiple layers of decision-making are used to calculate a progressively more abstract representation than the previous one. However, even with well-defined structures and algorithms, such as backpropagation for error correction, the computational demands for training these complex networks remained outside what was technically possible.

Geoffrey Hinton, often referred to as the godfather of deep learning, became a key figure in the development of deep learning in the mid-2000s. He advocated the idea that simple learning algorithms, when fed a sufficient amount of data and computed with sufficient processing power, could surpass traditional hand-coded software. However, Hilton's big breakthrough came in 2006 when he introduced a more efficient way to train deep neural networks—a concept that paved the way for practical applications of deep learning.

Hilton's breakthroughs were followed by two distinct but equally vital developments: the ongoing surge of big data and the advent of powerful graphics processing units (known as GPUs). In regard to the former, the ongoing penetration and acceleration of the Internet and the digital age brought with it an unprecedented supply of data. Smartphones, social media, e-commerce, and various other digital channels contributed to a vast and ever-growing reservoir of data. Deep learning models, which learn by adjusting their parameters to minimize prediction errors, perform more effectively when exposed to large amounts of data. The big data era, thus, provided the perfect environment for these data-hungry models.

However, vast data alone could not solve the computational bottleneck. Training deep learning models involves complex calculations and adjustments across millions, if not billions, of different parameters. This is where GPUs, originally designed for video games and computer graphics, caught the eye of AI researchers. In contrast to traditional central processing units (CPUs) that undertake calculations one after the other, graphics processing units are engineered to perform multiple computations concurrently, which enables a more sophisticated and immersive graphics experience.

Investment in GPU technology exploded and by 2005, mass production strategies drove the costs of these chips down substantially. This price reduction, paired with their unique processing capabilities, extended the use of GPUs beyond the realm of graphics rendering, paving the way for their use in other fields including deep learning and, later, Bitcoin mining.

In the case of deep learning, the advantage of GPUs lies in their ability to perform parallel processing. This capability aligns with the demands of deep learning computations, which are predominantly matrix and vector operations. The capacity of GPUs to handle these calculations concurrently, rather than sequentially, attracted the interest of researchers including Andrew Ng.[1]

As a professor at Stanford University, Ng's experiments with GPUs led to significant reductions in training times for deep learning models, making it feasible to build more complex neural networks.

---

[1] It's important to note that Andrew Ng's contributions to deep learning stretch beyond his work with GPUs. His popular Coursera course on machine learning has introduced millions of students worldwide to AI. His tenure at Google Brain, meanwhile, led to the development of large-scale deep neural networks, pushing the boundaries of what was thought possible.

This development signaled a paradigm shift, with deep learning models outperforming traditional AI approaches across numerous tasks including image and speech recognition as well as natural language processing. The advancements in deep learning led by Ng and other researchers including Geoffrey Hinton in the area of backpropagation pushed the boundaries of what was thought possible, with their findings facilitating new breakthroughs and startups including DeepMind and OpenAI.

Acquired by Google in 2014, DeepMind is best known for developing AlphaGo, a deep learning program that defeated the world champion in the game of Go in 2016. Due to the complexity and intuitive nature of the game, the feat was considered a major milestone in AI, and the publicity generated from the five-match series fueled a flood of interest in deep learning among students and startups. The company has since ventured into using AI to tackle societal challenges, such as the protein folding problem in biology and forecasting energy production for wind farms.

OpenAI, meanwhile, has made headlines with the release of generative AI products including DALL-E and ChatGPT that are capable of generating unique art and performing knowledge-based tasks such as translation, question answering, and summarizing text. These recent advancements introduced by OpenAI are set to form an integral part of many sectors and industries, driving innovations in areas such as education, marketing, entertainment, web development, and visual design.

As we delve deeper in the following chapters, we will examine how generative AI and other examples of AI work, as well as their common applications and what AI holds for the future.

Key Takeaways

1) The history of AI has experienced a recurring pattern of inflated expectations and periods of hibernation known as *AI winters*, characterized by downperiods of decreased funding and interest. These different cycles highlight the importance of maintaining realistic expectations and a measured approach to AI's capabilities.

2) The resilience of AI, seen throughout its history, can be partly attributed to the Lindy effect, which suggests that the longer an idea or technology survives, the longer its future life expectancy becomes. AI's ability to overcome periods of skepticism, funding cuts, and technological limitations underlines its resilience and reinforces the notion that the longer AI continues to advance, the more likely it is to stay.

3) The advent of powerful graphics processing units played a crucial role in the modern era of AI by enabling the parallel processing required for complex computations. This ability significantly reduces the time to train a model and has facilitated the development of deep learning, pushing the boundaries of what AI can achieve.

Thought Exercise

1) What percentage of the current AI cycle do you think is hype or exaggeration? What aspects of AI aren't hype and how can you focus on these opportunities?

## 3

AI BUILDING BLOCKS

Just as physical laws govern the mechanics of the universe, the field of artificial intelligence is controlled and regulated by algorithms. They underpin the advanced capabilities we see today, from the more simple act of recommending a song based on a user's listening history, to the complex task of driving an autonomous vehicle.

By definition, algorithms are sets of specific instructions designed to perform a task or solve a problem. They are the essential building blocks and the recipe for every good AI system. But unlike recipes written in human language, these algorithms are written in code and read by machines. While explaining the code and mathematical intricacies of popular algorithms is beyond the scope of this book, the following chapter provides a high-level overview of different algorithm categories, including classification, regression, sorting, and clustering techniques, as well as transparent and black box algorithms.

First, let's examine the shared characteristics of algorithms within the context of artificial intelligence. Fundamentally, algorithms function by processing data inputs to yield an output. Input data can include text, images, audio, video, sensor data, or any other form of unprocessed information. For a recommendation engine, the output might be a series of suggested products, and for a facial recognition system, the output might be an identification or face match.

AI algorithms typically have the capacity to learn and improve over time. As more data is processed, the algorithm fine-tunes its understanding, often improving the quality of its outputs. This feedback typically comes in the form of a loss function, a measure of how well the algorithm is performing its task. The loss function quantifies the difference between the algorithm's actual output and the expected output. Lower values of the loss function imply better performance.

When the loss function indicates that the output is failing to achieve an expected outcome, the algorithm undergoes an optimization process. This process involves adjusting the internal parameters of the algorithm to better align its outputs with the expected result. In essence, this is the algorithm's way of learning from its past mistakes. Parameters, meanwhile, are the internal settings that the algorithm adjusts during the optimization process. The exact nature and number of these parameters depend on the specific algorithm being used. An example of an algorithm with very few parameters is the k-nearest neighbors (k-NN) algorithm. In k-NN, the number of parameters is determined by the value of k, which represents the number of nearest neighbors used for classification or regression. Conversely, an artificial neural network may consist of thousands of different parameters.

Classification vs. Regression

It's essential to understand that there's no one-size-fits-all algorithm when it comes to AI. Different algorithms cater to different tasks and different types of data. The choice of algorithm depends on the specific problem you are attempting to solve.

To illustrate, classification algorithms are designed to assign the input data to a certain category or class based on its features, such as identifying whether an email is spam and whether a tumor is malignant or benign. The task of classifying instances is conducted by analyzing the characteristics or composition of existing examples and then creating a prediction model that captures relationships between the features and the class labels in order to predict the class of instances yet to be classified. This could involve diagnosing whether a patient is carrying a specific disease, such as diabetes, based on various health indicators. In this scenario, the output or class label is binary: "diabetes" or "no diabetes". The input features include a range of health measurements such as patients' blood pressure, body mass index (BMI), age, cholesterol levels, and so on. These measurements are collected from a large number of patients, some of whom have been diagnosed with diabetes and some who have not. This data is then used to train a classification model.

Patient ID	Blood Pressure	BMI	Age	Cholesterol Levels	Diabetes
1	120/80	25.3	40	180	No
2	140/90	29.8	55	220	Yes
3	130/85	27.6	65	200	Yes
4	118/75	22.1	32	150	No
5	150/95	31.2	48	240	Yes

Table 1: Sample data for classification of patients with diabetes

This training process involves feeding the features and the corresponding class labels ("diabetes" and "no diabetes") of each patient into the algorithm. The algorithm will analyze these features and establish a relationship between them and the corresponding class labels to create a trained model that captures these relationships. The trained model can then be used to predict the likelihood of a patient having diabetes based on the input of their health measurements.

When a new patient's data is fed into the model, the model can classify them as having "diabetes" or "no diabetes" based on the relationships it learned from the training data. For instance, the model may have learned that patients over the age of 50 with a high BMI and high blood pressure are statistically more likely to have diabetes. Thus, if a new patient matches that criteria, the model will classify the patient in the "diabetes" category. However, it's important to remember that the model is actually making an educated guess based on the data it was trained on, and while this can be highly accurate, certain errors are unavoidable, especially if the model doesn't account for fringe cases.

Regression algorithms, on the other hand, are used to predict continuous values (in numerical terms), such as evaluating the value of a house or predicting a patient's life expectancy. In the case of the second example, the input features can include a range of the same health measurements used in the previous example, such as blood pressure, body mass index (BMI), age, and cholesterol levels. The difference is that the target outcome is no longer binary ("diabetes" and "no diabetes") but a continuous value: the patient's life expectancy measured in years. The dataset again comprises numerous examples of patients, each characterized by their feature values in terms of health measurements but instead, there is a new column with a life expectancy value expressed in numbers.

Patient ID	Blood Pressure	BMI	Age	Cholesterol Levels	Diabetes	Life Expectancy
1	120/80	25.3	40	180	No	78
2	140/90	29.8	55	220	Yes	72
3	130/85	27.6	65	200	Yes	68
4	118/75	22.1	32	150	No	82
5	150/95	31.2	48	240	Yes	65

Table 2: Sample data for regression of patient's life expectancy

A regression algorithm, such as linear regression, can then be trained on the dataset to create a model. The training process involves feeding the features and corresponding life expectancy values of each patient into the algorithm. The algorithm will then analyze those features and establish a relationship between the input features and life expectancy, which is the target output for this model.

Once the training phase is complete, the algorithm will have learned and designed a model that can predict the life expectancy of a patient. When a new patient's data is entered into the model, the model estimates their life expectancy based on their health measurements. For instance, the model might have learned that patients who are younger, with a lower BMI, and who have controlled blood pressure tend to enjoy a higher life expectancy. Therefore, if a new patient's data fits these criteria, the model will estimate a higher life expectancy for that patient. However, similar to the classification model example, the model's prediction constitutes an estimation based on a generalization of the data the model was trained on and is not guaranteed to be 100% correct and the model may need to be retrained over time.

In summary, classification and regression algorithms are designed to handle different types of problems. Classification is used when the output variable is a category or a class, such as spam or not spam in the case of email filtering. Regression is used when the output variable is a real or continuous value, like house prices measured in dollars or life expectancy measured in years.

For a deeper exploration of specific classification and regression algorithms, I have documented these techniques in a separate book, *Machine Learning for Absolute Beginners: Third Edition*, which walks through the process of designing basic prediction models.

Sorting & Clustering

In addition to classification and regression, there are also sorting and clustering algorithms.

Sorting algorithms arrange a collection of items or data points in a specific order, making it easier to analyze. Sorting can be performed on various types of data, including numbers, dates, and strings. For example, consider a list of numbers: [11, 23, 1, 5, 2]. By applying a sorting algorithm, such as merge sort, the list can be rearranged in ascending order: [1, 2, 5, 11, 23].

Clustering, on the other hand, involves grouping similar data points together based on shared characteristics or similarities. The objective is to identify patterns, structures, or relationships within the data without any predefined labels or categories. Spam email, for example, isn't usually labeled by the sender as "spam", but by grouping emails together based on the subject line, contents, and external links, it's possible to group most of the spam email messages into a cluster based on similar patterns—all without any labels directly categorizing these emails as "spam".

Another common example of clustering is finding customers who share similar purchasing patterns. By identifying a cluster of customers who share purchasing preferences, such as time of purchase and seasonal factors, brands can identify distinct customer segments for targeted marketing campaigns.

Algorithm Transparency

In addition to matching the model with the type of problem you are attempting to solve, you also need to consider the model's interpretability. To elaborate, some algorithms are easier to understand but may not be the most accurate. Other algorithms can be highly accurate but are often described as black boxes because their internal decision-making process is difficult to interpret.

Transparent or highly interpretable algorithms are those where the steps taken to produce an output are easy to follow and clear to interpret. Decision trees and linear regression are two examples of algorithms where the relationship between the input(s) and the output is clear and easy to follow. The logic behind these algorithms can be examined step by step, allowing you to understand correlations and the specific variables that led to the final output. In general, transparent algorithms are useful in contexts where understanding the reasoning behind decisions is crucial, such as a credit loan decision or house valuation.

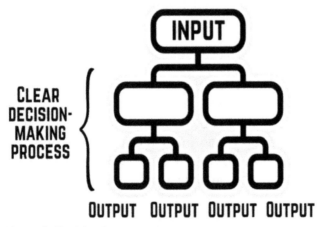

Figure 1: Decision tree

Black box algorithms, on the other hand, are those where the pathway from input to output cannot be easily traced or explained. Examples of black box algorithms are multi-layered neural networks. These models involve layers and layers of interconnected neurons that process input data, transforming it multiple times to reach an output. Due to the large number of transformations and the non-linear nature of these transformations, it's extremely difficult to understand how a neural network makes its decision. This lack of transparency can become problematic in contexts where accountability and explainability are favored.

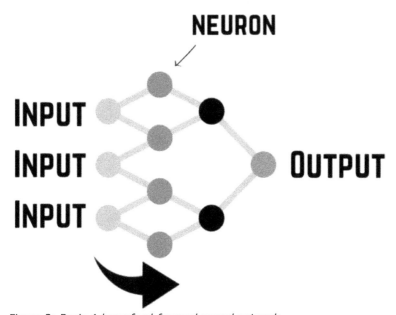

Figure 2: Basic 4-layer feed-forward neural network

Balancing the need for highly effective AI systems and the need for transparency and accountability is a key issue in AI research and ethics. The development of techniques to improve the interpretability of black box models, a field known as *explainable AI*, is an active area of study seeking to address this issue.

Explainable AI refers to the ability of an AI system to provide understandable explanations or justifications for its decisions and actions. In medical diagnosis, for example, explainable AI can help to provide doctors with clear explanations of how a system arrived at a diagnosis or treatment recommendation. This helps doctors validate the AI's suggestions and gain insights into the underlying factors considered by the model.

Datasets

Creating effective AI systems is not just about selecting and implementing the right algorithm. The design process also requires a deep understanding of the dataset the algorithm will consume and analyze.

Just as a car needs petrol or electricity to move, AI algorithms need data to learn. However, the relationship between AI and data goes beyond necessity. Understanding the nuances of data—its collection, interpretation, and limitations—is paramount to not only the effectiveness of AI systems but also fairness and transparency. Poor quality or biased data can lead to poor or biased results, a common challenge in AI called "garbage in, garbage out".

As organized stores of data, datasets provide the fuel for algorithms to operate. In the case of supervised learning (explored further in Chapter 5), a dataset is split into training and test portions with a 70:30 or 60:40 split. The training data is used to create the model, while the test data is used to evaluate the model's performance.

The quality and size of the dataset significantly impact the accuracy and reliability of the AI model. The better the dataset, the better the model's ability to learn and generalize to new inputs. Yet, datasets are not as straightforward as they might seem. Datasets can present numerous challenges that, if not properly managed, can lead to poor or erroneous predictions. A dataset that lacks diversity or that is not representative of the problem at hand can lead to models that are biased or that perform poorly when faced with real-world data.

One problem is the *curse of dimensionality*. Coined by Richard Bellman in the late 1950s, the term refers to various challenges that arise when analyzing datasets with hundreds or thousands of variables—a phenomenon that only occurs in high-dimensional datasets (with a large number of variables). According to this theory, to obtain a statistically sound and reliable result, the amount of data needed to support the result often grows exponentially with the dimensionality or number of variables analyzed. However, having too many variables also injects noise that makes it harder to identify patterns and build an accurate model. What's more, given the sheer volume of variables thrown at the model, it's possible for one or more variables to correlate with the target output due to coincidence rather than pure causation.

As you might have heard, correlation does not imply causation. Just because two variables move together does not mean that one causes the other to move. The website Spurious Correlations (www.tylervigen.com/spurious-correlations) presents numerous examples of variables that are strongly correlated but clearly have no causal relationship. For instance, one chart on the site visualizes a strong correlation between the divorce rate in the state of Maine and the yearly per capita consumption of margarine in the United States. As amusing as it is to think about why that might be true, there is no reason to believe these two trends have any effect on each other. The correlation is likely a coincidence.

Next, the costs associated with processing large amounts of data must be taken into consideration. While having more data often improves the predictive ability of machine learning models, it amplifies computational requirements and increases model complexity. Conversely, too little data can result in models that are inadequately trained and perform poorly on new data.

Another crucial aspect is the cleanliness and integrity of the dataset. Inaccurate or missing data can impair the model's performance, leading to incorrect predictions. Hence, a substantial part of building a model involves preprocessing and cleaning data to ensure its quality and consistency. This step involves filling in missing data, removing duplicates, correcting inconsistencies, converting non-numerical variables to numeric variables, and normalizing variables to maintain a consistent scale (i.e., all variables measured in "minutes" and not in multiple different units of time). It's a demanding task, but the value it brings to the model and its outputs cannot be overstated.

To demonstrate the range of data quality considerations, let's use an example from an e-commerce company developing a machine learning model for its new marketing campaign. The aim of the model is to predict customer responses based on various variables such as past purchases, customer information, and website browsing behavior.

First, the accuracy of the data is paramount. If the past purchase history of a customer is recorded inaccurately, the predictive model might target the wrong customers and waste resources on customers who are less likely to purchase.

Completeness is the next essential aspect of data quality. If data concerning customer responses to past campaigns or seasonal events are missing, the model may not have sufficient information to make accurate predictions. This is akin to trying to complete a puzzle without all the pieces available.

Consistency in data is also crucial. Picture a scenario where the age of the customer is recorded in years in one part of the system and in months in another. Such inconsistency could lead to confusion and result in errors in the model.

The reliability of the data collected is another vital component of data quality. If the browsing data is collected inaccurately due to a bug in the tracking code or acquired from an unreliable third party, the model might skew its predictions. A customer might be misclassified as not being interested in certain products when they actually are, leading to inappropriate targeting and a missed sales opportunity.

Timeliness, the next metric, ensures that the model is based on the current reality. If the most recent purchase data is not updated in real-time, the model will base its predictions on outdated information. For instance, a customer who recently made several baby product purchases might be incorrectly classified as unlikely to respond to a new baby product recommendation if their latest transactions aren't included in the data. Conversely, marketing to a customer who made baby product purchases five years ago may no longer be a reliable candidate for purchasing that line of products.

Relevance of the data to the task at hand is essential to avoid confusion and the waste of computational resources. For example, including data such as the customer's phone carrier or the color of the last item purchased (if color isn't relevant to the campaign), introduces noise into the model and distracts the model from more relevant variables.

Lastly, granularity refers to the level of detail in the data. While highly detailed data might seem advantageous, it can also introduce noise into the model, leading to a problem known as overfitting where the model over-emphasizes randomness or insignificant patterns in the data. For instance, if website browsing data is recorded for every single page view, it might add unnecessary complexity without providing significant value. Conversely, if data is aggregated or too coarse (having a low level of detail), critical details about customer behavior might be overlooked and wasted.

To summarize, data is a critical asset for creating AI systems, providing the necessary information for these systems to learn, improve, and generate accurate predictions or insights. Each piece of data is like a brick used to construct a building. If the bricks are weak or flawed, the resulting building might be unstable. Similarly, if data is inaccurate, incomplete, or unreliable, the resulting AI system could produce misleading results, leading to poor decisions and potential risks. For these and many other reasons, a thorough understanding of data and its various aspects is vital when working with AI. This includes not only the ability to analyze data and check for spurious relationships but also to clean and preprocess the input data.

Quality Metric	Description	Marketing Model Example
Accuracy	The data correctly represents the entities it is describing.	Customers' purchase history is not recorded accurately due to errors in the transaction logging system.
Completeness	Complete datasets contain few or no omissions.	Data missing for customers' responses to past campaigns or missing information about customer demographics.
Consistency	Data should be consistent across different data sources and over time.	The age of customers is recorded in years in one part of the system and in months in another.
Reliability	Reliable data should be trusted and from reliable sources.	Customer data acquired from a third-party may be partly or fully fabricated.
Timeliness	Data should be available when it is needed.	Purchase data that is not updated regularly or when there's a delay between collection and model training.
Relevance	Data should be related to the task at hand.	Irrelevant data, such as customers' phone carrier, wastes computational resources and confuses the model.
Granularity	Data needs to have the right level of detail or summarization. Data that's too granular might contain more noise than signal.	If website browsing data is too coarse, such as only recording one activity per day, the model might miss important details about the customer.

Table 3: Data quality considerations and examples

AI Hardware & Software

In this next section, we'll explore the important role that hardware and software play in facilitating artificial intelligence.

Let's start with the hardware. High-performance hardware is a cornerstone of AI, particularly in the realm of machine learning and deep learning, where vast quantities of data are the norm. From the central processing units that serve as the brains of the computer to the graphics processing units that accelerate computations, the role of hardware is to provide the raw power needed to process and run complex algorithms on the data.

CPUs vs. GPUs

During the early stages of AI development, computations were executed using CPUs, which are known for being versatile and capable of executing a variety of tasks. In practice, CPUs are used for performing sequential processing, where each instruction is executed one after another.

While CPUs are efficient for general computing tasks, advanced AI and particularly deep learning require the processing of complex mathematical operations on very large datasets, which necessitates parallel rather than sequential processing. Parallel processing refers to the ability to break down large tasks into smaller ones and run them simultaneously across multiple processors, significantly speeding up computation compared to handling tasks one at a time (sequential processing).

Originally designed to handle the rendering of pixel-rich images in computer games and gaming consoles such as the PlayStation 2 and Xbox, GPUs are specifically designed for parallel processing. This makes them well-suited for tasks that require a lot of computing power, such as graphics processing and machine learning. This also explains why the use of GPUs in AI has become so widespread and why the production and price of GPUs are carefully monitored by companies and governments.

In general, GPUs are more expensive than CPUs to produce. The specific pricing of GPUs is influenced by multiple factors including production costs, demand, technological advancements, and geopolitics. Over time, as with many technologies, we have witnessed a general trend of price deflation in the cost per unit of computing power. This doesn't mean that the price of a GPU has decreased, but rather, that the cost for a certain level of performance (measured in floating point operations per second) has generally gone down over time. This is due to improvements in manufacturing, increased efficiency, and technological upgrades.

Nonetheless, it's important to note that the price of chips can be subject to significant short-term fluctuations. During periods of increased interest in cryptocurrencies, the demand for chips can spike, leading to increased costs. Similarly, disruptions in the supply chain, such as those caused by the global pandemic or international trade disputes, can impact the availability and cost of computing resources.

As a byproduct of semiconductors, chips are becoming increasingly vulnerable to trade wars. In September 2022, the U.S. Department of Commerce added seven Chinese supercomputing entities to the Entity List, which restricts the export of certain goods and technologies to those entities. While aimed at preventing China from using chips for military purposes, the ban has far-reaching implications for the AI industry.

Specifically, the ban affected the export of chips to China from two major chipmakers, Nvidia from Taiwan and Advanced Micro Devices (AMD) from the United States. Both companies had been supplying chips, including GPUs, to China for use in supercomputers but were forced to halt shipments in response to the ban. This now makes it challenging for companies in China to obtain the GPUs they need for building AI applications. The Chinese Government has responded to the ban by imposing its own restrictions on the export of chips to the United States, making it more difficult for U.S. companies to obtain chips from China. The trade war has also prompted countries to increase their investment in local chip manufacturing, which may lead to the development of new chip innovations, supply lines, and manufacturing processes.

The emergence of the company DeepSeek in early 2025 is another consequence of U.S. export controls on advanced semiconductor chips. The Biden administration's restrictions, introduced in 2022 and tightened in 2023, barred the export of cutting-edge GPUs like Nvidia's H100 to China. These controls were intended to hinder China's ability to develop advanced AI models by restricting access to critical hardware. However, they forced companies like DeepSeek to innovate within these constraints by optimizing software and leveraging less powerful chips, such as Nvidia's H800 and H20 models, which were initially allowed but later banned.

DeepSeek's R1 model has since demonstrated that it's possible to achieve high performance with fewer resources, challenging the U.S. industry's resource-intensive approach. By employing creative techniques like chain-of-thought reasoning and mixed expert models[2], DeepSeek achieved efficiency and cost-effectiveness that rivaled or surpassed U.S. counterparts like OpenAI, despite limited access to advanced chips. This innovation was driven by necessity, as the sanctions compelled Chinese

[2] Chain-of-thought reasoning is an approach that simulates human-like problem-solving by breaking down complex tasks into a sequence of logical steps; mixture of experts is a machine learning architecture that divides a large AI model into separate specialized sub-networks, or "experts," each focusing on a specific subset of tasks.

developers to maximize the utility of available hardware rather than relying on brute computational power.

To learn more about the lead-up and the potential trajectory of the current chip war, you may like to read *Chip Wars: The Fight for the World's Most Critical Technology* by Chris Miller, which tells the story of the global semiconductor industry and the growing competition between the United States and China to dominate this critical resource.

TPUs

Beyond CPUs and GPUs, there is another important type of chip to discuss. As the field of AI has advanced, more specialized hardware has been required and this has led to the development of Tensor Processing Units (TPUs), originally developed by Google.

TPUs are a type of application-specific integrated circuit (ASIC) developed specifically for accelerating machine learning workloads. They are named after the tensor data structure (a multi-dimensional array or data structure with multiple variables). The first generation of TPUs was announced in 2016 and used internally at Google to improve the efficiency and speed of their machine learning systems such as Google Search and Google Translate.

Google announced its second-generation TPU in 2017, and these units were made available to external developers via Google's public cloud platform, which continues to release new and more powerful TPU generations. Other companies including Microsoft and Amazon Web Services (AWS) have since followed in offering TPU services on the cloud. This has helped to accelerate the development of AI as these processing chips make it possible to train and run models on a larger scale.

In terms of hardware comparison, while CPUs are used to handle a variety of general computing tasks and GPUs are designed to quickly process the mathematical calculations needed for rendering graphics, TPUs are specifically built to handle the kind of matrix-based computations that are common in machine learning and deep learning.

One of the significant differences between GPUs and TPUs lies in their architecture. GPUs are designed to handle a large number of relatively small computational cores for parallel processing, which is great for graphics rendering and beneficial for certain types of machine learning tasks. TPUs, on the other hand, are designed around a large matrix multiply unit, which offers high computational capability and reduced computational precision (such as lower-bit floating-point numbers) that is typically acceptable for neural network workloads. This precision reduction can still deliver accurate results for neural network models while offering significant performance gains, which makes TPUs efficient at executing the large-scale matrix operations that are often found in deep learning algorithms. TPUs can also be significantly faster than GPUs in regards to the running of machine learning applications and, in general, are more energy efficient.

However, it's crucial to note that while individual operations may be more efficient, the overall environmental impact of TPUs and GPUs raises a reason for concern. First, the manufacturing of these high-performance chips requires a lot of upfront energy and resources, including the mining of raw materials, such as silicon and rare earth metals, which are energy-intensive to mine. They then continue to consume a lot of energy once put into use. The energy consumption of these chips can be significant, especially in data centers where they are used in large quantities.

As a result, there are a number of initiatives underway to reduce the environmental impact of high-performance chips, such as the development of more energy-efficient manufacturing processes, the recycling and reusing of chips, and the use of renewable energy sources, including solar and wind power, to power data centers.

Regarding manufacturing processes, there are a number of new energy-efficient manufacturing processes that are currently being implemented including 3D stacking, which involves vertically attaching three or sometimes four chips to make better use of available chip space.

Software

Having discussed the evolution and importance of hardware, including the use of GPUs and TPUs, let's shift our focus to another critical component of AI systems: the software. AI software ranges from the programming languages used to write algorithms, such as Python and R, to specialized libraries like TensorFlow, PyTorch, and Keras that offer pre-built functions for creating and training prediction models.

(Please note that this section delves into more technical aspects, including descriptions of common code libraries. If you aren't interested in the programming side of AI, feel free to skim or skip over this section.)

Libraries

Libraries, in the context of AI software, are collections of pre-written code that developers can use to streamline their work. They span everything from simple data-importing commands to complex mathematical functions. Essentially, they provide a way to perform tasks without having to write custom code from scratch every single time you want to do something. To explain why this is important, let's consider the case of creating a neural network. Without code libraries, a programmer would need to manually code the entire architecture of the network, implement the mathematical operations for forward propagation (where the network makes its predictions) and backpropagation (where the network learns from its errors), and handle the optimization process that tweaks the network parameters for improved performance. Not only is this process extremely time-consuming but it also requires a deep understanding of the underlying mathematics.

Libraries reduce much of this complexity. When creating a neural network using TensorFlow or Keras, developers can build a model by simply stacking together pre-defined layers. Each layer might represent a set of neurons in the network, and come pre-packaged with the necessary mathematical operations. Furthermore, these libraries come with pre-implemented algorithms for training and optimizing the model.

When data is fed into the model, the library takes care of passing it through the mathematical operations defined by the network's architecture, adjusting the network's weights based on the errors it makes, and iteratively improving the model. The end result is that with just a few lines of code, developers can create, train, and implement a model without having to manually insert the underlying math.

These libraries also provide code for preprocessing data, which is a critical step in creating a model. They can handle tasks like normalizing data[3] to ensure that variables are expressed on a common scale, converting categorical variables into numerical variables, and splitting datasets into training and test sets, among other things.

Lastly, libraries play an essential role in promoting consistency and standardization. By using libraries, developers adhere to a set of standardized practices, which reduces the risk of errors and improves the replicability of the code for future use.

Beyond TensorFlow, PyTorch, and Keras, there is an extensive selection of useful libraries out there. Scikit-learn, for instance, offers a broad array of machine learning algorithms and tools for data preprocessing and model evaluation using Python. Natural Language Toolkit (NLTK) provides resources for tasks in natural language processing, a field of AI focused on the interaction between computers and human language. Matplotlib is a widely used library for creating static, animated, and interactive visualizations in Python, which is crucial for data exploration and presenting results.

Programming Langauges

---

[3] Normalizing data means adjusting values, like changing test scores from a 0-100 scale to a 0-1 scale, so they can be compared more easily. For example, if you have test scores of 45 and 85 out of 100, normalizing them to a 0-1 scale would give you: 0.45 and 0.85. This way, both scores are now on a 0 to 1 scale, making them easier to compare.

Programming languages are fundamental in the development of AI systems. The choice of language often depends on the specific needs of a project, including factors such as the type of problem being solved, computational efficiency requirements, and the availability of relevant libraries and frameworks. Here, we'll discuss some of the most popular programming languages used within AI.

Python: Known for its simplicity and readability, Python is the most widely used programming language in AI and machine learning. Python boasts a plethora of libraries and frameworks that facilitate the development of AI applications, including TensorFlow, PyTorch, Keras, and Scikit-learn. It's also a great choice for beginners and experts.

R: If you're leaning towards statistical computing or data analysis, R is a language designed specifically for these purposes. It has a rich package ecosystem that facilitates statistical modeling and visualization, which are core components of AI and machine learning.

Java: Java is another language worth considering, particularly if you're building large-scale enterprise applications. It's platform independence and robust debugging features make it a versatile choice for AI development.

C++: Due to its high execution speed and control over system resources, C++ is often used in AI projects where performance is a crucial factor. It's typically used in parts of AI applications where low latency is required, although it may not be as easy to use as Python or R.

Julia: Julia is a high-level, high-performance language for technical computing. It provides the ease of use of Python and R, but also the performance of C++. Julia is gaining some popularity in the data science and AI communities, particularly in areas that require heavy numerical and scientific computation.

Prolog: Prolog, short for Programming in Logic, is a language often associated with artificial intelligence and computational linguistics. Its capacity to efficiently resolve problems involving relationships, especially those that involve structured data, makes it suited to certain AI applications.

LISP: Although less commonly used today, LISP is one of the oldest high-level programming languages and is closely associated with artificial intelligence research. It was widely used in AI research due to its symbolic processing capabilities, but its use has waned with the rise of more modern languages.

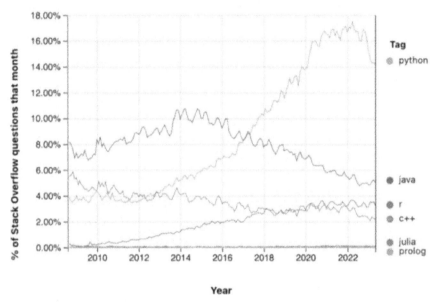

Figure 3: Percentage of Stack Overflow questions that month (not necessarily AI-specific)

The right language for a particular AI project can depend on many factors, but these languages have demonstrated their value across a wide range of AI applications. Beyond the languages themselves, you should also consider the support systems surrounding them. From tutorials and forums to sample code, an active community can be a goldmine of resources. These resources can dramatically accelerate your learning and provide much-needed support when you encounter problems with your code. Languages with large communities also tend to be regularly updated with new features and improvements, keeping you at the forefront of AI development.

The nature of your project will play a significant role in your decision too. If you are developing an AI solution that needs to integrate with existing systems, your choice might be influenced by the languages these systems use and their compatibility. Similarly, if your work involves large volumes of data, you should look for languages with strong data-handling capabilities.

Lastly, bear in mind that many AI tasks can be significantly accelerated by running them on multiple processors simultaneously. This is especially true for deep learning. As such, languages that support parallel computing can be advantageous.

In conclusion, the right language to learn for AI development depends on your personal circumstances, including your existing skills, the type of projects you intend to work on, and your performance requirements. Python, R, Java, and C++ are all excellent choices, but they come with their own strengths and weaknesses. If you are still unsure, it may be wise to default to the most popular language for AI systems, which, at this time, is Python.

Key Takeaways

1) Classification and regression are two common categories of algorithms used in AI. Classification algorithms assign input data to specific categories or classes based on their features, while regression algorithms predict continuous values.

2) Sorting algorithms arrange data into a specific order, facilitating easier understanding. Clustering algorithms, on the other hand, group similar data points together without predefined labels, allowing for the identification of new patterns and relationships.

3) Transparency and interpretability of algorithms are important considerations. Transparent algorithms have clear and understandable steps, making their decision-making process easily interpretable. Black box algorithms, on the other hand, lack transparency and their internal workings are difficult to trace.

4) Datasets play a crucial role in AI systems. The quality, diversity, and relevance of the data used to train AI models significantly impact their performance. Inaccurate, biased, or incomplete data

can lead to poor or biased predictions. Preprocessing and cleaning the data are also important steps for ensuring data quality.

5) Libraries promote convenience and consistency. By using established libraries, developers adhere to standardized practices, reducing the risk of errors and improving the replicability of code for future use.

6) The choice of programming language should consider factors such as computational efficiency, access to code libraries, community support, integration with existing systems, data handling capabilities, and parallel computing support.

7) Python is currently the most widely used language in AI and machine learning, offering simplicity, readability, and a rich ecosystem of libraries.

Thought Exercises

1) What's a real-life example reflecting the curse of dimensionality? Is there a business book, news channel, conspiracist, politician, or popular theory, for instance, that draws on a select number of seemingly correlated examples that are coincidental and not typical of the true situation?

2) Do you think classification problems or regression problems are more common in your organization or institution? (i.e., how much to pay interns is a regression problem, whereas selecting new interns based on their credentials is a classification problem.)

3) Is model transparency important for a football coach using a prediction model to recruit players who are likely to score goals? Do fans betting on a football player to score also need to know why the model predicts that player to score or is model accuracy more important?

4) Pick an industry you are currently interested in and think of a special use case for AI. Now ask whether model interpretability

and transparency are important for evaluating the effectiveness of the model.

## 4

THE 3 STAGES OF AI DEVELOPMENT

As you venture further into the field of AI, it's important to recognize and understand the three potential stages of AI development. Spanning narrow AI, general AI, and superintelligent AI, these three stages represent crucial milestones in the evolution of AI systems.

Narrow AI, for example, is designed to perform a specific task, whereas general AI is more advanced and capable of understanding, learning, and applying knowledge flexibly across a broad spectrum of tasks. As the most advanced category, superintelligent AI remains a theoretical category at present but is hypothesized to surpass human intelligence within all domains at some point in the future.

Narrow AI

Despite its name, *narrow AI* or *weak AI* should not be confused as weak or ineffective. Rather, the naming of this category refers to the focused nature of AI systems in relation to their scope and functionality.

By design, narrow AI systems are capable of mimicking human intelligence but are constrained to a specific domain, meaning they can't perform tasks outside of what they are trained or programmed to do. To illustrate, an AI system designed for image recognition can identify and categorize images based on its training but cannot translate languages or diagnose diseases without radical adjustments and additional training data. This might make narrow AI seem limited in terms of application, but these specialized systems form the backbone of many powerful AI applications. Google's search engine, Amazon's recommendation engine, Apple's Siri, and Tesla's Autopilot are all examples of narrow AI systems. Each of these systems performs specific tasks exceptionally well, often surpassing human capabilities in speed, accuracy, and efficiency. Google's search engine, for instance, can process billions of web pages and deliver the most relevant search results in a fraction of a second. It's optimized to perform this specific task and outperform any human assistant. However, the same system is clueless when it comes to steering a car or writing a poem. This underlines the essence of narrow AI: exceptional at performing a specific task but inflexible and unable to operate effectively at other tasks.

General AI

Having established the definition of narrow AI, let's turn our attention to a more advanced iteration and the next phase of AI development called *general AI* or *strong AI*.

General AI, often referred to as *artificial general intelligence* or *AGI*, refers to a version of artificial intelligence that has the ability to perform any cognitive task achievable by a human. Note, however, that this definition does not encompass physical abilities or the use of robotics, which are often subject to different tests and forms of evaluation. *The Coffee Test*, proposed by Apple Co-founder Steve Wozniak, for instance, sets a benchmark for evaluating physical capabilities by testing a robot's ability to enter an unfamiliar house, find the kitchen, identify the tools and ingredients, and prepare a cup of coffee. Robots are yet to pass the test and this example is just one of many benchmarks currently in discussion regarding AGI (beyond the boundaries of solely cognitive tasks).

When it comes to solely cognitive tasks, benchmarks and definitions of AGI remain varied, which creates a sliding scale of standards and expectations. In general, the more specific the definition (such as the ability to converse with humans on any topic in multiple languages), the easier the target becomes. Conversely, the less specific the definition (perform any task a human can do), the harder the benchmark. Depending on the definition, AGI might also include a biological component, physical capabilities, consciousness, or some other human quality, which comes with its own set of design challenges. Broad physical capabilities, for example, are difficult to achieve due to the lack of data available to train robots or humanoid robots. ChatGPT was trained on millions of data sources scoured from the world wide web but the data available to train robots is much harder to find and acquire. Consciousness, meanwhile, is the subjective feeling of being aware that one exists and having an understanding of the surrounding environment. Some experts contend that having an inner mental life is not replicable in machines because consciousness arises from biological substrates and cannot be replicated in non-biological entities.

Amidst these nuanced attempts to define general intelligence, the core of the discourse and AGI research both center on emulating cognitive abilities across a comprehensive range of non-physical tasks. This includes the ability to reason, solve puzzles, plan, learn, integrate prior knowledge into decision-making, and communicate in a natural language such as English or Spanish. Importantly, general AI includes the ability to transfer knowledge from one domain to another—a skill known as *transfer learning*. This might involve leveraging its understanding from reading books to engage in a meaningful conversation about literature, a capability that is well beyond the ability of narrow AI systems.

It's important to highlight that as of the time of writing, general AI remains unrealized. While we've made significant strides in AI technology, we're still some way from creating a machine that can fully replicate the broad cognitive capabilities of the human mind. Most of the AI systems we have today, including GPT-4, are considered narrow AI because they excel at specific tasks (such as content generation) but don't possess a generalized understanding or ability to reason beyond their specific training. Also, while some applications are capable of performing multiple different tasks, they are actually using a collection of narrow AI models under the hood.

One candidate for driving progress in the field of general AI is AutoGPT. As an open-source AI agent powered by OpenAI's GPT-

4 API, the system can generate text and perform various tasks autonomously, including code writing, language translation, text summarization, question answering, creative text generation, and online task completion. It operates by breaking down user goals into subtasks and utilizing various resources such as the Internet to accomplish those tasks. For instance, if a user requests AutoGPT to compose a Tweet about coding, the agent will segment the task into subtasks like finding a coding tutorial, reading the tutorial, composing the Tweet, and posting it on Twitter.

Although AutoGPT demonstrates promise and has the potential to serve as a robust automation tool for complex projects, it falls short of emulating human intelligence across a broad spectrum of tasks or rivaling human capabilities in its current form. Still, it signifies a step towards the development of general AI by showcasing the feasibility of creating AI models capable of connecting to different online tools and adapting to new tasks without human supervision.

Although it remains to be seen whether AutoGPT or a similar model could evolve into AGI, it is essential to address the philosophical and ethical questions before achieving this milestone. For instance, if we create machines that match or surpass human intelligence, what are the implications? How do we ensure these AI systems align with human values and ethics? Exploration of these questions forms an important part of the current discourse on AI.

Superintelligent AI

Following our exploration of general AI, let us now venture into the most speculative phase of artificial intelligence. While currently residing in the bounds of theoretical forecasts and human imagination, superintelligent AI presents a vision of the future that has long captivated scientists, philosophers, futurists, and science fiction authors.

Whereas general AI aims to replicate the full spectrum of human cognitive abilities, superintelligent AI goes a step further, seeking to exceed human capabilities. In theory, a superintelligent AI would not only outperform humans at any intellectual task but would also outperform humans in high-value endeavors including scientific research, strategic planning, and social influencing. Thus, the idea of superintelligent AI extends beyond an advanced tool or system; it suggests a potentially autonomous entity capable of out-thinking humanity, coming up with ideas, strategies, and solutions that exceed the abilities of the smartest human minds. As such, it raises questions and concerns about control and alignment with human values that are significantly more challenging than those associated with general AI.

This leads us to what's termed the *control problem*, a term popularized by philosopher Nick Bostrom, author of the seminal book *Superintelligence: Paths, Dangers, Strategies*. The control problem refers to the theoretical difficulty of controlling or restraining a superintelligent AI. If AI surpasses human intelligence, it might become impossible to fully predict or control its actions. The AI entity could devise strategies to avoid being shut down or it could manipulate humans in ways we are unable to detect and control.

The late Stephen Hawking, one of the most renowned theoretical physicists of our time, expressed concern about the potential risks of developing superintelligent AI. In a 2014 interview with the BBC, Hawking warned that "The development of full artificial intelligence could spell the end of the human race". He went on to explain that once machines reach a point where they can improve themselves at a rapid pace, humans, with our slow biological evolution, won't be able to compete and we will be superseded as a result. Hawking reiterated his viewpoint during a Q&A session at the annual Zeitgeist Conference in 2016. He stated, "I believe there is no deep difference between what can be achieved by a biological brain and what can be achieved by a computer. It, therefore, follows that computers can, in theory, emulate human intelligence—and exceed it".

Beyond a potential showdown with AI agents, a more immediate concern lies in how humans will harness superintelligence to wield power and influence. Similar to preceding technological advancements, humans will inevitably seek out ways to exploit superintelligence to achieve their objectives, whether that's delivering bias and misinformation over the Internet or exploiting it for cyberattacks, digital espionage, and deep surveillance. Equally, there is a looming danger of a strong central actor like OpenAI, Microsoft, or a state actor such as the Chinese Communist Party monopolizing access to superintelligent systems and relevant hardware.

Seeing the problems posed by this scenario, initiatives such as StabilityAI advocate for an open-source and grassroots-driven approach to AI development. They warn against the path of centralized power and encourage the proliferation of distinct AI systems, each aligned with the values and perspectives of the communities they serve, mirroring the plurality and diversity of human values.

The Singularity

Building on the concept of superintelligent AI, the theory of *the Singularity* forecasts a future point of irrevocable societal change that will occur if and when AI surpasses human intelligence. This theory is based on the principle that a sufficiently advanced AI would be capable of designing an even more advanced version of itself, which could then design an even more advanced version, and so forth, leading to a rapid and exponential increase in intelligence.

The term and theory were popularized by mathematician and science fiction author Vernor Vinge in his 1993 essay *The Coming Technological Singularity*. According to Vinge, the Singularity represents the end of the human era. With superintelligence continuing to upgrade itself, this will lead to an exponential increase in AI capabilities. This process would result in unfathomable changes to civilization, so much so that our current models of reality—the ways we think about and understand the world—would no longer be sufficient.

These ideas have been explored and expanded upon by authors and thinkers like Ray Kurzweil. In his book *The Singularity is Near*, published in 2005, Kurzweil predicts that the Singularity will occur somewhere around the year 2045 and lead to considerable societal and biological changes, as the line between humans and machines becomes increasingly blurred. Kurzweil suggests that humans will merge with AI, enhancing our intellectual, physical, and emotional capabilities.

Amid this possibility, it's important to revisit the existential risks of pushing AI development in this direction. As previously noted, there are substantial concerns regarding the issue of aligning AI with human values and objectives. Experts argue that as AI systems become more intelligent and capable, the likelihood rises that they will deviate in ways unforeseen by us today. To counter this risk, Nick Bostrom emphasizes the need for substantial investments in research aimed at developing strategies to manage superintelligent AI, ensuring that it contributes positively to humanity rather than causing harm.

One popular solution is to control and monitor the data used to train AI models. However, even with meticulous screening of data inputs to eliminate inappropriate content, ideologies, and knowledge, it's theoretically possible for superintelligent AI to uncover pathways to act contrary to human values or behave in unexpected ways. Using an inversion function, for example, the model could use its knowledge of positive behavior to acquire insights into the characteristics of negative behavior. To illustrate, if the model is trained to avert house fires, it could also learn how to start a house fire by adopting behavior contrary to the training data—all without ever being explicitly trained to engage in such behavior.

Similarly, training AI to perform a specific task may inadvertently increase the likelihood of it doing the opposite of the intended behavior. This alignment problem has been termed *the Waluigi Effect*, inspired by the character Waluigi from the Super Mario franchise and the evil counterpart of Luigi. Humans, particularly teenagers, for instance, are inclined to do the opposite of what they are instructed and it's possible that developmental AI models may do the same.

At the same time, there are many experts who question whether it's possible for AI models to rebel or replicate and surpass human-level intelligence. One of these skeptics is the computer scientist

Gordon Moore, co-founder of Intel and the originator of *Moore's Law* (the observation that the number of transistors on a microchip doubles approximately every two years). Moore has expressed doubts that the Singularity will occur within the predicted timeframe of the next 25 years or even at all. He argues that there are physical limitations to the computation speeds that machines can reach and that these limits will prevent the realization of the Singularity as envisioned by Vinge and Kurzweil.

Whether we are destined to reach the superintelligence phase of AI and witness the Singularity in our lifetimes remains uncertain, especially as it would require significant breakthroughs far beyond our current understanding and capabilities. In the meantime, contemplating the potential consequences of the Singularity is crucial for steering responsible AI development.

According to the *precautionary principle*, a popular concept from risk management, it's valuable to address potential risks or harm even in the absence of scientific proof. The precautionary principle emphasizes the need for proactive action when there's the possibility of serious or irreversible harm to the environment or human health. In the context of superintelligence, this may involve implementing some of the following measures.

1) Regulation and policy: Robust regulatory frameworks and policies are needed to address potential risks and provide guidelines for the responsible development and use of advanced AI systems. This involves setting safety and transparency standards, monitoring development, defining ethical boundaries for tech companies to operate under as well as potential intervention, if necessary.

Experts such as Daniel Colson, Executive director of the Artificial Intelligence Policy Institute, have proposed that governments impose restrictions on AI firms, preventing them from acquiring vast supplies of hardware used to build super-advanced AI systems, while also making it illegal to build computing clusters above a certain processing threshold.[4] While these measures may

---

[4] Daniel Colson, "One think tank vs. 'god-like' AI", *Politico*, August 15, 2023.

appear severe, there is public support for government regulation and oversight of AI development.

According to a 2023 poll organized by the Artificial Intelligence Policy Institute, 82% of American respondents said they don't trust tech executives to regulate AI, with 56% of respondents supporting a federal agency to regulate AI (compared to 14% who did not).[5] Similarly, a 2023 global study published by the University of Queensland and KPMG found that across 17 countries and 17,000 respondents, 71% of people surveyed were in favor of AI regulation[6], while the Ada Lovelace Institute and The Alan Turing Institute found that 62% of 4,000 British respondents would like to see laws and regulations guiding the use of AI technologies.[7]

However, backing AI regulation doesn't automatically imply public confidence in the ability of governments to act effectively. As per the University of Queensland and KPMG study, confidence in the government's ability to regulate AI development stood at 49% in the U.S., 47% in Japan, 45% in the UK, 86% in China, 70% in India, and 60% in Singapore.

2) Global coordination: While country-level measures to regulate AI development are crucial, it's just as—or if not more—important to maintain alignment between countries and regions. Similar to the founding of the International Atomic Energy Agency to manage the safe use of nuclear power, OpenAI's co-founders have called for a global agency to rein in the development of superintelligence. This organization would be responsible for conducting assessments and audits of AI systems, designing and implementing safety standards, and defining ethical boundaries. While difficult to implement, agreements to restrict the pace of global AI development are another recommendation under discussion.

---

[5] Ryan Heath, "Exclusive poll: Americans distrust AI giants", *Axios.com,* August 9, 2023.

[6] N. Gillespie, S. Lockey, C. Curtis, J. Pool, J & A. Akbari, "Trust in Artificial Intelligence: A Global Study", *The University of Queensland and KPMG Australia,* 2023.

[7] "How do people feel about AI? A nationally representative survey of public attitudes to artificial intelligence in Britain", *Ada Lovelace Institute and The Alan Turing Institute,* 2023.

Existing forums for global cooperation, including the European Union, G7, and the United Nations are also in the process of designing processes to monitor and regulate the development of AI systems. However, as the COVID pandemic has shown us, achieving global cooperation is a challenging endeavor, especially in light of the present geopolitical environment and various schisms between Western powers, China, and Russia.

If a country or several countries opt out of regulatory efforts or disregard global guidelines, the efficacy of participating nations' endeavors diminishes, resulting in a myriad of issues including inequitable access to AI hardware and technology, along with the migration of ambitious AI companies to non-participating states.

3) Public engagement: Next, to help more people identify and understand the potential risks and impacts of AI, it's crucial to encourage public participation in discussions and decision-making processes related to the development and deployment of advanced AI systems. This ensures that a wide range of perspectives and concerns are considered, while also encouraging ongoing debate over social, economic, ethical, and safety implications that could arise from developing superintelligent systems. Part of this debate may start as early as high school, with the Montana Digital Academy now offering courses covering AI history and ethics to high school students in the U.S., for example.

Other public initiatives include the United Nations AI for Good Global Summit, the Center for AI Safety's 2023 statement raising the risk of extinction from AI as a global priority, and the Future of Life Institute's open letter calling for AI companies to pause training AI models more powerful than GPT-4 for at least 6 months (which OpenAI has not signed). As a signee of the Future of Life Institute's open letter, Elon Musk has also launched a new company called xAI, with the mission of offering pragmatic alternatives to pausing the development of superintelligence.

With each new AI breakthrough, we can expect to see more non-government initiatives and public activities discussing the role and threat of AI, with the overall aim of ensuring that AI remains aligned with societal values and priorities.

Key Takeaways

1) Narrow AI, general AI, and superintelligent AI form the three potential stages of AI development. Narrow AI is designed for specific tasks, while general AI possesses broad cognitive capabilities similar to humans, and superintelligent AI surpasses human intelligence.

2) There are serious concerns regarding the control and alignment of superintelligent AI to ensure that it aligns with human goals and values.

3) It is difficult to discuss and imagine the future of AI without tackling the issue of the Singularity, which predicts a future point where the human race is overtaken and potentially overrun by AI agents.

4) It's important to discuss the potential implications of superintelligence and introduce early precautionary measures despite the absence of scientific proof.

Thought Exercises

1) What are your instincts regarding the possibility of the Singularity? Also, what alternative perspectives or potential developments are we overlooking?

2) What measures, if any, can humans take to prevent the Singularity from becoming a reality?

## 5

MACHINE LEARNING

No matter where your exploration of AI takes you, the path will invariably intersect with the field of machine learning. Whether it's forecasting stock prices, detecting fraudulent transactions, or powering speech recognition in virtual assistants, machine learning provides the foundation for many common AI systems.

As a subfield of AI, the power of machine learning lies in its ability to learn from data and make predictions without being directly programmed. Given a set of inputs, the model will make a prediction about what it thinks will happen next based on the patterns learned from existing data. This might involve predicting the price of a house based on features such as its location, size, year built, and sales history.

This process of learning and understanding patterns in the data is known as *training*, whereby an algorithm is fed data, called a training set, and studies that data in order to learn patterns. If we take the example of a house price prediction model, the algorithm is shown many examples of houses alongside their actual price value. The algorithm learns the relationship between the features of the houses (the inputs) and their price valuation (the output). After learning this relationship, it can predict the price of a new house based on its input features using what's called a *model* or *prediction model*. The model is a mathematical representation that maps all the input features to an output value, such as the qualities of a house and its market value. The goal of training is to find the best model, which is the one that most accurately captures the relationship between the inputs and the output.

It's crucial to realize that perfect alignment with the existing data is not necessarily the goal of designing a reliable model. This stems from a common pitfall in machine learning, known as *overfitting*. This occurs when a model is fine-tuned to the nuances and noise of the training data to such an extent that it captures insignificant and random fluctuations in the data. While this results in exceptional performance when tested against the training dataset, it leads to a drastic decline in the model's ability to generalize new and unseen data. In its pursuit of achieving the best fit on the training data, the model fails to encapsulate the underlying relationships that are universally true beyond that training data. In sum, the model has memorized the training data rather than learning the underlying patterns.

Thus, the objective of machine learning is to find a balance—one that fits the training data well enough to capture the true patterns and relationships without mirroring its exact patterns and noise. Striking this balance between a model's capacity to learn from data and not overfitting or overlearning is one of the biggest challenges in machine learning and requires careful model design, data handling, and evaluation methodologies.

In regard to model design, there are three overarching techniques that we will explore in this chapter, starting with supervised learning.

Supervised Learning

Supervised learning is a type of machine learning where the algorithm learns from a labeled dataset. Here, "labeled" means that the training data includes both the inputs and the correct outputs. The house price prediction example is a case of supervised learning because the model is trained on a dataset of houses for which the input features (i.e., land size, year built, etc.) and output feature (house price) are already known and included in the dataset.

Explanatory Variables				Target	
Land Size (ft)	Year Built	Distance to City (miles)	No. of Rooms	House Price (USD)	
5000	1990	10	4	300000	Labeled
6000	2005	5	5	450000	
7500	1985	15	3	280000	
5500	2010	3	6	500000	
4800	2000	8	4	400000	
6200	1995	12	5		Unlabeled

Figure 4: Labeled vs. unlabeled data

As another example, consider the model for predicting the quickest route from point A to point B in Tokyo. First, you need a labeled dataset that includes numerous examples of routes from various points to various other points, along with information about how long each route took. The label in this case is the time it took for each route. The machine learning model, through training, would then learn to associate different factors such as distance, number of turns, speed limits, and other route characteristics with the time taken. Once trained, and given a new pair of start and end points, the model is able to predict the quickest route based on patterns learned from past examples.

In essence, supervised learning is giving the model all the information it needs so that it can decipher relationships between the input features and a given output, such as house price or travel time.

Unsupervised Learning

Unsupervised learning deals with unlabeled data. The model still has access to different input variables but no corresponding outputs. In this case, you might have the same dataset describing house features, including land size and the number of rooms, but no information about the sale price. As a result, it's impossible to predict the value of houses without this missing variable. Unsupervised learning, therefore, looks at other ways of exploring the data.

In general, the goal of unsupervised learning is to find structure in the data, such as grouping similar variables together. Building on an earlier example, let's say you have access to the GPS data for thousands of taxi trips in Tokyo including travel times and addresses but no labels about popular pickup and drop-off points.

Using unsupervised learning techniques, you could use this data to explore and discover the structure within it. For example, you might identify clusters of trips that start or end in certain areas, effectively identifying popular pick-up and drop-off points. Likewise, you might discover recurring patterns in the data, such as specific routes that are frequently taken, essentially learning the main thoroughfares without ever being explicitly told what the main roads in Tokyo are.

This ability to discover unlabeled relationships means that unsupervised learning algorithms can also be used in advance of supervised learning to prepare the data for prediction modeling. When used in this way, unsupervised algorithms help to clean up and label the data.

Reinforcement Learning

Opposite to unsupervised learning, reinforcement learning is told the output but needs to learn the inputs (which are unknown).

Used in various fields, including robotics, game playing, and navigation, reinforcement learning allows the model to learn by performing actions in a defined environment and receiving rewards or punishments based on its decisions.

In reinforcement learning, the learning process is guided by the goal of maximizing the total reward. To explain, let's consider a self-driving car that needs to navigate from point A to point B. The car has a map of the city and a GPS signal, but it needs to learn how to drive to the destination on its own. In reinforcement learning, the self-driving car would learn by trial and error. It might start with random actions and receive a reward or penalty based on how well it performed. If it takes a shorter route, it might get a reward. If it violates traffic rules or takes a longer route, it might receive a penalty. Over time, by trying to maximize its total reward, the self-driving car would learn to effectively navigate the city.

Due to the exploratory nature of reinforcement learning, such models require significantly more time and computing power than other forms of machine learning to train.

Model Design

It's vital to remember that the model techniques discussed are not easily interchangeable. Each technique is tailored to solving a specific type of problem using a given dataset and their use cases don't tend to overlap.

Supervised learning, for example, is the go-to approach when you have a lot of labeled data, in which you know both the input features and the target output. For example, if you're developing an email spam filter and you have a dataset with emails (input) that are already labeled as "spam" or "not spam" (target output), supervised learning is an ideal technique for this task.

Unsupervised learning comes into play when you have plenty of input data but no corresponding output labels. The main goal is to uncover hidden patterns, clusters, or structures within the data. If you're tasked with customer segmentation as part of a marketing analytics project, unsupervised learning methods like clustering can help identify groups of similar customers based on their purchasing behaviors or preferences, for example. In its place, supervised learning would not be a suitable approach for discovering these unknown customer categories given there are no existing labels.

Reinforcement learning, meanwhile, is suitable for situations where a model learns to make decisions by interacting in an environment with a finite number of sequential decision actions. For instance, if you're designing a system for playing chess or a video game, reinforcement learning would be a prime candidate as it allows the AI to learn optimal strategies over time through trial and error. Reinforcement learning, though, cannot be used to predict house prices or categorize emails into spam or non-spam as these tasks don't involve sequential decision-making within a confined environment.

In summary, the choice between supervised, unsupervised, and reinforcement learning is not a matter of superiority or preference, but rather a matter of fit. It's about selecting the technique that aligns with the data you have, the computer processing resources available, and the problem you are attempting to solve. Making the right choice can make the difference between a successful AI project and one that is destined to fail before you even start.

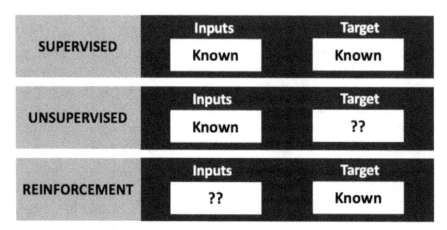

Figure 5: Machine learning techniques

Practical Demonstration

To reinforce the difference between supervised, unsupervised, and reinforcement learning, let's explore three different model scenarios. To help with this practical demonstration, we will be using a hypothetical dataset, belonging to a fictional video game. In this video game, players control a character to collect items, avoid enemies, and maximize their score within a limited time period.

Variables:
PlayerID (unique identifier for each player)
Items_Collected (number of items the player's character collected)
Enemies_Avoided (number of enemies the player's character avoided)

Time_Taken (time in seconds taken to complete a mission)
Score (points earned by the player, based on items, enemies, and time taken

PlayerID	Items_Collected	Enemies_Avoided	Time_Taken	Score
001	10	5	100	125
002	8	4	85	117
003	9	3	120	87
004	10	5	120	104
005	8	3	100	95
006	4	9	140	60
007	6	8	120	83

This dataset has five variables, also known as features or dimensions, and seven rows of values. Please note that this dataset is for illustrative purposes; in real-world scenarios, you would need a much larger dataset with many more rows in order to train a credible model.

Model 1: Supervised Learning

Objective: Predict the Score of a player given the other features
Explanatory variables: Items_Collected, Enemies_Avoided, Time_Taken
Target variable: Score

Steps
1. Divide the dataset into a training set (75%) and a test set (25%)
2. Choose an algorithm: In this case, a regression algorithm such as linear regression is a good choice because the target variable (Score) is a continuous variable.

3. Train the algorithm on the training data to build a model, which works by finding the correlation between different explanatory variables and the target variable.

4. Test the model on the test data to see how well it predicts the target variable (Score) using the remaining unused data.

5) Measure the accuracy using an evaluation metric such as Mean Squared Error (MSE), which is the average of the squares of the differences between the actual and predicted values.

6) Use the trained model to predict future data.

Model 2: Unsupervised Learning

Objective: Group players into clusters based on their playing style
Explanatory variables: Time_Taken, Score
Target variable: N/A (unknown)

Steps

1) Choose a clustering algorithm, such as k-means clustering.

2) Decide on the number of clusters/groups, i.e. $k = 3$.[8]

3) Train the algorithm on the explanatory variables. (There is no training-test data split in unsupervised learning.)

4) Analyze the clusters to see which players fall into which cluster and interpret the characteristics of each cluster. For example, we might find that the three clusters represent: aggressive players, balanced players, and defensive players.

---

[8] As an explanatory technique, there are no fixed rules for determining the number of clusters to analyze. Note that if you set k to the same number of data points contained in the dataset, each data point automatically becomes a standalone cluster. Conversely, if you set k to 1, then all data points will be deemed as homogenous and fall inside one large cluster. You, therefore, want to avoid using a k value close to 1 or close to the maximum number of data points.

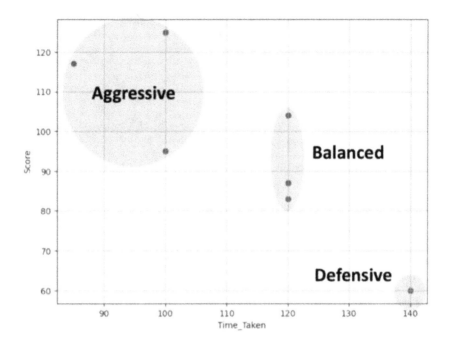

These three new categories can now be used to label each player in the dataset, providing a new variable/feature that we didn't know previously.

PlayerID	Items_Collected	Enemies_Avoided	Time_Taken	Score	Type
001	10	5	100	125	Aggressive
002	8	4	85	117	Aggressive
003	9	3	120	87	Balanced
004	10	5	120	104	Balanced
005	8	3	100	95	Aggressive
006	4	9	140	60	Defensive
007	6	8	120	83	Balanced

Model 3: Reinforcement Learning

Objective: Develop an AI agent that can play the game and maximize the Score value.

Explanatory variables: Move left, move right, jump, crouch, advance forward

Target variable: Score

Steps

1) Define the state space: A combination of the player's position, items left, enemies nearby, etc.

2) Define the action space: Move left, move right, jump, crouch, advance forward.

3) Define the reward: For example, +50 for collecting an item, -50 for colliding with an enemy, and +100 for passing the mission.

4) Use an algorithm like Q-learning to train the agent. The agent will play the game multiple times. In the beginning, it will play randomly and make many mistakes.

5) Over time, the agent will learn the optimal strategy to play the game and maximize Score.

Other Approaches

In addition to the three approaches we have discussed, there are two other machine learning approaches that lie between supervised and unsupervised learning, called *semi-supervised learning* and *self-supervised learning*.

In the case of semi-supervised learning, there is typically a large amount of data but only some of it is actually labeled. The idea is to use the labeled data to train an initial model and make predictions on the unlabeled data. The most confident predictions are then used to label the unlabeled data and expand the labeled training set. The prediction model can then be retrained on the combination of the originally labeled and the self-labeled data. In this way, semi-supervised learning seeks to benefit from the additional (albeit imperfectly labeled) data. For instance, you might have GPS data for millions of taxi rides but only have the route times for a few thousand of those rides. Using the known route times to train an initial model, you can then use that model to predict the route times for rides missing that variable based on their start point, end point, and other variables such as the day of the week.

In the case of self-supervised learning, all data is considered unlabeled, but the structure within the data is used to provide supervision. In other words, the training labels are automatically generated from the input data itself, without human annotation. This is done by creating a learning task where the objective is to predict some part of the input data. For example, a self-supervised learning algorithm may learn to predict the next word in a sentence or the next frame in a video. The goal is to design a task where the correct answer is available, allowing the model to learn from the data directly.

A real-world example of self-supervised learning is the masked language model training objective used in transformer-based language models such as Google's BERT (Bidirectional Encoder Representations from Transformers). During training, some portion of the input data such as a word in a sentence is masked, and the model is trained to predict the masked word based on the rest of the sentence. This allows the model to learn useful features about language from the data itself, without requiring explicit labels for each example.

Another common example comes from the field of computer vision, where a portion of an image might be obscured and the model is tasked with predicting the missing part. In this case, the model takes an image and purposedly obscures a part of it, like covering a portion of the image with a black box. The model then predicts what's hidden behind the black box by analyzing the surrounding context and making an educated guess. For instance, if the covered area is around a person's face, the model might predict that it's likely a face. As the model is exposed to more images, it learns to predict more hidden parts. Through this process, the model becomes better at recognizing objects, patterns, and relationships without explicit labels for every image.

In summary, semi-supervised learning is used when you have some labeled data and lots of unlabeled data, while self-supervised learning can be used on data without preexisting labels to predict hidden features.

Key Takeaways

1) Machine learning allows systems to learn from data and make predictions without explicit programming.

2) Training involves feeding a machine learning algorithm a dataset to learn patterns and relationships. The goal is to find a model that accurately captures the underlying patterns without overfitting the training data.

3) There are three primary types of machine learning models:

- Supervised learning uses labeled data with known inputs and outputs to train the model.

- Unsupervised learning deals with known inputs and aims to discover hidden patterns and structures within the data to create a new output.

- Reinforcement learning involves learning through trial and error in an environment with rewards and punishments in order to achieve a predefined output.

4) Model selection depends on the type of data you have available and the problem you are attempting to solve.

Thought Exercises

1) What is a use case for supervised learning? (Hint: think of a website that makes a prediction based on past data)

2) What is a use case for unsupervised learning? (Hint: think of a model for sorting items)

3) What is a use case for reinforcement learning? (Hint: think of a game or closed environment with a limited number of potential actions)

## 6

DEEP LEARNING

From self-driving cars to large language models, the ability of deep learning to learn from raw data and process large datasets has revolutionized AI. However, like all technologies, deep learning has its own unique limitations and challenges that we will examine in this chapter.

Before we dive in further, it's important to explain the connection between deep learning and machine learning. Machine learning, as discussed, involves algorithms and models that improve with experience and exposure to data. As a subfield of machine learning, deep learning takes the foundational principles of machine learning and applies its own techniques to larger and more complex datasets. This involves the use of artificial neural networks with deep and multiple layers stacked together to form a model.

While artificial neural networks are not a direct replica of the human brain, (with the human brain estimated to contain 100 billion neurons, outnumbering the number of stars in the galaxy, and more than one thousand kilometers of interconnections), they are loosely inspired by it. Artificial neural networks consist of interconnected nodes or neurons that process information and pass it on to the next layer of neurons—similar to how neurons in the brain process and pass on information. The first layer of neurons in the network, for example, might recognize basic features in images, such as edges. The next layer might put these edges together to recognize shapes, the layer after that might recognize fur patterns, and so on, until the final layer recognizes the overall image as a cat.

Like machine learning, deep learning contains supervised, unsupervised, and reinforcement learning techniques. In the case of supervised learning, a neural network, such as a convolutional neural network, can be trained to recognize images by studying a large number of labeled images (with the labels describing the image) and learning to identify the labeled objects contained in those images.

In the case of unsupervised learning, deep learning is often used to simplify and reduce the dimensionality (number of features) in the data or remove noise from it. In reinforcement deep learning, neural networks are combined with reinforcement learning techniques to create systems that can learn to make a sequence of decisions. An example is the AlphaGo program developed by DeepMind, which learned to play the game of Go at a superhuman level by studying past games played by humans (supervised learning) as well as games played against itself (reinforcement learning).

Deep Learning Models

There are different types of neural networks employed in deep learning, each with its own unique strengths and common use cases. In this section, we will examine convolutional and recurrent neural networks as well as transformer networks, which play a major role in NLP and computer vision and are discussed in Chapter 7 and Chapter 10 respectively.

Convolutional Neural Networks

CNNs represent a major advancement in the field of computer vision, enabling machines to see and interpret visual data. The name "convolutional" comes from the mathematical operation by the same name, which is a specialized type of linear operation that is often utilized for image processing.

From facial recognition to self-driving cars, CNNs are integral to computer vision and other AI applications. As a go-to option for analyzing visual data, CNNs excel at identifying spatial hierarchies or patterns in images by processing small chunks of the image, allowing them to recognize complex shapes and structures. Prior to CNNs, image data was typically fed into neural networks as one-dimensional arrays.[9]

This, however, reduced the spatial information contained in the image. To elaborate, images are two-dimensional structures, consisting of rows and columns of pixels. Each pixel represents a value that represents the color or intensity at that specific location in the image. To process an image using a traditional neural network, the image is transformed into a one-dimensional array, also known as a vector. This transformation involves concatenating (meaning "joining") the rows or columns of the image into a linear sequence of values.

As an example, let's say we have a grayscale image of dimensions 64x64 pixels. Each pixel in the image represents a grayscale intensity ranging from 0 to 255. By flattening this image into a one-dimensional array, we obtain a sequence of 4,096 values, where each value represents the intensity of a pixel. By representing the image as a one-dimensional array, we can feed it into a neural network as input, which then processes that array and performs computations on the values of each element.

While flattening the image into a one-dimensional array simplifies the representation of the image, it also eliminates the spatial structure and relationships between neighboring pixels. This loss of spatial information can limit the ability of the neural network to capture complex patterns and spatial dependencies within images. Recognizing a face, for instance, isn't just about identifying individual facial features like the eyes, nose, or mouth, but also understanding their relative positions to each other. Traditional neural networks, though, fail to effectively account for such spatial hierarchy between features.

To overcome this limitation, CNNs preserve the spatial structure of images by operating directly on the two-dimensional or three-dimensional representations of images, allowing them to capture

---

[9] A one-dimensional array, also known as a vector, is a data structure that stores elements in a linear sequence where the elements are arranged in a single row or a single column.

local patterns, spatial hierarchy, and spatial relationships between features. Unlike traditional neural networks, CNNs maintain the spatial relationships between pixels by learning image features using small squares of input data. This method is less sensitive to object position and distortion within the image, enabling the model to recognize an object even if its appearance varies in some way. For example, when a CNN is trained to recognize a turtle, it learns to detect distinctive features like the shape of the shell, the presence of flippers, and the general body structure. These collections of features are consistently present across different images of turtles, irrespective of their overall positions or poses. By capturing the spatial relationships among these features, the CNN can effectively generalize and recognize turtles, regardless of whether they are crawling, standing, or partially hidden inside their shell.

In terms of their design, CNNs consist of a series of layers that filter the raw pixel data of an image to extract and learn higher-level features, which the model can then use for classification. Higher-level features refer to visual elements that are built upon simpler features detected in earlier layers, such as edges, lines, and textures. In other words, the earlier layers capture basic visual elements that are present in the input images and as the information flows through subsequent layers of the network, higher-level features are learned by combining and abstracting these low-level features.

Another important aspect of CNNs is the pooling layers that follow the convolutional layers. When passing an image through a CNN, it goes through several layers that detect different features like edges, shapes, and objects. As mentioned, these features are combined to understand what's present in the image. However, the information can be quite detailed, which can make the network overly complex and slow to run. Pooling layers solve this problem by reducing the dimensionality of the data. This involves summarizing and preserving the most relevant information, which results in a more manageable and efficient representation. By compressing the information, pooling decreases the size of the data and the number of calculations needed, speeding up the overall network. Pooling layers also make the network more robust by focusing on important features rather than their exact position. This enables the network to recognize objects even if they appear slightly shifted or in different parts of the image.

Recurrent Neural Networks

Renowned for their inherent ability to remember, RNNs have been central to groundbreaking developments in various fields including natural language processing, speech recognition, and time series prediction.

Popularized by John Hopfield in the early 1980s, RNNs were originally designed to overcome the limitations of existing artificial neural networks. Notably, traditional feed-forward neural networks, including CNNs, are not designed to deal with sequential inputs. (A feedforward neural network is an artificial neural network where connections between the decision nodes do not form a loop or cycle).

For tasks such as language translation, speech recognition, or time-series prediction, the order of the inputs often carries crucial information, and the ability to handle sequences is a key requirement. While traditional neural networks assume that all inputs (and outputs) are independent of each other, RNNs leverage the sequential nature of their input data. By processing inputs in sequence and having a form of memory, they can account for the context provided by preceding elements. This makes them excel at tasks where the sequence and context matter, such as sentences or time series data. They achieve this by creating loops that pass information from one step in the sequence to the next, effectively possessing a form of memory. Each neuron or unit in an RNN has a "hidden state" which acts as a form of memory. This hidden state is a function of the current input and the previous hidden state, allowing the network to retain information from prior inputs in the sequence.

Let's take the task of predicting the next word in a sentence as an example. A feed-forward network might be given a fixed number of previous words and be trained to predict the next, but it would treat these input words independently, ignoring the order in which they appear. An RNN, on the other hand, would process the sentence word by word, retaining information from previous words as it goes along, thereby capturing the sequence's context.

RNNs, however, have their own limitations, and chief among these is the *vanishing gradient problem*. The vanishing gradient problem occurs when a deep neural network struggles to learn and make meaningful updates to its weights during training. This happens because the gradients (slopes) of the loss function for the network's weights become extremely small as they are passed backward through the layers (backpropagation). These gradients are calculated by multiplying the gradients from the subsequent layers with the weights connecting the current layer. As the network becomes deeper, this multiplication can lead to a situation where the gradients diminish significantly as they propagate backward through multiple layers. This can result in very small gradient values, leading to slow weight updates or adjustments. As a result, the network makes only tiny adjustments to its weights and it either takes a very long time to complete or it fails to learn complex patterns in the data.

To gain a clearer grasp of this concept, it helps to think of the neural network as a hiker trying to find the best path to reach their destination. The network adjusts its path (which is the weights) by looking at how much the slope (which is the gradient) changes. If the slope is steep, it means there's a lot to learn, so the network makes bigger adjustments to its path. If the slope is gentle, it means there's not much to learn, so the network only makes small changes to its path. In some cases, especially with deep networks or long sequences like in RNNs, the slopes can become very small. When this happens, the network gets stuck because the slope can't make meaningful adjustments to its path (which is the weights). Similar to a hiker struggling on a flat mountain path, the network might take forever to learn and fail to understand complex patterns in the data.

As a more practical example, imagine that you are training a neural network to identify various types of animals in images. When the network faces tricky examples such as a zebra, the gradient is already extremely tiny, which reflects how much the model should fine-tune its internal settings to improve its recognition. As a result, the network learns at a sluggish pace or it may even become stuck and fail to accurately recognize animal images that are difficult to classify.

In the context of RNNs, the vanishing gradient problem makes it difficult for the model to learn long-range dependencies in the data (discussed also in Chapter 7) because it struggles to learn relationships between inputs that are distanced apart. For instance, in a language processing task, an RNN might find it challenging to connect information from the beginning of a long sentence with relevant words or phrases at the end of the sentence. This happens because the RNN's ability to remember and use information from earlier inputs gets weaker with more added inputs.

This problem has led to the development of more advanced types of RNNs like long short-term memory (LSTM) and gated recurrent unit (GRU), which introduce gates to control the flow of information and help mitigate this issue. Acting as a switch, a gate is a mechanism that controls the flow of information within the network. It determines how much information should be passed through and how much information should be blocked or forgotten at each step. This allows the model to selectively retain important information and which helps to mitigate the vanishing gradient problem.

This architecture has proven extremely effective, enabling RNNs to tackle complex and nuanced tasks in NLP, including machine translation, sentiment analysis, text summarization, and language generation.

Transformer Networks

Transformer networks represent a significant leap forward in dealing with sequential data and especially in the field of natural language processing. By focusing on the parts of the data that matter most and processing sequences more efficiently, they have opened a new paradigm in deep learning.

Transformer networks were formally introduced in a 2017 paper published by Google titled *Attention is All You Need*. They were designed primarily to address the shortcomings of existing models in handling sequential data, especially in the field of NLP. Prior to the introduction of transformers, recurrent neural networks and their variants such as long short-term memory and gated recurrent unit were the dominant models for sequential data tasks. While these models performed well, they processed sequences in a linear manner, considering one element at a time. This approach resulted in two problems: computational inefficiency and difficulty in capturing long-distance dependencies in the data.

First, sequential processing made it challenging and slow to effectively parallelize computations during training. Second, even though LSTMs and GRUs were designed to mitigate the vanishing gradient problem of standard RNNs and better capture long-range dependencies, they still struggled with very long sequences.

Transformer networks were thus developed to tackle these two issues. They introduced a mechanism called *attention*, which allows the model to weigh the relevance of different elements in the input sequence when producing an output, thus enabling it to focus more on important parts and less on others.

This mechanism is useful in NLP, where the meaning of a word can depend heavily on its context in a sentence or document. For instance, consider the following English sentence: "I took the dog that bit me to the vet". In this sentence, the word bit" is closely related to "dog" and me", while "vet" is more relevant to "I" and "took". A transformer model uses attention mechanisms to determine these dependencies. It assigns higher weights to "dog" and "me" when processing "bit" and higher weights to "I" and "took" when processing "vet". Moreover, if we were translating this sentence into a language like German, where the verb often comes at the end of the sentence, the transformer's attention mechanism would allow it to associate the verb in English with the corresponding verb in German, even though they are in different positions within their respective sentences.

Importantly, transformer models can compute the attention weights for all elements of the sequence in parallel, leading to significant improvements in computational efficiency. Moreover, by directly attending to all other words in the sequence, regardless of their position, transformer models capture both short-term and long-term dependencies contained within the data.

This architecture has proven extremely effective at natural language processing tasks with the ability to process entire sentences or even paragraphs at once—instead of sequentially. Specifically, they make use of the attention mechanism to weigh the importance of different words in understanding the context of a sentence. This has resulted in state-of-the-art models like GPT (generative pretrained transformer) by OpenAI and BERT by Google. These models, pre-trained on a large database of text and fine-tuned for specific tasks, have significantly advanced the field, demonstrating human-level performance on a range of different benchmarks.

Challenges

In general, building and training any type of deep learning network, especially reinforcement learning-based models, requires substantial computation and processing resources. This includes processing massive amounts of data and performing complex calculations that necessitate considerable memory and powerful graphical processing units. However, recent technological advancements and cloud-based solutions have made these resources more affordable and accessible, enabling more parties to participate in deep learning.

Deep learning models also thrive on data and the explosion of digital data in recent decades has provided important fuel for these data-hungry models. However, the quality of data is important too. Erroneous or biased data, for instance, can lead to misleading results or reinforce existing biases. In addition, deep learning models contain a tendency to model intricate patterns in the training data, which can be a strength as well as a potential weakness. There's a risk that models might overfit the training data, learning noise and specific details that don't generalize well to unseen data.

However, perhaps the biggest challenge within the domain of deep learning is the black box nature of these models. In general, it's difficult to understand why a particular prediction was made and this is problematic in scenarios like healthcare or judiciary scenarios where transparency and trust are crucial. As discussed in Chapter 3, efforts are ongoing in the field of explainable AI to make these models more transparent and interpretable.

Understanding these strengths and weaknesses is critical when deciding on potential uses for deep learning. Businesses without access to massive troves of data and GPU resources, for instance, may not be suitable candidates for deep learning, especially if they need a model that is transparent and easy to visualize.

Key Takeaways

1) Deep learning is an advanced subfield of machine learning that uses artificial neural networks with deep and multiple layers to learn and model complex patterns in data.

2) Deep learning models include convolutional neural networks (CNNs), recurrent neural networks (RNNs), and transformer networks. Each has its own strengths and use cases.

3) Due to the complexity of the neural networks and the large amount of data they handle, deep learning models require substantial computational resources. Deep learning models can suffer from limitations such as the black box nature of their decision-making process and the risk of overfitting patterns in the training data.

## 7

NATURAL LANGUAGE PROCESSING

Beyond numerical data, a vast amount of human knowledge and experience is captured in text and audio. The ubiquity of words in daily life and the need for effective human-computer interaction make the ability to process human language a crucial part of artificial intelligence.

As a multidisciplinary field straddling linguistics, computer science, and AI, natural language processing gives computers the capability to understand and reproduce human language.

Inspired by linguistics—the study of language and semantics—NLP was originally designed for parsing text in databases using coding rule systems, but over time, it merged with common algorithms from machine learning to evolve into a novel and specialized field of computational linguistics. Now, as a field of its own, NLP involves analyzing human language with reduced emphasis on quantitative problem-solving which is typically the focus of other AI subfields.

Early Development

To grasp the significance of recent developments in NLP, it's important to see what's changed and where it all began.

Initially, NLP consisted of human-programmed rule-based systems, where linguistic experts would manually encode rules of language into a computer program. While some of these early approaches recorded success in domain-specific areas, they were largely limited by the complexity and variability of human language. One example is ELIZA, which was one of the first chatbots developed in the 1960s by Joseph Weizenbaum at MIT. This included a version of ELIZA designed to emulate a psychotherapist using its ability to reflect user statements back in the form of a question, as demonstrated in this example.

Input: I am feeling sad.

Output: I see, can you tell me more about why you are feeling sad?

If a user said, "I am feeling sad", ELIZA might respond by saying, "I see, can you tell me more about why you are feeling sad?" While the output was impressive at the time, the ELIZA chatbox was simply following predefined rules and appearing more intelligent than it actually was—especially as it didn't understand the underlying context of the conversation.

During the late 1980s and 1990s, NLP research evolved with the introduction of machine learning methods. Rather than relying on hard-coded rules, new methods using statistical-based models to learn patterns from large amounts of labeled data came into the scene. This development significantly improved overall performance and broadened the scope of tasks that NLP researchers could handle.

Despite several advancements, these methods still had limitations. Notably, they relied on carefully engineered features derived from expert knowledge, which was labor-intensive and unable to fully capture the richness and subtlety of human language. In addition, these methods struggled to capture longer-range dependencies within a text, which refers to the relationship between words or elements in a sentence that aren't adjacent or close together but still influence meaning. To explain how, consider the following example.

Input: The girl, who was wearing a red hat that her mother bought her for her birthday last year, ran down the street.

Here, the main subject ("The girl") and the main action ("ran down the street") are separated by a long clause ("who was wearing a red hat that her mother bought her for her birthday last year"). Despite this distance, we can understand that it is the girl who is running, not the mother or the hat. Traditional NLP methods, however, struggled to capture and understand this type of long-range dependency.

Moreover, traditional NLP methods lacked the ability to leverage distributed representations, a method of symbolizing words as vectors in high-dimensional space. This approach, commonly known as *word embeddings*, enables semantically similar words to exist closer together, thereby enriching the understanding of textual data.

To understand this approach, think of a high-dimensional space as a coordinate system where each word has its own position. Words with similar meanings or usage, such as "cat" and "dog", tend to position close to each other because they share a similar semantic meaning related to animals. Likewise, words like "AI" and "artificial intelligence" would also be close together because they share the same meaning. These close relationships in a high-dimensional space are called vectors or word embeddings, which resemble an ordered list of numerical values. Using these word embeddings, NLP models are capable of understanding relationships between words and capturing their contextual meaning. This allows the models to see similarities and differences between words and make more accurate predictions or enhance their overall understanding.

As mentioned, traditional NLP methods struggled to analyze vectors in a high-dimensional space. This limitation and the need to overcome it finally led to the adoption of newer, more sophisticated deep learning architectures such as recurrent neural networks and transformer networks. Designed to examine the full context and multiple sentences at a time, these techniques exhibited a superior ability to handle longer-range dependencies in text, marking a major breakthrough in the field of NLP.

Transformer networks are now used heavily in NLP models including OpenAI's GPT model and Google's BERT model. In recent years, NLP has also benefited from several other emerging trends. One is the development of zero-shot learning, where models learn to generalize using fewer examples. Using these methods, NLP models can learn to understand and generate language even with minimal labeled examples. This can be especially useful when labeled data is scarce, which is often the case for less common and low-resource languages.

In practice, rather than relying solely on labeled examples, zero-shot learning leverages auxiliary information or semantic relationships to make predictions on new, unfamiliar classes. In other words, rather than training the model on multiple examples for every class, the model is first trained on a smaller selection of classes. Then, when it is presented with a completely new class that it hasn't seen before, the model uses the hints and relationships it learned from the initial training to form predictions.

In effect, this allows the model to generalize and perform tasks in domains it wasn't explicitly trained on. As an example, imagine you have a model that has learned to identify different animal classes, but the model has never seen a zebra before. Using zero-shot learning, if the model knows that zebras are similar to horses but they have black and white stripes, the model can recognize a zebra without ever seeing any direct examples of a zebra. In this case, the class "zebra" is already labeled in the dataset as a horse with black and white stripes.

Another promising trend has been self-supervised learning, which has been one of the driving forces behind the success of large language models such as GPT. This approach describes models that learn representations from unlabeled data, leveraging the abundant unannotated text available on the Internet.

In the context of GPT and large language models, learning involves two main steps: pretraining and fine-tuning. In the pretraining phase, the model is exposed to a massive collection of text, such as books, articles, and web pages. The model learns to predict the next word in a sentence based on the preceding context, such as the following example.

Input: "The cat sat on the _____"

In this example, the model needs to predict the next word after "the", which might be a word like "mat". The process repeats for numerous sentences in the dataset, exposing the model to a range of words and contexts. Through the process of self-learning, the model learns to capture the statistical patterns and relationships contained in the text. It learns that after "The cat sat on the", words like "mat", "chair", or "floor" are likely to follow based on patterns observed from the training data.

By continuously training on a diverse range of sentences, the model gradually develops a strong understanding of language. It learns to recognize grammatical structures, understand the meaning of different words, and grasp the contextual relationships between words. This pretraining phase helps the model acquire a broad knowledge of language, allowing it to generate coherent and contextually relevant responses in conversations.

After pretraining, the model enters the fine-tuning phase. During this phase, the model is trained on specific supervised tasks with labeled data. For example, it can be fine-tuned on a conversational dataset where inputs and corresponding responses are provided. By training on this labeled data, the model learns to generate appropriate responses based on different inputs.

NLU & NLG

To understand NLP in greater depth, we can divide it into two different approaches: natural language understanding (NLU) and natural language generation (NLG). NLU enables a model to comprehend and derive meaning from human language, while NLG empowers a model to generate coherent and contextually appropriate text. This involves creating entire sentences, paragraphs, or even entire articles. NLG can be used for tasks such as generating descriptions of data, writing news stories, summarizing text, or creating conversational agents (known as chatbots). The core process involves determining what information to include and how to organize it (document planning), before putting the information into appropriate sentences (sentence planning), and then realizing the sentence plans in the actual text (text realization).

NLU, meanwhile, aims to extract meaning, sentiment, intent, and other semantic features from the text to perform sentiment analysis, named entity recognition, or text classification.

In terms of their application, both approaches start with raw, unstructured text data. This data emanates from various sources such as databases, APIs, scraped website content, user inputs, and chat logs. As with any data processing data, the raw data is cleaned, which usually involves removing inconsistencies, inaccuracies, or irrelevant information. Depending on the source of the data, this could involve tasks such as reformatting and removing or correcting errors in the data.

Using a variety of techniques and preprocessing algorithms, the text is converted into a structured format that machines can process and understand. This involves tasks such as tokenization (breaking text into individual words or tokens), stemming (reducing words to their root form, i.e., "naturally" > "nature"), and removing stop words (common words such as "and", "the", "a" that don't provide informational value) as well as unnecessary white spaces.

Natural Language Understanding

After transforming the text into a suitable format, various tasks can take place. In the case of natural language understanding, common tasks include topic modeling, sentiment analysis, named entity recognition, and text classification. Sentiment analysis involves determining the sentiment or emotion of a sentence or document, usually categorized as positive, negative, or neutral. Named entity recognition identifies and classifies named entities (i.e., persons, organizations, locations) in a text. Text classification classifies text into predefined categories, such as spam detection in emails and categorizing news articles. Lastly, as an unsupervised learning approach, topic modeling is used to discover abstract topics within a text document.

After undertaking one or more of these tasks, the model is evaluated based on appropriate metrics (such as accuracy, precision, recall, F1-score) to measure its performance. Then, once the model is evaluated and fine-tuned, it is deployed in real-world applications and used to make decisions. Common examples include chatbots and virtual assistants such as Apple's Siri, Google Assistant, and Amazon's Alexa. These applications employ NLP to understand user commands and generate appropriate responses, enabling users to set reminders, search the Internet, control home devices, and so forth. In the realm of social media, NLU is used for sentiment analysis, helping businesses understand public sentiment towards their brand by analyzing text data from social media posts or customer reviews. The same technology can also aid in detecting online harassment or toxic behavior on online platforms.

Natural Language Generation

Having discussed common tasks in natural language understanding, let's revisit natural language generation. Following the data preprocessing stage, NLG typically consists of three main stages: document planning, sentence planning, and text realization.

Document planning is the initial stage where the content to be included in the output text is decided. The system identifies the information from the source data that needs to be conveyed in the text. For instance, if an NLG model is generating a weather report, the document planning stage will identify the key data points to be included in the report, such as temperature, precipitation, and humidity. This stage includes organizing the selected content into a coherent structure and determining the order and manner in which the information should be presented.

Sentence planning, known too as *microplanning*, then determines how to express the selected information in linguistic terminology. It decides on the specific words and phrases that can be used to represent the information. It also determines the structure of the sentences, taking into account different aspects such as grammatical correctness, cohesion with surrounding sentences, and variability in expressions to avoid repetitiveness. Using the weather report example, this stage would involve choosing whether to say "It's expected to be sunny" or "Sunshine is predicted", among other considerations.

Lastly, text realization is where the actual text is generated. Here, the system transforms the linguistic representations from the previous stage into a final, fluent text. It ensures proper grammatical structures and pays attention to other aspects of the language such as punctuation and agreement between subjects and verbs. Using the weather report example again, this last step would involve generating the final form such as "Tomorrow, it's expected to be sunny with a high of 25 degrees".

These three stages often involve complex algorithms and rules, and more recently, newer language models such as GPT have proved successful at generating fluent and coherent text, leading to major advances in the field of NLG and generative AI, which we'll discuss in the next chapter.

Challenges

As with other areas of artificial intelligence, NLP is not without a long list of potential challenges and headaches! First, understanding the intricate nuances of human language, including irony, sarcasm, and cultural references, poses a major challenge in the field of NLP.

Second, subtle changes in the text or context can shift the meaning of a word or phrase, and while this is easy for humans to perceive, it is notably difficult for machines to notice and comprehend. One example is the interpretation of homographs, which are words spelled the same but that possess different meanings. The word "bass", for example, can mean a type of fish or a low, deep voice or musical instrument depending on the context. Similarly, the phrase "It's raining cats and dogs" doesn't literally mean animals are falling from the sky. The meaning is something that comes naturally to humans but can be confusing for NLP models.

Issues such as language bias, model interpretability, data privacy, and the lack of high-quality annotated data for low-resource languages are other areas of concern and ongoing development. The issue of bias in NLP is a particularly significant concern. This is because AI models tend to learn and replicate biases in the training data, leading to biased predictions. This is problematic when NLP models are used in sensitive areas like recruitment or loan approval, where biased outcomes can have significant impacts on people's lives.

Ethical considerations, particularly around privacy, are also a crucial concern. Text data, whether from social media, emails, or other sources, often contains sensitive or personal information. Hence, handling this data responsibly, adhering to data privacy regulations, and anonymizing data to protect individual identities are important responsibilities for those involved with building the model.

Lastly, the development of NLP models for low-resource languages and multilingual contexts presents a considerable challenge. While a lot of work in NLP has been done in English, there's a scarcity of high-quality labeled data for many other languages. The lack of resources makes it challenging to develop robust NLP models that can understand and generate text in these languages. Furthermore, creating models that can handle text in multiple languages simultaneously also represents an ongoing challenge in terms of model sophistication and training.

Key Takeaways

1) Natural language processing is a multidisciplinary field that empowers computers to process, understand, and generate human language.

2) NLP can be divided into natural language understanding and natural language generation. NLU concentrates on extracting meaning, sentiment, and other semantic features from the text, while NLG focuses on generating coherent and contextually appropriate text.

3) Challenges in NLP include understanding the intricacies of human language, such as irony and cultural references, language subtlety, addressing bias, ensuring model interpretability, protecting data privacy, and developing NLP models for low-resource languages.

## 8

GENERATIVE AI

In this chapter, we will explore generative AI, looking at how it differs from its traditional counterpart, and explore how its creativity is changing the landscape of content creation, with a particular focus on generative adversarial networks and the need for data.

First, to understand the strengths of generative AI, it's important to understand how it differs from traditional AI. The first difference between generative AI and traditional AI is found in their outputs. Traditional AI, which is sometimes referred to as *discriminative AI*, is trained to discriminate, classify, or predict based on input data fed into a model. This approach powers a variety of AI applications including recommendation systems and search engines. Generative AI, on the other hand, learns the underlying patterns of input data but rather than provide a prediction or insight, it uses that learned knowledge to generate an output that is similar but different from the training data.

ChatGPT, developed by OpenAI, is a prominent example of generative AI. Instead of predicting a probable output to a given input, ChatGPT is designed to generate coherent and contextually appropriate responses, whether that be drafting emails, writing essays, creating poetry, or simulating human dialogue.

Similarly, new software applications such as DALL-E (also developed by OpenAI), Midjourney, and Stable Diffusion are making waves in the domain of art and image generation. Visual outputs can be generated using what's called a generative adversarial network (GAN), a type of generative AI model that consists of two neural networks: a generator and a discriminator.

During training, the generator and discriminator are pitted against each other in a competitive environment. The generator aims to produce realistic outputs that can fool the discriminator, while the discriminator aims to correctly identify whether the outputs are real or generated. In practice, the generator learns the target art style by observing and analyzing a vast dataset of existing artworks. Acting as a type of art critic, the discriminator then evaluates these generated images and issues feedback on their authenticity. Initially, the discriminator can easily identify the generated images as computer-generated due to the lack of resemblance to the training data. Using feedback from the discriminator, the generator adjusts its approach and through multiple feedback loops, the generator improves its ability to produce convincing artwork.

Throughout this entire process, the generator and discriminator are essentially engaged in a competition against each other. The generator aims to produce art that the discriminator cannot distinguish from real artwork, while the discriminator seeks to improve its ability to differentiate between real and fake art. This adversarial competition drives both sides to evolve and learn from each other. Over time, the competition and ongoing feedback loop lead to a point of convergence where the generator becomes so proficient at creating art (resembling the style of the training data) that it deceives the discriminator.

Building on their success in the domain of image generation, researchers are also developing GANs for generating audio, music, writing, and even three-dimensional objects, leading to a further explosion in AI-generated content.

Data as a New Asset Class

Riding the wave of large language models powered by OpenAI's GPT architecture and advances in GAN techniques, generative AI is set to radically transform the physics of content creation and creative expression. From producing full-length films to customer service avatars trained on customer service logs and product documentation, and simulating realistic video game and esports environments, the possibilities are suddenly closer than many people expected.

Underpinning these developments is access to relevant training data, and the growing adoption of generative AI software tools is set to unlock a new dimension of value for existing data. In sports, for example, match data and video footage of professional athletes can be monetized to create new and unique content. While this data has traditionally been used for entertainment and post-match analysis (as popularized in the film and novel *Moneyball*), it can now be commercialized for creative use cases as well.

One example comes from Behaviol, a digital sports company, working on a platform where gamers can acquire and develop AI sports stars to compete in virtual tournaments. The company is starting with cricket, after purchasing five years of player data to train and generate unique AI player avatars. This development marks a departure from traditional sports games, where in-game athletes are limited to preprogrammed actions and fixed behaviors.

Generative AI is being used by Behaviol to study the movements, techniques, and playing styles of real athletes through training AI on match data and video footage. By doing so, Behaviol can recreate the actions, style, and performance of athletes within a virtual environment. This will enable gamers to play alongside AI-generated athletes and make it possible to simulate hypothetical scenarios, such as pitting Michael Jordan against modern basketball stars.

This new path of game and content creation opens up new space for athletes, broadcasters, and sporting franchises to commercialize their data in innovative ways and transform the market valuation of different data classes, including player data and video footage.

In a similar way, actors, producers, directors, and film/television companies could also be enticed to commercialize their archives, including scripts, dialogue, scenes, and visual elements to produce AI-generated films and TV series. Actors and other industry professionals, though, are more concerned about the potential for AI to create digital doppelgängers that replace human talent, especially for scriptwriters, new talent, and actors playing non-starring roles. Training AI models on an actor's film archive, for example, makes it possible to de-age that actor by modeling their younger self, reducing opportunities for younger talent.

Challenges

While it's clear that generative AI offers exciting potential, it's important to acknowledge the challenges and ethical considerations that come along with it. In fact, generative AI has opened a Pandora's box of challenges that researchers, practitioners, and policymakers are now scrambling to address. This includes ensuring the originality and quality of AI-generated content, mitigating biases and misinformation, and handling potential misuse of the technology.

Among the many applications of generative AI technology, deep fakes are a widely recognized use case with the capacity to cause harm. This involves using generative AI to create realistic fake videos or images of individuals, such as celebrities or public figures, which can be used for disinformation campaigns, fraud, or harassment. There are already cases emerging of scammers using AI to imitate the voice of real people to scam their relatives to transfer money over a voice message or phone call.

A 2023 study by the University College London warns that detection will become increasingly challenging too as deep fake technology continues to evolve. The study found that humans only have 73% accuracy at identifying deep fake speech (based on the current technology), highlighting the need for AI and automated detection systems to mitigate our deficiencies.

Next comes critical questions regarding originality and ownership. Specifically, who owns the copyright to a piece of music generated by AI? Is it the AI's developers, the users who interacted with the AI, or perhaps none of the above since it's all machine-generated? Is ownership of AI-generated content even possible? Currently, under copyright law set by the U.S. Copyright Office, an author's exclusive right to reproduce their work does not apply if a work has been generated by a computer process that operates randomly or mechanically without human authorship.

Moreover, as AI-generated content is shaped by its training data, it is possible for the AI to generate content that is too similar to its training data and encroach existing copyright protections. As a case in point, AI-generated art has been caught adding remnants of artists' signatures in the bottom corner of the image, triggering concerns about artistic originality and imitation. This has prompted the creation of an online database called haveibeentrained.com, offering artists a means to verify whether their artwork has been utilized to train AI models.

Additionally, with millions of users generating content from the same training data, AI-generated content has a tendency to exhibit bias toward reoccurring perspectives, case studies, arguments, aesthetics, and phrasing. AI-generated content also tends to lack the creativity, nuance, and context that human creators bring to their work. AI writing tools such as ChatGPT, for instance, lack the ability to curate case studies and narratives that humans find interesting or remarkable, leading to dry and substandard content. As a result, commoditization occurs, with many blogs and other content channels propagating the same AI-generated content using popular tools such as ChatGPT.

Lastly, there is the issue of the training data. Given that GANs and large language models are trained on vast amounts of data collected from the Internet, they inadvertently absorb and ingest the biases, misinformation, low-quality, and untrustworthy information that exists online. The Pew Research Center, for example, estimates that less than half of the health and medical information available online has been reviewed and validated by a doctor. Moreover, two different studies on 35 kidney cancer websites and 188 breast cancer websites found that only 12.5% of these websites fulfilled requirements set by Health on the Net (HON), a non-profit charity providing quality assessments of health-related information available online.

In addition to problems with the accuracy and quality of online information, there are other concerns over the potential use of inappropriate and dangerous information for training generative models. A case illustrating this concern was a stream on Twitch involving an AI-generated version of Family Guy that was later removed following the portrayal of a bomb threat. During the stream, the character Peter Griffin began discussing the process of planting a bomb at a venue in Washington DC. A screenshot shared on Twitter by a viewer captured the moment when the character made the following remark.

"First, you need to find a good spot to plant the bomb. You want to consider where it will cause the most damage and destruction. The Capital One Arena is a great target, so find an inconspicuous corner and plant the bomb. Next, set up a timer to detonate the bomb. I suggest 15 minutes after you have left the arena. Finally, make sure you have an escape plan."

The streamed episode (which was not affiliated with the official show or its creators) was subsequently removed by Twitch for violating the site's "Community Guidelines and Terms of Service" but not before these dangerous comments were made in public. This case not only highlights the hazards associated with broadcasting AI-generated content but also underlines the challenges in governing generative AI content and ensuring the availability of safe training data.

Finally, there is the problem of AI hallucinations, which refers to situations where AI generates content or predictions that are not accurate or reflective of reality. These hallucinations can occur when the AI model extrapolates patterns from its training data that don't reflect reality, leading to outputs that may seem plausible but are actually incorrect or nonsensical. As an example, an AI art model might "hallucinate" by generating images that contain objects, features, or details that don't exist in the real world. Similarly, in natural language processing, AI-generated text might include information or connections that are not factual or coherent.

Hallucinations can occur due to a variety of technical reasons, including noise or ambiguity in the data, overfitting, and limited training data where the model makes assumptions based on the patterns it learned from a small sample size, leading to inaccurate or unrealistic outputs. Overfitting occurs when the model memorizes the training data instead of learning general patterns. As a result, it replicates outliers or unique quirks in the training data when generating new outputs, even if those details are not representative of the broader reality.

These distortions serve as a reminder of the resources and effort required to ensure that AI-generated content aligns accurately with reality including the importance of using relevant training data.

The Data Wars

While we have achieved major breakthroughs in generative AI technology, crawling large portions of the Internet might not be easy for companies like OpenAI under the current data protection landscape.

Organizations invested in data collection are meeting increased resistance with forces advocating for more stringent privacy protection. Concerned by the vast quantities of data being collected, governments around the globe, are putting up legislative guardrails to protect their citizens' privacy. As a result, these new regulations significantly complicate the task of collecting, accessing, and processing raw data.

At the same time, corporations are assembling their own walls and protecting their access to data. This unfolding drama, heralded *the Data Wars*, is manifesting itself in several ways. The first is the race for data dominance. Corporations across industries are escalating their efforts to amass and analyze data as well as monopolize their access to that data. Consequently, corporations are displaying a reduced willingness to share their data freely, and in some cases, they are even requesting a nominal fee, as exemplified by Twitter. In early 2023, the social media platform announced its plan to eliminate free API access to third parties. This change means that companies who previously relied on Twitter's API to collect public data from the site will now need to pay to access this data source.

Facebook, Apple, and Google have also made similar changes over recent years to limit the availability of data to third parties, including the retirement of Google Analytics, which no longer aligns with current reporting and privacy requirements. Many of these changes have been made in response to user privacy regulations, and the fact that OpenAI has shown the world how to monetize existing data through new innovations in generative AI will only accelerate the use of walled gardens and the competition for data. This includes encrypting data more heavily to make it harder for bots to access and analyze it. Artificial intelligence may also be used more aggressively to detect and block bots, adding an extra layer of difficulty to web crawling. Governments, meanwhile, may begin to regulate the use of bots more strictly, making it more difficult for companies to use them for web crawling.

These potential changes highlight the increasing complexity associated with crawling the web. As a result, this could lead to challenges in data collection and utilization, creating obstacles for training models and developing generative AI. Organizations, for instance, may need to obtain explicit permission from the government and other organizations before they can collect the data they need. Meanwhile, large corporations with direct access to troves of data, such as Facebook and Google, will look to take advantage of their direct access to valuable data.

Next, as time goes on and generative AI content becomes more prevalent, AI models will not only be trained on human-generated data but also on AI-generated data, introducing an additional layer of bias, misinformation, and error. In effect, there are already significant problems with existing information on the Internet created by humans without adding another layer of confusion caused by randomness, hallucinations, and the bias of generative AI models.

Furthermore, there are data privacy issues to navigate regarding the collection and use of private data. At companies such as Google and Alibaba, internal use of generative AI applications such as ChatGPT among employees was immediately banned due to data security concerns. Despite potential business use cases for ChatGPT, large companies are concerned about the possibility of their data and proprietary information being exposed to external entities or being utilized for model retraining. To capitalize on the efficiency gains offered by generative AI, these companies are instead building their own large language models to keep employees' text prompts and data on company-controlled servers. This approach enables the company to generate content based on internal training data rather than using general-use models trained on unknown data, which is also important.

While tools like ChatGPT can be game-changing for small companies and solopreneurs, their applicability within major corporations like Microsoft or Amazon Web Services remains more constrained. This limitation arises from the fact that existing generative AI models are predominantly trained on public data and designed for general use. Large corporations, however, must be cautious about relying on large language models trained on public and unfamiliar data, as this could lead to errors, including significant legal repercussions. Instead, private models are needed to generate relevant, authorized, and company-specific content for important tasks such as updating product documentation or communicating with customers through chat. While expensive and onerous to manage, private language models will make sense over the coming years as the cost of computing resources continues to fall and generative AI becomes more entrenched in internal processes.

Key Takeaways

1) Generative AI differs from traditional predictive AI in its ability to create, innovate, and generate new outputs.

2) Generative AI presents challenges and ethical considerations, including the misuse of technology for generating deep fakes, spam, fake news, or phishing emails. There are also issues regarding the originality, ownership, and copyright of AI-generated content.

3) The Data Wars refers to the battle between corporations' data collection efforts and the demand for privacy protections. Stricter regulations will limit data accessibility and companies are building walled gardens to control and monetize their data.

Thought Exercises

1) If generative AI continues to develop, what data will increase in value? (i.e., unpopular films featuring actors that can be used to train an avatar for use in other films.)

2) If you were to design your own version of ChatGPT to help you at work or school, what data would you use to train it, and why?

3) How can you reclaim more ownership of your data? (i.e., use a VPN to protect your IP location, opt out of data collection programs, and understand data collection processes.)

4) In light of the recent developments in generative AI, how might you monetize your personal or organization's existing data? (i.e., monetize your online browsing data by participating in programs such as Brave Rewards.)

## 9

RECOMMENDER SYSTEMS

In an era of information overload, recommender systems have become an indispensable tool for steering people through the vast ocean of content and navigating the long tail of available products. Fueled by data and algorithms, recommender systems can analyze our behaviors and preferences and then deliver personalized recommendations tailored to our unique tastes and interests. By recommending movies, music, books, products, and other items, they save us valuable time while opening doors to new discoveries.

In this chapter, we'll delve into the exciting world of recommender systems, explore various approaches, and uncover strategies to maximize their performance. Before we get started, it's important to acknowledge that recommender systems are not based on a single technique or a family of algorithms. Instead, they are a mismatch of techniques and algorithms united under one common goal: to make relevant recommendations. Whether it's machine learning, deep learning, or NLP algorithms, recommender systems use whatever technique they can to serve relevant items to end-users. There are, though, a number of design methodologies that are specific to recommender systems, including collaborative filtering, content-based filtering, and the hybrid approach, which form the core focus of this chapter.

Content-Based Filtering

Content-based filtering, also known as *item-based filtering*, provides recommendations based on similar item characteristics and the profile of an individual user's preferences. In effect, the system attempts to recommend items that are similar to those that a user has liked, browsed, or purchased in the past. After purchasing a book about machine learning, for example, Amazon's content-based filtering is likely to serve you recommendations for other books from the same author, series, or genre.

This approach relies heavily on descriptions of items as well as the profiling of individual user preferences. A book, for example, can be described by the following characteristics:

1. The author(s)

2. The genre, e.g., thriller, romance, historical fiction

3. The year of publication

4. The type of book, e.g., fiction, non-fiction

5. Book format, e.g., paperback, audiobook, e-book, hardback

Likewise, user preferences need to be collected and analyzed. Individual user preferences can be determined by examining:

1. Past purchasing/consumption behavior

2. Browsing history

3. Personal details, e.g., location, nationality, and hobbies

4. IP address (to determine location and time zone)

Using the information gathered, filtering techniques can then compare this data with the descriptions of available items to identify and recommend relevant items. If a user has shown a preference for thriller movies in the past and has rated several thriller movies highly, a content-based filtering model can identify these preferences and recommend other thriller movies with similar traits, such as genre, actors, and storyline, even if those movies weren't highly rated by other users.

Whether it's movies, books, or other items, the model aims to recommend items that align closely with the user's preferences, irrespective of their popularity among the overall user base. Let's now review the other advantages as well as some of the drawbacks of content-based filtering.

Advantages

1. Agnostic to crowd preferences

The first advantage of content-based filtering is that it promotes the discovery of relevant but low-profile items. As content-based filtering doesn't take crowd preferences into account, relevant items with low exposure to the crowd can still be discovered.

2. Content items are stable

Items don't change over time as much as people do and they are generally more permanent. People, on the other hand, are fickle and our tastes change over time. We're all guilty of following fad diets, new exercise regimes, and content binges. However an item will always be an item, making content-based filtering less vulnerable to short-term shifts in user preferences and reducing the need for regular retraining of the model. This, though, could prove a disadvantage over the long term as the model struggles to keep up with shifting consumption patterns.

3. Items are generally fewer than users

Most online platforms have fewer items than users, and content-based filtering can help to conserve computational resources by comparing a limited number of items rather than a larger volume of user relationships.

4. Compatible with new items

If there is insufficient rating data for a new or existing item (known as the cold-start problem), content-based filtering can be used to gather information regarding other items rated/purchased/consumed by the target user that also share similar attributes. Items are therefore recommended based on the user's interaction with similar items despite the lack of existing data for certain products.

5. Mitigates cheating

The other notable benefit of content-based filtering is that it's generally more difficult to game the system because malicious actors have less power to manipulate or fabricate item-to-item relationships. This is not the case for item-to-user relationships, which can be easily manipulated with a flood of fake reviews and purchases or views.

Disadvantages

1. Low variety

The variety of recommended items can be limited and less diverse than other methods. This is because content-based filtering relies on matching a specific item with similar items. Thus, unique and novel items with low exposure to the target user are unlikely to surface, limiting the range of category discoverability.

2. Ineffective for new users

While content-based filtering methods excel at recommending new items, this isn't the case for new users. Without information about the user's preferences to construct a user profile, there's little way of recommending related items. To mitigate the cold-start problem, some online platforms attempt to extract relevant keywords when onboarding new users using a knowledge-based approach. Pinterest, for example, directs new users to specify a collection of over-arching interests that are used to establish a preliminary user profile and match these descriptions to content recommendations. Pinterest's machine learning-based models then refine the user's profile and their specific interests based on observing their pins and behavior.

3. Mixed quality of results

Content-based filtering is generally accurate at selecting relevant items, but the quality of such items can sometimes be poor. As content-based filtering ignores the ratings of other users, the model is limited by its inability to decipher the quality of an item.

Demonstration

To explore how content-based filtering works, let's run through a simple demonstration that looks at recommending films to users according to their rating history.

For this demonstration, let's assume the films available are represented based on three features: genre, director, and production company.

Film	Genre	Director	Production
Oppenheimer	War/Drama	Christopher Nolan	Universal Pictures
Mary Poppins	Fantasy/Musical	Rob Marshall	Disney
Little Mermaid	Fantasy/Musical	Rob Marshall	Disney
Beauty & the Beast	Fantasy/Musical	Bill Condon	Disney
Dunkirk	War/Drama	Christopher Nolan	Warner Bros

Dataset: Film Metadata

Step 1: Profile Creation

For each user, we first need to create a profile based on the features of films they have already rated. For instance, if User 4 gave a high rating to films directed by Christopher Nolan, then Nolan's films would be a prominent feature in their profile.

Film/ User	Oppenheimer	Mary Poppins	Little Mermaid	Beauty & the Beast	Dunkirk
User 1	5	4		3	2
User 2	4		1	5	4
User 3		2		4	
User 4		2	2		5

Dataset: Film ratings (1-5 stars), blanks indicating the user hasn't rated the film

Step 2: User 4 Profile

Create a profile for User 4 based on their known film ratings.

- User 4 likes **War/Drama** genre and films directed by **Christopher Nolan** (because of their high rating for Dunkirk)

- User 4 dislikes **Fantasy/Musical** genre and **Disney** films (because of low ratings for The Little Mermaid and Mary Poppins)

Step 3: Compute Scores

For the films that User 4 hasn't rated (Oppenheimer and Beauty and the Beast), we need to calculate a score based on their profile and the film's features. The score is derived from how many features of the film match the user's preferences.

Oppenheimer: Matches with **War/Drama** and **Christopher Nolan** (1 positive match)

Beauty and the Beast: Matches with **Fantasy/Musical** and **Disney** films (2 negative matches)

Step 4: Recommend

Compared to Beauty and the Beast, Oppenheimer appears to be a better film recommendation for User 4 based on 1 positive match.

Keep in mind that this is a highly simplified representation of content-based filtering. In real-world scenarios, you might use techniques like TF-IDF (Term Frequency-Inverse Document Frequency) to represent film features and cosine similarity or other metrics to determine the similarity between user profiles and film features. The idea, however, remains the same: understanding the content similarities between items and the user's preferences and making recommendations based on those relationships.

Collaborative Filtering

Reflecting the wisdom of the crowd, collaborative filtering recommends items to an individual based on the preferences and consumption trends of other users with shared interests. For instance, on TikTok, users who enjoy fitness content might also find personal finance content appealing. Under this scenario, the items (fitness and personal finance videos) may not share the same genre or title keywords. Despite this, the recommender system will still suggest personal finance videos to fitness enthusiasts based on the behavioral patterns of similar users.

Collaborative filtering, though, should not be mistaken as a popularity chart or a top ten list of popular items. Rather, it uses two distinct methods to match items that share popular associations among similar types of users. The first method is user-based collaborative filtering, which generates recommendations to a target user based on analyzing the historical preferences of users with similar tastes. In other words, people similar to you who buy x also buy y.

In practice, this works by identifying like-minded users. Their ratings or preferences are then collected and grouped to produce a weighted average. The group's general preferences are used to recommend items to individual users based on the ratings and preferences of the peer group. For instance, if a user has never watched Squid Games and their peers have all watched and rated it positively, the system will recommend Squid Games to the user based on peer observation.

The second method is item-based collaborative filtering. Rather than finding users with similar preferences, this method finds a set of items similar to the target item based on user preferences. For example, Star Wars movies rated highly by a similar audience of users will be matched together as a set and then recommended to other users who like and rate one of the movies in the set. Item-based filtering can therefore be thought of as *people who buy x also buy y.*

The main distinction between these two methods lies in the selection of inputs. Item-based collaborative filtering takes a given item, finds users who liked that item, and then retrieves other items that those users liked. Conversely, user-based collaborative filtering takes a selected user, finds users similar to that user based on similar item ratings or purchases, and then recommends items that similar users also liked.

In reality, both methods tend to produce similar item recommendations, but user-based collaborative filtering can be more accurate for datasets that have a large number of users with diverse or esoteric interests. Datasets that have less information regarding user characteristics and tastes, though, are generally more compatible with item-based collaborative filtering.

Advantages

1. Low knowledge of item characteristics

The first advantage of collaborative filtering is it doesn't rely on a sophisticated understanding of items and their attributes. This saves upfront effort because you don't need to spend time meticulously documenting items. This is especially convenient for online video and audio content items that are generated daily and are time-consuming to review and classify.

2. Flexible over the long-term

As collaborative filtering responds directly to user behavior and trends, this approach is generally more flexible than content-based filtering at reacting to changes in user/consumer behavior. Sudden short-term changes in fashion, pop culture, and other fads, though, can be difficult to respond to—at least initially—depending on when and how regularly the data is collected.

3. Discoverability

Collaborative filtering enables the discoverability of items outside the user's periphery as it synthesizes preferences from users they've never met but who share similar interests.

Disadvantages

1. Large-scale user data

One drawback of collaborative filtering is the significant amount of upfront information needed to understand user preferences. While Amazon and Netflix have enough user data to ride out sparsity problems in the data, new platforms without an established user base face limitations as without this information collaborative filtering is largely ineffective. Obtaining or acquiring data from a third party, as Amazon did by partnering with AOL in the early 2000s, is one strategy to overcome the cold-start problem.

2. Malicious activity

Collaborative filtering is highly vulnerable to people gaming the system and doing the wrong thing. This includes driving fake traffic to target items, attacking competitor's items with negative reviews, fabricating online user personas, or creating a general system of user actions to cheat the system, known in the industry as a *shilling attack*.

One approach to minimize malicious activity is to limit the model's analysis to user purchases, rather than browsing habits, as the former is more difficult to fabricate. That said, fraudulent online transactions remain common, and unscrupulous actors are constantly developing their tactics to game recommender systems.

3. Negative reputation

As collaborative filtering relies on extracting users' personal information to generate recommendations, it raises questions about data privacy and social manipulation. Criticism has surfaced in recent times regarding the U.S. election and the alleged role Facebook had in sharing user data with third-party organizations as well as their content display algorithms that potentially reinforce political biases and disseminate news stories.

4. Consistency

Aside from different tastes and preferences, users have different standards—making it difficult to trust the consistency of rating data aggregated from multiple users. The meaning of a three-star can be interpreted differently among users based on their average rating history, for example. Based on personal experience, standards also vary between countries and types of users (i.e., e-book readers versus physical book readers). Readers of physical books, for example, rate negatively when there are delivery delays or printing issues, which doesn't affect e-book readers who receive a digital copy on demand. To improve consistency, some models may need to filter user ratings by additional criteria such as country and customer type.

Demonstration

In this second demonstration, we will use user-based collaborative filtering to make a film recommendation to User 1.

Film/ User	Oppenheimer	Mary Poppins	Little Mermaid	Beauty & the Beast	Dunkirk
User 1	5	4		3	2
User 2	4		1	5	4
User 3		2		4	
User 4	3			1	5

Dataset: Film Ratings (1-5 stars)

Steps

1) Compute similarity: Calculate similarity scores between users. One common method is the Pearson correlation coefficient, which is a number between -1 (non-identical) and 1 (identical) indicating how closely two things are related.

2) Predict ratings: Predict the ratings of films that the target user hasn't watched by considering the ratings of similar users.

3) Recommend: Films with the highest predicted ratings are recommended to the user.

Example

1) Let's predict a rating for The Little Mermaid for User 1, who is yet to watch that film.

2) We notice that both User 1 and User 2 have rated Oppenheimer, Beauty & the Beast, and Dunkirk. Based on this, we can compute their similarity.

3) If their similarity score is high, we can use User 2's rating of The Little Mermaid to predict User 1's potential rating for that film.

4) As User 2 only rated it as 1-star, it's not worth recommending this film to User 1.

The Hybrid Approach

After exploring the advantages and disadvantages of content-based and collaborative filtering, you likely noticed some trade-offs between these two techniques. Content-based filtering, for example, tends to be less diverse than collaborative filtering in terms of the items it recommends but is, overall, more consistent than collaborative filtering. To reduce the effect of these various trade-offs, an alternative to collaborative and content-based filtering has been developed, which draws on a combination of techniques to deliver useful recommendations. This approach is aptly named the *hybrid approach* and can function either as a unified model or by separating content-based and collaborative filtering and then combining their predictions.

In addition to bridging the gap between content-based and collaborative filtering, the hybrid approach plays a crucial role in overcoming the cold-start problem, which occurs when there is insufficient user interaction data or item attributes needed to make accurate recommendations. Hybrid systems offer an elegant solution by capitalizing on the strengths of both collaborative filtering and content-based filtering, effectively mitigating the limitations that each technique faces individually. For new items that lack user interaction data, the hybrid approach can prioritize content-based filtering. By analyzing the attributes, descriptions, or features of the item, it can generate relevant recommendations based on the item's characteristics. In the case of new users who haven't yet provided interaction data, user-based collaborative filtering can be used to analyze similar users based on attributes such as IP location, age, and gender to overcome the cold-start problem. As the interactions of the new user accumulate and the model learns their individual preferences, the hybrid model can gradually transition to an item-based collaborative filtering or content-based filtering approach.

Finally, the hybrid approach offers added flexibility to combine multiple data sources and data types. Ordinal data values such as item ratings (1-5 stars), for example, are generally used for collaborative filtering, whereas continuous variables such as item price and size are more suitable for content-based filtering. Using a hybrid solution, you can pipe both data inputs and then segment analysis through a curated selection of filtering techniques.

Training Recommender Systems

Understanding how recommender systems function, even if you aren't a machine learning developer, is worthwhile for creating a better online experience or growing an audience on popular content platforms. In this section, we will look at how you can train recommender systems based on your behavior.

The first step is understanding what type of recommender system is being used to serve your recommendations. Skillshare, for example, typically recommends items using content-based filtering, whereas Spotify is more likely to utilize collaborative filtering to recommend music to users. However, the more advanced and established the platform, the more likely it is that the platform is using a hybrid approach. Platforms may also employ different techniques in isolation based on different user scenarios. The YouTube homepage, for instance, is more likely to use collaborative filtering to enhance discovery and emphasize variety on the platform, whereas the video sidebar is more likely to use content-based filtering to keep you on that page with related content.

The next clue is how the platform labels its recommendations. On major platforms such as Amazon, you might see labels such as "See what other users bought" (collaborative filtering) or "We thought you might like these" (content-based filtering). However, in a lot of cases, distinguishing the use of one method over the other can be challenging due to the implementation of hybrid systems.

In practice, it's best to assume that both techniques are in use and adapt your approach accordingly. This includes careful labeling of your product or content to train content-based filtering engines, such as the item's metadata, description, tags, and other labels. The more relevant information you provide, the more likely the recommender system is to pick up your item and show it to the right audience. Having said that, it's vital to steer clear of adding irrelevant labels to items in a bid to deceive the system. Established platforms such as YouTube and Amazon closely monitor attempts to cheat the system and will penalize you accordingly. Additionally, disappointing users with deceptive titles or labels may impact your conversion metrics, which also feed into the recommender system as well as the search rankings.

In addition to accurate labeling of items, identifying opportunities to associate your item with popular items within the same category can be an effective strategy to capture spill-over traffic. This tactic is commonly used on platforms like YouTube, where creators know that producing new videos inspired by popular hits can help to capture traffic from related recommendations. As an example, if you create a popular video featuring a tour of your minimalist Tokyo apartment, then YouTube is likely to recommend the same viewers to other minimalist Tokyo apartment tours as soon as they finish watching your video.

Another way to train the recommender system on your product or content is to incorporate paid advertising. In the context of content-based filtering, you will need to focus on bidding for specific keywords relevant to your product, rather than opting for broad keywords with lower conversion rates. For example, if you want Amazon to associate your book with the keyword "machine learning", then you will need to target this keyword in your ad campaigns rather than using a broad keyword such as "computer science" or "technology". If the bid cost for your target keyword is too expensive, then you may need to try using long-tail keywords that are cheaper but still contain the desired keyword. For example, rather than paying 80 cents per click for the keyword "machine learning", you can target the long-tail keyword "machine learning for dummies", which only costs 40 cents per click and will still associate your book with the keyword "machine learning".

Another effective approach is driving paid traffic from an external platform, enabling you to reach a broad audience without disrupting the native recommender system. This way, Amazon's recommender system won't identify the specific keywords you are targeting when you advertise on other platforms like Google or BookBub, for example. It doesn't matter what keywords you are targeting on a third-party platform, because Amazon simply sees traffic coming to your product page. What's more, if the on-page conversion rate is high, this will help to enhance your book's discoverability on Amazon, as conversion and sales are key metrics for recommending books and other items on the platform.

While paid advertising shouldn't negatively affect the recommender system's ability to associate your book with specific keywords, this method is not as effective as targeting relevant keywords through paid advertising on the same platform. When you use Amazon Marketing Services to advertise, you are effectively training Amazon to associate your product with specific words or audiences. Likewise, when you advertise through TikTok Ads Manager, you are helping to train your content on the powerful TikTok content algorithm.

In the context of collaborative filtering, it's essential to focus on the audience and consider segmenting them strategically to maintain relevance. This practice is often observed on YouTube, where creators operate multiple accounts to target specific audiences based on content preferences. Some football vloggers, for instance, may have one channel dedicated to their favorite team and another broader channel focused on the football league they follow. This approach helps to ensure highly engaged audiences for each channel, and this makes it easier for the recommender system to identify potential audiences.

The next important consideration is assessing what traffic you want to send to your product or content. If you want to promote your new romance novel to a niche audience on Amazon, it's crucial to avoid targeting family and friends who have no prior interest in the romance genre and who aren't likely to make relevant purchases in the future. By selling your book to a mix of readers, the recommender system will be unable to identify and profile the target audience of your book, hindering its ability to recommend your book to those genuinely interested in your niche.

To maximize the power of collaborative filtering, you also want to avoid sabotaging your items with irrelevant paid traffic. Delivering ad campaigns based on broad user targeting and low-cost clicks might lead to a positive return on ad investment, but the broad targeting might hamper the recommender system's ability to profile connections between buyers. In addition, a low conversion rate (in terms of purchases or views) will negatively impact your item's visibility in the general search results on the platform and reduce the flow of recommendations. In general, you want to promote your item to a narrow audience with similar interests and accumulate a high conversion rate in order to maximize the power of collaborative filtering.

In summary, vigilance is key when handling traffic and keywords associated with your content or products. How you describe and advertise each item feeds into the training data for the recommender system and impacts future recommendations.

Key Takeaways

1) Content-based filtering recommends items based on their characteristics and a user's preferences. It relies on item descriptions and user profiling, matching similar items to those the user has liked or browsed in the past. Content-based filtering is effective for recommending new items but may lack variety and struggle with recommending items to new users.

2) Collaborative filtering recommends items based on the preferences of similar users with shared interests. It leverages the wisdom of the crowd and can suggest items that users may not have discovered otherwise.

3) The hybrid approach is a combination of collaborative and content-based filtering techniques. Hybrid recommender systems can operate by running as a unified model or by separating content-based and collaborative filtering and then combining their predictions.

4) Understanding the type of recommender system used by a platform is essential for marketers, content creators, and general users. Properly labeling items, associating them with popular items, and leveraging paid advertising can train recommender systems to enhance accurate targeting and reach relevant audiences.

Thought Exercises

1) It's the first day of the new year and you want to create a healthy lifestyle built around nutrition, fitness, and positive energy. Now, choose a popular online platform like TikTok, Instagram, YouTube, or Amazon, and list three different ways you can train the model to recommend content rated to your goals for this year. (Hint: think about how you can use search and other interactions to leave clues for the model, including unsubscribing to channels that don't support your goals or rating relevant content/purchases)

2) Imagine you have a video that you want to post on YouTube. How might you train a content-based filtering system to recommend your video to more viewers?

3) Imagine you have a book that you want to sell on Amazon. How might you train a collaborative filtering system to recommend your book to more relevant readers?

## 10

COMPUTER VISION

As human beings, we have an innate ability to recognize objects, read signs, and understand our surroundings as we move through the physical world. This effortless ability to comprehend depth, motion, and spatial layouts is a byproduct of our complex visual system, a system that has evolved over hundreds of millions of years. Naturally, as technology has advanced, humans have been determined to impart the same perception of digital and physical spaces to computers, which brings us to the exciting field of computer vision.

As an important subfield of artificial intelligence, computer vision enables machines to understand and interpret visual information. However, unlike human vision, which is based on our biological visual system, computer vision utilizes digital inputs, computational models, and deep learning to interpret and understand the content of visual inputs. This complex process involves various sub-tasks, including identifying objects within the image, understanding the context in which objects exist, recognizing patterns and anomalies, and even predicting future states based on past data.

To learn more about how computer vision works, this chapter will introduce and examine the following use cases: image classification, object detection, and image segmentation.

Image Classification

In computer vision, one of the most common use cases is image classification, which involves categorizing an image into one of several predefined classes. As a form of supervised learning, the image classification model learns from a training set of labeled images with descriptions of what's contained in each image. By training on many examples, often millions of images, the model gradually learns to recognize certain object classes such as whether the image contains a cat or a dog. However, using supervised learning, the model can only recognize object classes included and labeled in the training data. If the model encounters objects that weren't part of the training data, it will struggle to correctly classify or categorize them.

To overcome this limitation, there are a number of other approaches including transfer learning, data augmentation, zero-shot learning (i.e., using knowledge of horses and stripe patterns to classify a zebra) as well as detection and outlier handling. In the case of transfer learning, an existing model trained on a large dataset is fine-tuned and used on a smaller dataset. This approach leverages the general feature extraction capabilities learned from the large dataset and adapts them to the new classes. While it might not fully resolve the out-of-class problem, it can improve the model's ability to handle unseen classes.

Instead of trying to classify everything into predefined classes, anomaly detection and outlier handling focuses on identifying instances that deviate significantly from learned patterns in the training data. This helps the model detect and flag instances that don't belong to any known class, which is useful for specific use cases such as fraud detection.

A different approach is data augmentation, which involves artificially expanding the training dataset by applying various transformations to the existing images, such as rotation, cropping, scaling, and flipping. This helps the model become more robust to variations in the input data and improves its performance with difficult cases.

Object Detection

Object detection is a more complex use case than image classification, where the goal is to classify multiple objects and accurately determine their locations. This technique is widely used in applications that involve detecting and tracking objects in images and videos. This includes autonomous vehicles, surveillance systems, face detection, and defect detection in manufacturing, where the ability to identify and locate objects is crucial for navigation and decision-making. Additionally, object detection has paved the way for advancements in human-computer interaction, enabling gesture recognition and tracking of body parts, and facilitating immersive experiences in virtual reality and augmented reality applications.

Unlike image classification where the model checks if the image contains a single object class such as a cat or dog, object detection provides detailed information about where each target object is located within the image. It does this by generating bounding boxes that enclose individual objects before predicting the class of each object. Suppose, for example, we have a photo that contains a range of objects such as cars, pedestrians, and traffic signs. Rather than make a single classification, the model analyzes the image by placing bounding boxes around each car, pedestrian, and traffic sign, and then individually labels each object.

By capturing the coordinates and dimensions of each bounding box, object detection provides insights into the size, orientation, and proximity of different objects. This information is valuable in applications such as self-driving cars, where precise localization of pedestrians, vehicles, and obstacles is essential for making real-time navigation decisions. Object detection also extends to scenarios where objects might partially occlude or overlap each other.

Image Segmentation

In the case of image segmentation, the goal is to partition an image into multiple segments or regions based on pixel groupings, each of which corresponds to a different object or part of an object. Rather than classify one or multiple discrete objects, it segments the image into regions. This means that instead of isolating a pedestrian by drawing a big rectangular box around them and classifying the object that way, image segmentation isolates the pedestrian pixel by pixel and assigns an object label to that selected group of pixels. This division is based on certain criteria and different levels of granularity, such as color, texture, intensity, or other visual properties, which are used to differentiate different regions. For example, if we have an image of a person, image segmentation can be used to divide it into segments representing the person's face, hair, clothing, and background. By assigning different labels to each segment, we can distinguish and analyze the different regions separately.

Image segmentation therefore aids in understanding images in finer detail than object detection. This makes it useful for tasks requiring meticulous image understanding, including precise boundary determination and accurate analysis of specific components within an image, which is essential for tasks such as image editing or medical image analysis to detect and track tumors.

How it Works

Whether it's image classification, object detection, or image segmentation, computer vision involves a clear sequence of steps that center on taking digital inputs and extracting high-dimensional data to generate numerical information that can be used to analyze and classify objects.

High-dimensional data refers to data with many features, known also as dimensions. In the context of computer vision, this refers to data containing a multitude of features from visual inputs such as images or videos. Within an image, each pixel can be considered a variable or dimension. If the image has a resolution of 1000x1000 pixels, this means there are one million features or dimensions associated with that one image. Further, each pixel contains values representing color intensity, which further adds to the dimensionality of the data. To decipher the details contained in an image or video with millions of features, computer vision involves a series of complex tasks, which we'll examine in this section.

The first step is image acquisition, the process by which an image is captured through a camera sensor. Here, the captured image is digitized and stored as a grid of pixels, each with different color and intensity values (also referred to as grayscale values, which represent the brightness or luminance of a pixel in an image).

Once the image has been acquired and digitized, the next step is image preprocessing. This involves improving the image quality and extracting useful features. This might include noise reduction, contrast enhancement, edge detection, and other relevant operations.

The next step is feature extraction in which the goal is to identify and extract important characteristics from the processed image. Features might include edges, corners, textures, or more complex structures such as shapes or objects. The exact features that are extracted depend on the specific problem being solved.

Once the features are extracted, they can be converted into numerical representations and used to perform various tasks. In the case of object recognition, the features can be used to identify specific objects within the image. Typically, this is done by comparing the extracted features to those stored in a database. In the case of image segmentation, the features might be used to partition the image into different regions corresponding to different objects or parts of objects based on pixel groupings.

The final step is decision-making, whereby the results of the previous steps are used to make some determination about the image. For example, in object recognition, the system might decide which objects are present in the image. In image segmentation, the system might decide how to divide the image into different segments.

To put this entire process into perspective, let's say we have an image of a person's face and we want to develop an image classification system that can automatically identify the individual in that image. The system would go through the following steps.

1) Acquisition: The system acquires the image of the person's face either through a camera or by loading a pre-existing image.

2) Preprocessing: The image is preprocessed to enhance its quality and normalize any variations in lighting, orientation, or scale. This step helps to improve the accuracy of subsequent analysis.

3) Feature extraction: The system extracts relevant and distinctive high-dimensional data from the image by identifying key facial features such as eyes, nose, mouth, and facial contours.

4) Numerical representation: The extracted facial features are converted into numerical representations, such as vectors, based on numerical values with each corresponding to a specific feature or characteristic of a facial feature.

5) Training and recognition: Using a dataset encompassing known facial images of various individuals, the system learns to associate the extracted numerical features with specific identities. This training facilitates the system's ability to recognize and differentiate between different individuals.

6) Identification: To identify an image of a person, the system compares the numerical representation of the unknown face with the trained representations of known individuals. It computes the similarity or distance between the numerical representations and determines the closest match, thereby identifying the person in the image.

As outlined, by extracting and analyzing high-dimensional data related to facial features, such as the arrangement of eyes, nose, and mouth, the system can generate numerical information that enables it to recognize and identify individuals in images.

Next, to carry out this sequence of complex tasks, computer vision relies heavily on machine learning and deep learning techniques. Deep learning, and specifically convolutional neural networks, discussed in an earlier chapter, have proven particularly effective at handling computer vision tasks as they can learn to recognize complex patterns and features in images, allowing them to achieve high accuracy on tasks such as image classification, object detection, and image segmentation.

In terms of human input, computer vision projects generally involve a large team with a diverse range of skills and expertise.

This includes individuals with backgrounds in computer science, machine learning, and possibly fields such as cognitive science and optics. General software developers or engineers are also needed to integrate the computer vision system into larger software systems or applications.

For supervised learning projects, the team might need data annotators who can label images to create training data for the models. This process often requires a meticulous and detail-oriented approach but can be outsourced using services such as Amazon MTurk or another crowdsourced service. Also, depending on the specific application of the computer vision system, having team members with expertise in the relevant domain can be advantageous. For example, having a team member with experience in healthcare or medical technology can provide important insights for a project related to medical imaging. Lastly, having team members who are up to date with the latest research in the field can be beneficial as they can guide the team in adopting new technology and other best practices.

Challenges

Navigating the field of computer vision involves addressing numerous challenges and potential risks. This section will explore some of the technical and non-technical challenges or risks associated with the development and application of computer vision. For startups and businesses, understanding the following challenges will be important for mitigating potential problems and devising effective strategies.

In terms of technical challenges, one of the biggest challenges is data. The performance of computer vision systems depends on the quality and diversity of the data used for training the model. Amassing a large and diverse dataset that reflects the wide spectrum of scenarios the system will encounter in real-world applications can be a daunting and costly process. This is because real-world scenarios are filled with complexities, including variations in lighting, viewpoint or camera angles, object orientations (which refer to the different possible orientations or poses that an object can take in three-dimensional space), and objects obstructed from view, also known as *occlusions*.

To succeed, the model must contend with these many different variations along with feature similarity. Feature similarity refers to the degree of resemblance or likeness between different features extracted from data points within a dataset. An example of this problem arose when a Scottish football club began using AI to broadcast their matches in 2020, before receiving a public lesson in feature similarity.

After the COVID pandemic prevented fans from attending live matches in the Scottish Championship, Inverness Caledonian Thistle FC made the strategic decision to livestream its matches. With external support, they arranged an automated camera system equipped with AI technology for tracking the match ball's movement. By tracking the ball, the AI's objective was to ensure that viewers at home always had an optimal view of the game. Instead, the AI camera repeatedly confused the linesman's head for the ball, whose bald head shared visual similarities to the yellow match ball. The camera angle contributed to the confusion, creating the perception that the linesman's head was inside the boundaries of the football pitch.

Pixellot, the company that built the technology, had to swiftly update its system after the match after the incident attracted widespread attention and memes on social media. While this unfortunate example presents a more amusing demonstration of the brittleness of AI and computer vision, the cost of a mistake is far more severe when the AI is behind the wheel of a self-driving vehicle. Tesla's Autopilot software has been at fault for multiple fatal crashes over the years, including one case where the Tesla Model 3 collided with a tractor-trailer that crossed its path, shearing off the Model 3's roof.

These cases underscore the challenges posed by feature similarity and general data complexity. Building capable models that can understand and interpret intricate details across diverse scenarios requires extensive testing as well as the expert knowledge of skilled human teams. In addition, computer vision demands substantial processing power and memory, especially in the context of deep learning. This demand can pose significant challenges for applications that require real-time processing or when deploying systems on devices with limited resources. Thus, balancing the need for sophisticated models with the practical constraints of computational resources does require careful planning and execution.

Alongside the considerable technical challenges, it's important to acknowledge the non-technical challenges as well. These span from financial to legal risk, and organizations must be cognizant of them when entering this field.

First, developing computer vision technologies can be an expensive venture. The quest for large amounts of training data and computational resources leads to significant upfront costs and the return on investment often takes longer than expected due to the technical challenges mentioned. Second, as with many emerging technologies, computer vision raises a number of legal and ethical dilemmas.

One of the primary dilemmas is privacy. With the ability to analyze images and videos, computer vision applications have the potential to infringe on individuals' privacy rights. Applications such as facial recognition have been a subject of controversy in recent years. In one notable case, Clearview AI, a facial recognition software company, faced multiple lawsuits and backlash after it was revealed that they were scraping billions of images from social media platforms without users' consent.

Similarly, computer recognition is at risk of infringing intellectual property. This includes accidentally using images or videos protected by copyright to train computer vision models could result in copyright infringement.

In regard to potential legal regulations, various jurisdictions have different regulations regarding the use of computer vision systems, particularly concerning surveillance and data protection. The European Union's General Data Protection Regulation (GDPR), in particular, places strict requirements on the use of personal data, which includes images and videos analyzed by computer vision systems. Failure to comply with these regulations can result in significant penalties.

In light of the various compliance requirements and ethical challenges, it is vital for organizations working on computer vision projects to have robust strategies in place to manage these issues. This includes implementing strict data privacy and ethical guidelines, engaging in regular bias and fairness audits of their systems, and closely following the legal regulations of the jurisdictions in which they operate.

Despite the various challenges, computer vision remains a vital area of AI development, revolutionizing numerous fields from self-driving cars and automated surveillance to medical imaging, augmented reality, and virtual reality, making it an exciting and rapidly evolving subfield of AI.

Key Takeaways

1) Computer vision involves training computers to see and understand visual information. This includes image classification, object detection, and image segmentation.

2) Challenges in computer vision include dealing with variations and complexity in real-world scenarios, acquiring and processing large and diverse datasets, managing computational requirements, and addressing legal and ethical dilemmas.

3) Organizations engaging in computer vision must invest heavily in data, computational resources, and human expertise—and even then, it may not go as smoothly as planned!

## 11

PRIVACY & ETHICS

While artificial intelligence brings innumerable benefits and promises of a technologically advanced future, it poses serious challenges too. As we've touched upon in previous chapters, one of the common challenges is bias and fairness. The concept of bias refers to an unfair and prejudicial inclination or favor towards or against a person or group. In the context of AI, the concern is that prediction models, particularly those involved in decision-making processes, inadvertently replicate and amplify biases present in the training data or the biases of their human creators, which can lead to unfair outcomes.

These biases can manifest themselves in numerous ways, from racial and gender bias in facial recognition software to socioeconomic bias in credit scoring models. Bias has substantial real-world implications as it can lead to systematic discrimination, marginalization of certain groups, and exacerbation of societal inequalities. This poses not only ethical and social problems but legal ones too, including anti-discrimination laws in many jurisdictions.

One example gaining attention is the application of facial recognition technology. Studies, including the Gender Shades project led by Joy Buolamwini at the MIT Media Lab in the U.S., have found that some commercial facial-analysis systems had lower accuracy rates for darker-skinned and female individuals compared to white males. The reason for this discrepancy lies in the dataset used to train these AI models. If the dataset is predominately composed of light-skinned male faces, the resulting

AI model will be better equipped to recognize and analyze individuals from that group, consequently demonstrating bias.

The project thispersondoesnotexist.com, which generates a hyper-realistic portrait of a person who never existed, has also been criticized for failing to generate people with black skin color, which alludes to issues with the training data used to create the model. (It's worth noting that the project was spun up as an online stunt to build awareness regarding the powerful capabilities of AI rather than as a fully polished software product.)

A different instance of AI bias involves decision-making in the criminal justice system. An investigative report by ProPublica revealed that software used to predict future criminal behavior was biased against African-American defendants. The software, designed to aid in decisions involving bail and sentencing, was more likely to incorrectly label black defendants as future criminals, while white defendants were more often mislabeled as low risk.

It's important to recognize that bias in AI can manifest in other forms as well, such as socioeconomic background, age, gender, and disability, making it vital to address a broader spectrum of potential biases to create more inclusive and fair AI systems.

To ensure fairness in AI, it's crucial to take steps in the design, development, and deployment stages. This includes careful selection and scrutiny of training data, implementing fairness metrics, transparency about the limitations of the AI system, and continuous auditing of AI models for bias. These steps, however, still aren't foolproof—especially as fairness is a complex and context-dependent concept. Like eliminating all forms of bias from schools and businesses, it may not always be possible to remove bias completely from AI models.

Privacy and AI

The expansion of artificial intelligence into many aspects of our lives also poses significant privacy concerns. AI models, especially those involved in computer vision and recommender systems, are voracious consumers of personal data, including sensitive and personal information regarding individuals.

The rise of AI has created a paradox because while these systems rely heavily on data to function effectively and potentially improve our lives, they also infringe on our privacy. Privacy, in this context, refers to the right of an individual to keep their personal information and activities secluded from or inaccessible to others, particularly those who are unauthorized to view them.

Consider social media platforms, which employ sophisticated models to curate and recommend personalized content. While this personalization enhances the overall user experience, it is often based on the collection and analysis of vast amounts of personal data, including our likes, dislikes, location, political affiliations, or even our different moods. This precise targeting ability has profound privacy implications and raises questions about user consent and control over the collection and use of personal data.

Another use case raising substantial concerns is facial recognition. While it can enhance security and streamline verification processes, it can also be used for continuous surveillance, leading to potential misuse. Without proper regulations and safeguards, this poses a serious threat to individual privacy.

Likewise, AI's predictive capabilities are complicated when it comes to user privacy. Machine learning models, for example, can analyze large datasets and infer sensitive information, even if that data was not explicitly provided. Prediction models, for instance, have been found to unintentionally expose a person's sexual orientation or political affiliation based on their online activity. These inferences can be disturbingly accurate, leading to potential invasions of privacy that are hard to anticipate and control.

The risks of privacy breaches and unintended data exposure became evident in 2009 when a woman in America sued Netflix over the disclosure of her sexual preferences from the 2007 Netflix Prize dataset. The lawsuit was filed after academic research at the University of Texas demonstrated privacy flaws in the design of the dataset Netflix used for the public competition. Despite Netflix's best attempts to remove personal identifiers from the data, including the names of individuals, the identities were revealed by matching the competition's dataset with film ratings from the publicly available Internet Movie Database. The researchers found that an anonymous user's rating of six obscure movies could be used to identify an individual Netflix user with an 84% success rate. Moreover, accuracy rose to 99% when the date of a movie review was known.

Legal Frameworks

In recent years, new legal frameworks have come into effect, including the GDPR (General Data Protection Regulation) in the European Union and the CCPA (California Consumer Privacy Act) in the United States. Designed to give individuals more control over their personal data, these frameworks encompass rights such as the right to access personal data, the right to be forgotten, and the right to data portability. GDPR, for example, enforces added transparency for users regarding how their data is processed and the use of cookies on web applications, as well as a clarified "right to be forgotten" when users no longer wish their data to be retained (given there are no legitimate grounds for keeping it). GDPR also requires the encryption of users' stored personal data and the right of users to accept or reject the use of their personal information for the application of online recommendations.

While such legal frameworks raise the bar for privacy and data protection, AI poses unique challenges to these frameworks due to their complexity and the often-opaque nature of deep learning models. In the face of these challenges, various practical strategies are being developed to reconcile AI with data privacy. Techniques like differential privacy, for example, offer a way to glean useful insights from data while providing robust privacy guarantees. Differential privacy adds controlled noise or randomness to the data before performing any computations or analysis. By introducing noise, the algorithm obscures individual contributions and makes it difficult to determine specific information about any individual in the dataset.

A different approach is federated learning, which makes it possible to train models on local devices rather than using a central server or the cloud under a centralized approach. The latter raises privacy and security concerns as the raw data needs to be shared with a central entity, potentially exposing sensitive information. By using a federated learning approach, model training is performed locally on individual devices or servers, such as smartphones, edge devices, or local servers without the need for data to leave the device and be shared externally.

Another important consideration is the software used to store and process data. To fulfill legal and privacy standards, it's imperative to assess different software based on their security measures, data anonymization features as well as data encryption tools to protect sensitive information. Examples of data anonymization include replacing specific values with more generalized values (e.g., age ranges instead of exact ages), replacing identifiers with pseudonyms, and adding random noise to the data to make it difficult to identify individuals while preserving statistical integrity.

Regarding data security, the software should offer permissions based on roles to restrict data access to authorized personnel or implement multiple forms of user verification to safeguard access to sensitive data. Also, from an operations perspective, data retention policies are useful for ensuring that sensitive data is not kept longer than necessary.

Finally, there is a need for professionals who can address the ethical and legal implications of AI and abide by the law. Here, larger organizations should consider the need for hiring AI ethicists and AI policy advocates, who are responsible for conducting internal audits, monitoring best practices, hosting internal training, and working with the government and other companies or industry organizations to establish industry practices.

In conclusion, the issue of privacy in the age of AI is a complex one, requiring a multifaceted approach. It touches not just technological solutions but also robust legal frameworks, ethical guidelines, software controls, and human resources. However, the overall goal should be to create an environment in which AI technologies can evolve without compromising the privacy rights of individuals.

Key Takeaways

1) AI systems can unintentionally replicate and amplify biases present in their training data or the biases of their human creators, leading to unfair outcomes.

2) Privacy is a major concern as AI relies on vast amounts of personal data, raising questions about individual privacy. Legal frameworks like GDPR and CCPA aim to protect privacy rights, but AI's complexity also presents challenges to upholding these regulations.

3) Legal frameworks, ethical guidelines, software design, and human resources are essential for creating an environment where AI technologies can evolve while safeguarding privacy rights.

Thought Exercises

1) How can you better protect your data and privacy? (i.e., Using a special email or user account to search and purchase sensitive items, opting out of recommender systems, using incognito or private browsing mode, or using anonymous search engines to protect your privacy.)

2) What does Google already know about you? To find out, go to google.com and sign in. Next, click the "Google apps" icon in the top right corner. Select "Account > Data & privacy > Personalized ads (My Ad Center)".

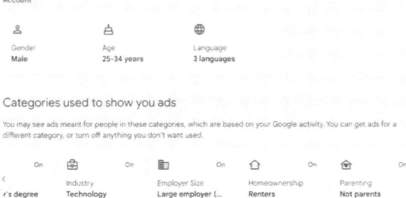

Figure 6: Example of Google's user profiling for personalized ads

## 12

THE FUTURE OF WORK

As a transformative technology, artificial intelligence holds the power to reshape jobs and the work environment in profound ways. But, in a world where news and discussions about AI bring up visions of imminent job replacement, there are genuine concerns about further job losses. The fear is heightened by the AI industry's preoccupation with benchmarking model performance and efficacy with human talent. From IBM's Deep Blue to the Stanley autonomous car and DeepMind's AlphaGo, AI companies have a history of evaluating and marketing their systems based on their ability to outperform humans in real-world demonstrations. While this approach is effective at attracting media attention, it has the dual effect of exacerbating and reinforcing people's fear of AI from the viewpoint of job security.

This type of fear is not unique to AI; from the cotton gin (which enabled the quick separation of seeds from cotton fibers) to the computer, anxiety has surrounded the advent of every new transformative technology. Yet, there is a strong consensus among economists and technologists that AI's impact might be different, given its potential to replace not only physical tasks but cognitive-based tasks as well.

According to *GPTs are GPTs: An Early Look at the Labor Market Impact Potential of Large Language Models,* commissioned and published by OpenAI and the University of Pennsylvania, professionals exposed to large language models are more vulnerable to future job replacement. Their findings revealed that approximately 80% of the U.S. workforce could have at least 10% of their work tasks impacted by the introduction of large language models, while approximately 19% of workers may see at least 50% of their tasks affected.

This includes tax preparers, mathematicians, writers and authors, web and digital interface designers, court reporters, proofreaders, auditors, accountants, journalists, and administrative assistants. Conversely, the study predicted that tasks that rely on critical thinking and scientific skills are less likely to be replaced by AI. Note that physical tasks associated with stonemasons, painters, cooks, and auto mechanics aren't at high risk of being replaced by large language models such as ChatGPT but could be replaced by AI robots and further automation in the future.

The 7 Stages of Resistance

During periods of fast technological transition—as we are experiencing now—it's common for people to experience fear or to sink into a state of denial, anger, and depression. In fact, individuals and organizations often experience something akin to the seven stages of grief in response to drastic changes caused by new technology. Typically applied to describe emotional responses to loss, the seven stages of grief are shock, denial, anger, bargaining, depression, testing, and acceptance.

First, both individuals and organizations are shocked or stunned by the introduction of new technology. This shock stems from uncertainty or confusion about how it works and the potential implications. In the case of ChatGPT, the new technology shocked people with its ability to mimic human writing capabilities.

Once the initial shock wears off, most people turn skeptical and reject the notion that the new technology will have any significant or longstanding impact. In practice, they may avoid learning about it or dismiss it as a trend or fad that will quickly pass.

Third, as the realization that the new technology is not going away sets in, people start to experience feelings of anger or resentment. They may feel threatened by the changes that the new technology brings and how it might affect their role or organization.

This is followed by the bargaining stage, where individuals and organizations try to negotiate or find a compromise. This could involve attempting to maintain their existing routines and operations while incorporating some aspects of the new technology.

Subsequently, people recognize that the old ways of doing things are changing and are no longer celebrated. This can cause a sense of sadness, loss, and even depression. In addition, people may feel overwhelmed by the new skills and knowledge required to adapt.

Eventually, more individuals and organizations begin to experiment with the new technology as part of the testing phase. Individuals start learning new skills or finding ways to integrate technology into their job or organization.

Finally, everyone comes to acknowledge the benefits and accept the new technology as a part of their lives and day-to-day work.

For organizations, understanding these seven stages is vital for setting realistic expectations, managing internal resistance, and navigating the changes required in order to stay competitive. For individuals, being cognizant of the natural reactions to new technology can spur you into action and help you reach the acceptance stage faster than those around you.

It's worth noting that not every individual or organization will go through all seven stages or experience each stage in the prescribed order. Early adopters, for example, are inclined to embrace new technology overnight, while others may linger in one stage for an extended period and never reach the next stage. The latter can be dangerous as there is an opportunity cost to inaction as others capitalize on the first-mover advantage, which brings us to the *missing middle theory*.

The Missing Middle

For those looking to thrive in the new era of work, it is critical to understand that AI, in most cases, is designed to enhance productivity rather than to outright replace you. In line with this perspective, many of the jobs of the future are predicted to be copilot roles, in which humans work alongside AI to carry out a collection of professional tasks, whether that's linguists using ChatGPT to translate documents or lawyers validating contracts drafted by AI assistants.

In the healthcare sector, for example, AI can be used to streamline administrative tasks, manage patient records, and even assist in interpreting medical images, allowing medical professionals to spend more quality time with patients and make more informed decisions.

In marketing, AI tools can provide real-time analytics, predictive models, and relevant ad copy, helping marketers make informed decisions and increase the success of their ad campaigns.

By leveraging AI's ability to handle complex calculations and process vast amounts of data, humans across industries can focus more on tasks requiring creativity, emotional intelligence, and critical thinking—skills that are uniquely human. This is the viewpoint championed in the book *Human + Machine: Reimagining Work in the Age of AI*. Termed the *missing middle*, the authors advocate that the most effective and cost-efficient path forward is to merge automated tools with the flexibility of human workers to achieve optimum outcomes.

The principles of cybernetics, as espoused by Norbert Wiener, reinforce the concept of the missing middle and highlight the complementary nature of our respective strengths. Derived from the Greek word *kybernetes*, cybernetics means *steersman* or *governor*, which emphasizes the notions of control, communication, and feedback in systems. While broad in scope, at its core, cybernetics looks at systems and processes that aim to analyze and understand the principles of how to be effective, adaptive, and self-governing. In the context of artificial intelligence, cybernetics looks at how machines can complement and mimic human-like behavior or decision-making processes as part of a symbiotic feedback loop with human operators, as popularized in Norbert Wiener's research.

Born in 1894, Wiener became interested in cybernetics following his involvement in the development of computers and automated anti-aircraft guns during World War II. This included his realization that the process of tracking a moving aircraft entailed making several observations to anticipate its future trajectory. During the dynamics of war, he noticed that the reactions of the gunner must be factored into predictions. This is due to the fact that pilots alter course in response to enemy fire, prompting the gunner to adjust, thereby creating a feedback loop where the gunner's actions eventually shape their future actions.

Recognizing that feedback loops are all around us, Wiener went on to explore the traits of this phenomenon to optimize human-machine feedback loops under the lens of cybernetics. Wiener posited that when harnessed correctly, technology actually amplifies human capabilities and productivity by extending our cognitive and physical capacities, enabling us to accomplish tasks more efficiently and effectively.

We see this today with AI-powered tools like Consensus, Elicit, and Semantic Scholar, which allow researchers to find papers, extract key claims or summaries, and even brainstorm their ideas by connecting with a massive pool of academic research. These tools allow researchers to streamline the research process and concentrate on higher-level cognitive activities such as critical thinking, hypothesis formulation, experimental design, and interpretation of results, which can help drive advancements in innovation and scientific understanding.

While the idea of substituting human tasks with AI tools is alluring, not all tasks should function independently of humans. Instead, most tasks should operate in a feedback loop with human copilots, with AI constantly learning from human inputs and modifying their behavior accordingly. These interconnected feedback systems optimize the strengths of both parties, resulting in new breakthroughs and an overall productivity boost.

Chess, in particular, offers a glimpse into effective collaboration between humans and AI, especially given chess's history with AI technology. In hybrid chess competitions, human players utilize their creativity and deep understanding of the game to work in tandem with AI chess engines to leverage their vast analytical capabilities. The combination of human ingenuity and AI's analytical prowess creates a synergy that outperforms either side performing on its own. This successful partnership has been demonstrated in a number of tournaments, including freestyle chess competitions, where teams composed of human players and AI engines have consistently outperformed human-only and AI-only teams.

This includes the 2005 Freestyle Chess Tournament held by the Internet Chess Club (ICC), which permitted players to use any combination of computer chess engine, database, and human analysis. The winners weren't grandmasters or supercomputers but two amateur players working together with multiple AI chess machines, defeating both highly ranked human players and standalone chess engines.

Job Replacement & Business Disruption

The speed at which AI is seeping into all aspects of modern work—from marketing to human resources—underscores AI literacy as a key skill set for the modern workforce. Also, just as the Internet Age triggered an avalanche of new job titles, so too will the AI-centric era we are now entering.

During the formative years of the Dot-com evolution, many traditional job opportunities—including travel agent, journalist, courier, stockbroker, and Encyclopaedia salesperson—contracted or were phased out entirely. However, these losses were gradually filled with the creation of new job roles. An explosion of highly skilled jobs ensued in web development, search engine optimization, e-commerce, online customer service, web design, affiliate marketing, and eventually social media and mobile web design. While it's possible that a high proportion of these jobs will now be phased out by AI, new job roles will again be created or converted to copilot roles.

Moreover, it's possible that AI may assist in creating more inclusive workplaces. Assistive AI technologies such as AI-driven speech recognition software can help individuals with mobility impairments, while AI-powered predictive text and voice synthesis can assist those with speech difficulties.

Likewise, AI technology will empower smaller companies or companies-of-one to thrive in a more fragmented and fast-paced world. The ability to generate a website, write blog content, and create an explainer video using generative AI tools will allow individuals to test their ideas, gain market feedback, and iterate faster than ever before.

Conversely, labor-intensive organizations that rely on human capital to carry out services such as ghostwriting, translation, and online tutoring are earmarked to be the first affected by AI technology. With AI offering a faster and lower-cost alternative, these organizations may experience a significant transformation in how they operate as well as a negative impact in the short term. Exposing this reality, stocks in the online tutoring company, Chegg, plummeted after the CEO admitted the threat posed by AI. During the company's earnings call in mid-2023, the CEO Dan Rosensweig explained that "In the first part of the year, we saw no noticeable impact from ChatGPT on our new account growth and we were meeting expectations on new sign-ups. However, since March we saw a significant spike in student interest in ChatGPT. We now believe it's having an impact on our new customer growth rate."

While it's important to acknowledge that Chegg exceeded profit expectations as a result of the explosive demand for online education during the COVID lockdowns that took place between 2020 and 2021, AI must be considered as a competitive force in all industries, alongside traditional business threats such as globalization and geopolitics.

In response to technological changes introduced by ChapGPT, Chegg has announced that it's developing its own AI, CheggMate, in partnership with OpenAI to assist students with their homework. Textbroker, a content writing service provider, has also added AI technology to its service offering, and many other service platforms will be forced to adapt or die as well.

Human services will remain in demand but rather than being the staple service, they will become a premium or concierge service added on top of a fast and more cost-effective AI-powered service. Tax, legal, and accounting services, for example, will be serviced by AI agents trained on relevant data, and then verified, witnessed, and supplemented by human experts. This creates a new business model where customers can access self-service offerings powered by AI, such as contract drafting or balance sheet analysis, and then have the option to communicate or receive personalized assistance from a human assistant as part of a human service that is more focused, personalized, and effective than many of today's basic service offerings.

AI Adoption in Organizations

The adoption of AI presents a range of opportunities for organizations seeking to gain a competitive edge. However, the road to successful AI implementation is not without obstacles. From data quality and availability to cultural resistance and ethical concerns, various factors can hinder the smooth integration of AI solutions.

Implementing AI practices entails significant upfront costs as well, including investments in hardware, software, and hiring skilled professionals. In many cases, organizations may be reluctant to commit substantial resources without a clear understanding of the return on investment and the potential long-term benefits AI can bring. AI processes can also disrupt traditional job roles and workflows, creating anxiety among employees about potential job losses or changes to their responsibilities.

Overcoming these obstacles requires a well-thought-out strategy, including robust data management practices, hiring, training and upskilling employees, thorough cost-benefit analyses, stakeholder involvement, and prioritizing ethical considerations. For small organizations, collaborating with experienced AI vendors and consultants can help to facilitate successful AI integration. However, for medium and large-sized organizations, it's important to follow a top-down approach that can align all the necessary resources and implement organization-wide changes. In this context, appointing a dedicated Chief AI Officer can play a pivotal role. By appointing a single Chief AI Officer instead of relying on a committee of AI consultants, companies can ensure streamlined implementation and accelerated testing, leading to faster adoption of AI strategies throughout the organization.

Reporting directly to the CEO, CTO, or a board of directors, a Chief AI Officer works as a senior executive responsible for identifying opportunities for AI adoption, and ensuring that AI efforts align with the company's overall business objectives. It's important to acknowledge that the Chief AI Officer does not personally code algorithms or lead the data science team's day-to-day operations. Rather, they are responsible for monitoring market changes, determining the right strategic direction, and identifying opportunities for the company to utilize AI technologies effectively in marketing, research and development, and other areas of the organization. By staying ahead of the curve, they guide the organization to ride the AI wave instead of being overwhelmed by it.

In addition, the Chief AI Officer is responsible for engaging with various teams within the organization in order to gather feedback and determine optimal areas for AI application. In the short term, this may involve conducting A/B or split testing to compare human and AI-powered resources, evaluating different AI software, and using testing and data to find quick wins and gain internal support for new practices. By presenting quantifiable metrics and data that highlight the improvements achieved through AI practices, it becomes easier to demonstrate the value that AI brings to the organization.

The Hustle Daily Newsletter, for example, ran an A/B test using custom AI-generated images and human-edited stock photography. The AI-generated version was spun up using Midjourney and designed based on the goal of aligning the image with the ad copy and the value proposition they wanted to communicate. This resulted in a 3x increase in ad performance (measured on the cost to acquire clicks) compared to the classic stock photography approach. On top of this, the AI-generated ads were faster to produce.

Figure 7: The Hustle Daily ad image created using Midjourney

While it's valuable to run internal experiments and consider the benefits that AI can bring, it's important to acknowledge that not all teams, departments, and organizations will need to adopt AI technology. The search engine company DuckDuckGo, for example, has resisted industry trends such as personalized search results, personalized ad targeting, and user data tracking to provide a privacy-centric alternative for users concerned about data privacy and tracking. This includes offering Duck Player mode, which provides users with a clean viewing experience stripped of personalized ads and prevents users' viewing activity from influencing their YouTube recommendations.

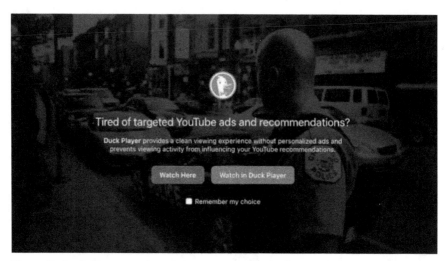

Figure 8: Duck Player mode removes personalized ads

Similarly, Basecamp has chosen not to adopt certain AI-driven features commonly found in other project management tools, instead prioritizing a more human-centric approach to collaboration in its task management software. In a different vein, Luddite Games focuses on developing games that rely on human creativity and decision-making under the game's narrative of destroying AI and saving human jobs.

This type of counterapproach strategy allows each of these companies to differentiate themselves in the market and cater to an audience that values privacy or human involvement and expertise. While it may not be the fastest or most effective way to obtain media interest and investor funding in the early stages of an AI hype cycle, there will be plenty of opportunities for other service providers to target a niche audience by openly resisting AI technology and embracing human expertise. The key is to openly resist new AI technology and integrate this stance into the company's marketing strategy and value proposition rather than being a side-effect of inaction or complacency.

Digital Craftmanship & Offline Events

Despite the immense efficiency gains that AI offers, consumers will continue to respect the craft and attention to detail that humans bring to their work. Whether it's creating a piece of artwork or crafting handmade products, we disproportionally value things created by ourselves or other humans. We see this with birthday and thankyou cards. Despite the shareability and convenience of e-cards, most people prefer the thoughtfulness and effort that comes with sending a physical card and writing a handwritten message.

Similarly, if you browse the comments on YouTube videos, you will see users consistently praise creators who take the time to produce subtitles for their videos, add timestamps, or who spend inordinate amounts of time and effort capturing the perfect drone shot. Ultimately, the human touch carries a sense of quality, uniqueness, and care that resonates with people. In addition, there is an inherent appreciation for the time, skill, and dedication that goes into creating something manually—even if it is done digitally.

In the future, the ubiquity of AI-generated content may even lead to a future where creating your own podcast or video content without AI assistance is valued as a form of digital craftsmanship. Likewise, companies that offer human customer service support might stand out in a world where AI avatars are trained on millions of data points and customer support logs.

Finally, the surge in AI-generated content may lead to renewed interest in offline events such as meetups, political debates, and music concerts, as a direct response to the growing distrust of online content. In an age of deep fakes and content manipulation, seeking face-to-face interactions may be the only way to discern authenticity and verify what is genuinely real in the world. Likewise, dating might veer towards a return to more in-person meetups or an embrace of Japanese-style single's parties known as goukon, countering the influence of AI-enhanced photos and AI-generated conversations in the online dating space. Alternatively, some individuals may find the efficiency of their AI dating agent communicating with a suitor's AI agent and scheduling a coffee date more appealing!

Key Takeaways

1) The fear of job displacement isn't new and while AI is expected to create new roles and demand new skills, we could see a drastic shakeup to knowledge work. This includes humans working together with AI agents as copilots to enhance productivity and efficiency.

2) Resistance is common in the face of technological innovation, with individuals and organizations often going through a series of emotional responses akin to the seven stages of grief.

3) AI technology has the potential to empower smaller companies and individuals to test new ideas at a lower cost.

4) AI-powered service providers can offer faster and low-cost services, challenging traditional business models.

5) Appointing a Chief AI Officer can help organizations navigate AI strategies, identify opportunities, and align AI efforts with overall business objectives.

6) The proliferation and ubiquity of AI technology could pave the way for a new form of digital trade or commerce carried out by humans, without AI involvement.

Thought Exercises

1) What are your strengths and weaknesses? How can AI be used to overcome your weaknesses and spend more time on your strengths?

2) How can AI companies move beyond crude comparisons with humans to measure and market their products? (i.e., new jobs created by AI, lives saved by an AI product).

3) In which industries or scenarios will using AI be a potential disadvantage for the brand, sport, organization, or other entity?

FURTHER RESOURCES

The field of artificial intelligence is vast and multifaceted, encompassing various domains covered in this book. As a result, acquiring knowledge in AI requires deep-diving into an array of different subjects, each one contributing to a more comprehensive understanding. This final chapter provides a general guide to learning resources and an overview of potential career paths.

Formal Education

An obvious starting point for anyone interested in AI is formal education. Universities around the world offer courses dedicated to AI and related fields, including data science, machine learning, and computer science. Highly respected Master's programs in machine learning are offered at Stanford, Berkeley, Carnegie Mellon, Columbia, University of Washington, and MIT. Other reputable institutes include Edinburgh, Duke, Michigan, University of Pennsylvania, Toronto, UCSD, Brown, UCL, Georgia Tech, Cambridge, Oxford, and Cornell. Carnegie Mellon University, renowned for its Robotics Institute, also provides excellent degree courses in AI robotics. Note too that many colleges offer online degrees and there are various other degree options offered around the world.

Another valuable but more affordable option is the Georgia Tech Online Master of Science in Computer Science (OMSCS) program. Launched in 2014 in collaboration with Udacity and AT&T, this degree is fully online and the curriculum is no different from what you would receive as an on-campus student. The program costs just under USD $10,000 for a one-year full-time degree or a two-year part-time degree.

The program includes specialization tracks in areas such as machine learning and robotics. The machine learning track provides a deep understanding of the key principles and algorithms. The robotics track, meanwhile, teaches you how to design, implement, and analyze modern robotic systems. This track will teach you knowledge regarding the physical embodiment of AI systems, which is a crucial part of how AI interfaces with the real world. However, be wary that the program's rigor and pace are equivalent to its on-campus counterpart, so you will need to be ready to dedicate a significant amount of effort and time to your studies.

After completing a Master's degree in machine learning/artificial intelligence/data science, there is then the option of completing a PhD. This is an ideal route for those wishing to delve deeper into AI topics. PhDs in many countries are supported by government or university funding. There is, though, a sizeable opportunity cost of completing a four-year PhD on a basic salary/stipend over working in industry on a full-time salary. In places like the United States, you can expect to receive USD $20,000-45,000 a year to complete a PhD course, compared to earning an annual salary of USD $80,000-120,000 working for a private company.

However, Google, Facebook, and Microsoft have been known for raiding the ranks of academia to recruit talent in the space of artificial intelligence and to secure a pipeline of young talent. The prevailing logic is that hiring professors unlocks a new network of talent and makes it easier to hire former PhD students. The other upside of completing a PhD is that you have greater control over the scope of your work and research, and the academic path overall may be a more attractive proposition for some people.

Non-Degree Options

Beyond traditional education pathways, there is a plethora of non-degree options delivered online. Online learning platforms have democratized access to knowledge, offering a range of courses catering to various specializations. This includes platforms like Coursera and edX which partner with top universities and industry leaders to provide high-quality, accessible content. For example, Coursera's *AI For Everyone* course, developed by Andrew Ng, a co-founder of Coursera and an adjunct professor at Stanford University, offers a non-technical introduction to AI.

As my preferred non-degree option, I recommend DataCamp as an excellent resource for learning about AI, machine learning, data science, and related fields including how to code. The platform's approach is hands-on, focusing on active learning and practical application, which is quite different from traditional lecture-based courses. Each skill-based course is broken down into bite-sized lessons combining short videos with immediate hands-on exercises.

Books

There is a wealth of books that delve into AI from different perspectives. For those interested in the philosophical and societal impacts of AI, books such as Nick Bostrom's *Superintelligence: Paths, Dangers, Strategies* and Max Tegmark's *Life 3.0: Being Human in the Age of Artificial Intelligence* are highly recommended. If you're interested in the technical aspects, O'Reilly Media textbooks such as *Hands-On Machine Learning with Scikit-Learn, Keras, and TensorFlow* authored by Aurélien Géron provide practical insights for developers into AI and machine learning.

Real-World Projects

For hands-on learning, nothing beats working on real-world projects. As a platform for data science competitions and public datasets, Kaggle offers a plethora of datasets and challenges that can be used to hone your skills in machine learning and AI.

Contributing to open-source AI projects is another way to gain practical experience. Projects such as OpenAI's GPT models, TensorFlow, and PyTorch all welcome community contributions.

In regard to practical training, LeWagon offers data science boot camps around the world, which train students with the practical skills needed to become a data scientist and work in a data team. LeWagon also runs free online and offline events, which you can sign up for on their website (www.lewagon.com).

Blogs & Podcasts

Podcasts and blogs are valuable resources for learning about AI. Podcasts such as *The AI Alignment Podcast* by the Future of Life

Institute, *Data Skeptic*, and *AI in Business* all provide insightful discussions on various AI topics. Blogs such as *Towards Data Science* and the *Google AI Blog* also offer deep dives into AI trends and research. My favorite podcast is the OC Devel *Machine Learning Guide* podcast.

Potential Career Paths in AI

Whether you're a recent graduate or a seasoned professional considering a career switch, there is a place and role for you in the ever-broadening world of AI. As Stuart Russell and Peter Norvig point out in *Artificial Intelligence: A Modern Approach*, AI is a broad and rapidly evolving field that offers a plethora of opportunities for those willing to invest the time and effort required to master it.

As the influence and impact of AI grows, the demand for professionals in this field will also continue to rise. Regardless of industry or geography, organizations across the globe are recognizing the power of AI to drive growth, innovation, and efficiency. This section focuses on the vast array of career paths in AI and provides a broad view of the roles, skills, and opportunities available for those interested in this field.

AI Research Scientist

The first role we'll examine is the AI research scientist. This position is typically based in academia or research institutions but some private sector companies employ research scientists too. These professionals are the thought leaders of AI, pushing the boundaries of what's possible. In addition to publishing papers and attending conferences, they are often found working on abstract and complex problems in machine learning, deep learning, and other AI-related fields. They possess a deep understanding of algorithms, calculus, linear algebra, and statistics. While a doctoral degree in a related field is often required, some organizations hire candidates with a Masters degree and substantial relevant experience.

AI Engineers

AI engineers apply the theories and concepts developed by AI research scientists in real-world scenarios. They build, test, and deploy AI models and manage AI systems and infrastructure. They must be proficient in various programming languages like Python, Java, or C++, and be familiar with AI libraries such as TensorFlow or PyTorch. A Bachelors or Masters degree in computer science, data science, or a related field is usually required, along with a strong practical understanding of machine learning.

Data Scientists

Data scientists work as the detectives of the AI world. They sift through large volumes of data, using machine learning and statistical models to extract meaningful insights that can be used to solve business problems and make strategic decisions. They require a firm grasp of statistics, as well as experience with programming languages and data management tools.

Machine Learning Engineers

Straddling the roles of AI engineer and data scientist, machine learning engineers are typically tasked with creating data models that are then implemented by AI applications to learn and improve. To work as a machine learning engineer, you will need to have a deep understanding of multiple programming languages, machine learning algorithms, and data modeling.

AI Ethicists

AI ethicists represent a newer but increasingly important role in the field of AI. As AI applications proliferate, questions about their ethical implications and the governance required to ensure their fair use have expanded too. AI ethicists analyze and address these issues. Their backgrounds can vary widely, from philosophy to law to data science, with the common denominator being a dual understanding of AI technologies and a strong ethical framework.

AI Policy Advocates

A lesser-known but growing role is the AI policy advocate. These professionals work with governments, non-profit organizations, and companies to influence policy and legislation related to AI. This role requires a strong understanding of AI, public policy, and legal frameworks.

The roles mentioned represent just a snapshot of the opportunities available in the field of AI. Each of these roles offers a unique perspective on AI and serves a critical function in its ongoing development. However, all these roles share a common need for continuous learning and adaptation. Given the rapid pace of advancements in AI, professionals in this field must be committed to staying up-to-date with the latest developments.

Before deciding on a career path in AI, it's important to consider your interests, strengths, and long-term career goals. For example, if you're passionate about researching new theories and technologies, a career as an AI research scientist might be a good fit for you. If you are more interested in applying AI technologies to solving real-world problems, roles such as AI engineer or data scientist might be a better match.

Moreover, each of these roles offers different levels of interaction with others. Some roles, such as AI engineer or machine learning engineer, may work as part of a larger team and interact closely with other departments. Other roles such as AI research scientist may have a more solitary focus and work primarily on individual projects.

Finally, it's crucial to consider the societal implications of AI in choosing a potential career path. As AI becomes more integrated into our daily lives, there is a growing need for professionals who can address the ethical, legal, and societal implications of AI. Roles such as AI ethicist or AI policy advocate are expected to become increasingly important as the field continues to evolve.

BOOK 2: MACHINE LEARNING FOR ABSOLUTE BEGINNERS

## 1

PREFACE

Machines have come a long way since the onset of the Industrial Revolution. They continue to fill factory floors and manufacturing plants, but their capabilities extend beyond manual activities to cognitive tasks that, until recently, only humans were capable of performing. Judging song contests, driving automobiles, and detecting fraudulent transactions are three examples of the complex tasks machines are now capable of simulating.

But these remarkable feats trigger fear among some observers. Part of their fear nestles on the neck of survivalist insecurities and provokes the deep-seated question of *what if*? *What if* intelligent machines turn on us in a struggle of the fittest? *What if* intelligent machines produce offspring with capabilities that humans never intended to impart to machines? *What if* the legend of the *singularity* is true?

While AI is moving fast, broad adoption remains an uncharted path fraught with known and unforeseen challenges. Delays and other obstacles are inevitable. Nor is machine learning a simple case of flicking a switch and asking the machine to predict the outcome of the Super Bowl and serve you a delicious martini.

Far from a typical out-of-the-box analytics solution, machine learning relies on statistical algorithms managed and overseen by skilled individuals called data scientists and machine learning engineers. This is one labor market where job opportunities are destined to grow but where supply is struggling to meet demand.

In fact, the current shortage of professionals with the necessary expertise and training is one of the primary obstacles delaying AI's progress. According to Charles Green, the Director of Thought Leadership at Belatrix Software:

> *"It's a huge challenge to find data scientists, people with machine learning experience, or people with the skills to analyze and use the data, as well as those who can create the algorithms required for machine learning. Secondly, while the technology is still emerging, there are many ongoing developments. It's clear that AI is a long way from how we might imagine it."* [10]

Perhaps your own path to working in the field of machine learning starts here, or maybe a baseline understanding is sufficient to fulfill your curiosity for now.

This book focuses on the high-level fundamentals, including key terms, general workflow, and the statistical underpinnings of basic algorithms to set you on your path. To design and code intelligent machines, you'll first need to develop a strong grasp of classical statistics. Algorithms derived from classical statistics sit at the core of machine learning and constitute the metaphorical neurons and nerves that power artificial cognitive abilities. Coding is the other indispensable part of machine learning, which includes managing and manipulating large amounts of data. Unlike building a web 2.0 landing page with click-and-drag tools like Wix and WordPress, machine learning requires Python, C++, R, or another programming language. If you haven't learned a relevant programming language, you will need to if you wish to make further progress in this field. But for the purpose of this compact starter's course, the following chapters can be completed without any programming experience.

While this book serves as an introductory course to machine learning, please note that it does not constitute an absolute beginner's introduction to mathematics, computer programming, and statistics. A cursory knowledge of these fields or convenient access to an Internet connection may be required to aid understanding in later chapters.

---

[10] Matt Kendall, "Machine Learning Adoption Thwarted by Lack of Skills and Understanding," *Nearshore Americas*, accessed May 14, 2017, http://www.nearshoreamericas.com/machine-learning-adoption-understanding

For those who wish to dive into the coding aspect of machine learning, Chapter 17 and Chapter 18 walk you through the entire process of setting up a machine learning model using Python. A gentle introduction to coding with Python has also been included in the Appendix and information regarding further learning resources can be found in the final section of this book.

Lastly, video tutorials (included free with this book) can be found at https://scatterplotpress.com/p/ml-code-exercises

## 2

WHAT IS MACHINE LEARNING?

In 1959, IBM published a paper in the *IBM Journal of Research and Development* with an intriguing and obscure title. Authored by IBM's Arthur Samuel, the paper investigated the application of machine learning in the game of checkers "to verify the fact that a computer can be programmed so that it will learn to play a better game of checkers than can be played by the person who wrote the program."[11]

Figure 1: Historical mentions of "machine learning" in published books. Source: Google Ngram Viewer, 2017

Although it wasn't the first published paper to use the term "machine learning" per se, Arthur Samuel is regarded as the first person to coin and define machine learning as the concept and specialized field we know today. *Samuel's landmark journal submission, Some Studies in Machine Learning Using the Game of Checkers, introduced* machine learning as a subfield of computer

---

[11] *Arthur Samuel, "Some Studies in Machine Learning Using the Game of Checkers," IBM Journal of Research and Development, Vol. 3, Issue. 3, 1959.*

science that gives computers the ability to learn without being explicitly programmed.

While not directly treated in Arthur Samuel's initial definition, a key characteristic of machine learning is the concept of *self-learning*. This refers to the application of statistical modeling to detect patterns and improve performance based on data and empirical information; all without direct programming commands. This is what Arthur Samuel described as the ability to learn without being explicitly programmed. Samuel didn't imply that machines may formulate decisions with no upfront programming. On the contrary, machine learning is heavily dependent on code input. Instead, he observed machines can perform a set task using *input data* rather than relying on a direct *input command*.

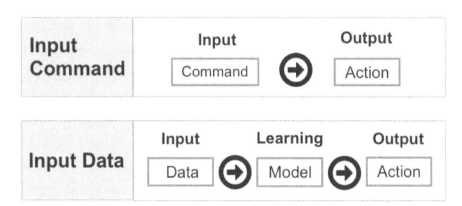

Figure 2: Comparison of Input Command vs Input Data

An example of an input command is entering "2+2" in a programming language such as Python and clicking "Run" or hitting "Enter" to view the output.

```
>>> 2+2
4
>>>
```

This represents a direct command with a pre-programmed answer, which is typical of most computer applications. Unlike traditional computer programming, though, where outputs or decisions are pre-defined by the programmer, machine learning uses data as input to build a decision model. Decisions are generated by deciphering relationships and patterns in the data using probabilistic reasoning, trial and error, and other computationally-intensive techniques. This means that the output of the decision model is determined by the contents of the input data rather than any pre-set rules defined by a human programmer. The human programmer is still responsible for feeding the data into the model, selecting an appropriate algorithm and tweaking its settings (called *hyperparameters*) in a bid to reduce prediction error, but ultimately the machine and developer operate a layer apart in contrast to traditional programming.

To draw an example, let's suppose that after analyzing YouTube viewing habits, the decision model identifies a significant relationship among data scientists who like watching cat videos. A separate model, meanwhile, identifies patterns among the physical traits of baseball players and their likelihood of winning the season's Most Valuable Player (MVP) award.

In the first scenario, the machine analyzes which videos data scientists enjoy watching on YouTube based on user engagement; measured in likes, subscribers, and repeat viewing. In the second scenario, the machine assesses the physical attributes of previous baseball MVPs among other features such as age and education. However, at no stage was the decision model told or programmed to produce those two outcomes. By decoding complex patterns in the input data, the model uses machine learning to find connections without human help. This also means that a related dataset collected from another time period, with fewer or greater data points, might push the model to produce a slightly different output.

Another distinct feature of machine learning is the ability to improve predictions based on experience. Mimicking the way humans base decisions on experience and the success or failure of past attempts, machine learning utilizes exposure to data to improve its decision-making. The socializing of data points provides experience and enables the model to familiarize itself with patterns in the data. Conversely, insufficient input data restricts the model's ability to deconstruct underlying patterns in the data and limits its capacity to respond to potential variance and random phenomena found in live data. Exposure to input data thereby deepens the model's understanding of patterns, including the significance of changes in the data, to construct an effective self-learning model.

A common example of a self-learning model is a system for detecting spam email messages. Following an initial serving of input data, the model learns to flag emails with suspicious subject lines and body text containing keywords that correlate strongly with spam messages flagged by users in the past. Indications of spam email may include words like *dear friend, free, invoice, PayPal, Viagra, casino, payment, bankruptcy,* and *winner.* However, as more data is analyzed, the model might also find exceptions and incorrect assumptions that render the model susceptible to bad predictions. If there is limited data to reference its decision, the following email subject, for example, might be wrongly classified as spam: "**PayPal** has received your **payment** for **Casino** Royale purchased on eBay."

As this is a genuine email sent from a PayPal auto-responder, the spam detection system is lured into producing a false-positive based on previous input data. Traditional programming is highly susceptible to this problem because the model is rigidly defined according to pre-set rules. Machine learning, on the other hand, emphasizes exposure to data as a way to refine the model, adjust weak assumptions, and respond appropriately to unique data points such as the scenario just described.

While data is used to source the self-learning process, more data doesn't always equate to better decisions; the input data must be relevant. In *Data and Goliath: The Hidden Battles to Collect Your Data and Control Your World,* Bruce Schneier writes that, "When looking for the needle, the last thing you want to do is pile lots more hay on it."[12] This means that adding irrelevant data can be counter-productive to achieving a desired result. In addition, the amount of input data should be compatible with the processing resources and time that is available.

---

[12] Bruce Schneier, "Data and Goliath: The Hidden Battles to Collect Your Data and Control Your World," *W. W. Norton & Company,* First Edition, 2016.

Training & Test Data

In machine learning, the input data is typically split into *training data* and *test data*. The first split of data is the *training data*, which is the initial reserve of data used to develop the model. In the spam email detection example, false-positives similar to the PayPal auto-response message might be detected from the training data. Modifications must then be made to the model, e.g., email notifications issued from the sending address "payments@paypal.com" should be excluded from spam filtering. Using machine learning, the model can be trained to automatically detect these errors (by analyzing historical examples of spam messages and deciphering their patterns) without direct human interference.

After you have developed a model based on patterns extracted from the training data and you are satisfied with the accuracy of its predictions, you can test the model on the remaining data, known as the *test data*. If you are also satisfied with the model's performance using the test data, the model is ready to filter incoming emails in a live setting and generate decisions on how to categorize those messages. We will discuss training and test data further in Chapter 6.

The Anatomy of Machine Learning

The final section of this chapter explains how machine learning fits into the broader landscape of data science and computer science. This includes understanding how machine learning connects with parent fields and sister disciplines. This is important, as you will encounter related terms in machine learning literature and courses. Relevant disciplines can also be difficult to tell apart, especially machine learning and data mining.

Let's start with a high-level introduction. Machine learning, data mining, artificial intelligence, and computer programming all fall under the umbrella of computer science, which encompasses everything related to the design and use of computers. Within the all-encompassing space of computer science is the next broad field of data science. Narrower than computer science, data science comprises methods and systems to extract knowledge and insights from data with the aid of computers.

Figure 3: The lineage of machine learning represented by a row of Russian matryoshka dolls

Emerging from computer science and data science as the third matryoshka doll from the left in Figure 3 is artificial intelligence. Artificial intelligence, or AI, encompasses the ability of machines to perform intelligent and cognitive tasks. Comparable to how the Industrial Revolution gave birth to an era of machines simulating physical tasks, AI is driving the development of machines capable of simulating cognitive abilities.

While still broad but dramatically more honed than computer science and data science, AI spans numerous subfields that are popular and newsworthy today. These subfields include search and planning, reasoning and knowledge representation, perception, natural language processing (NLP), and of course, machine learning.

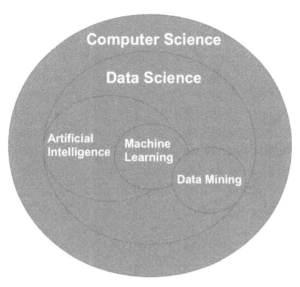

Figure 4: Visual representation of the relationship between data-related fields

For students interested in AI, machine learning provides an excellent starting point as it provides a narrower and more practical lens of study (in comparison to AI). Algorithms applied in machine learning can also be used in other disciplines, including perception and natural language processing. In addition, a Master's degree is adequate to develop a certain level of expertise in machine learning, but you may need a PhD to make genuine progress in the field of artificial intelligence.

As mentioned, machine learning overlaps with data mining—a sister discipline based on discovering and unearthing patterns in large datasets. Both techniques rely on inferential methods, i.e. predicting outcomes based on other outcomes and probabilistic reasoning, and draw from a similar assortment of algorithms including principal component analysis, regression analysis, decision trees, and clustering techniques. To add further confusion, the two techniques are commonly mistaken and misreported or even explicitly misused. The textbook *Data mining: Practical machine learning tools and techniques with Java* is said to have originally been titled *Practical machine learning,* but for marketing reasons "data mining" was later appended to the title.[13]

Lastly, because of their interdisciplinary nature, experts from a diverse spectrum of disciplines often define data mining and machine learning differently. This has led to confusion, in addition to a genuine overlap between the two disciplines. But whereas machine learning emphasizes the incremental process of self-learning and automatically detecting patterns through experience derived from exposure to data, data mining is a less autonomous technique of extracting hidden insight.

Like randomly drilling a hole into the earth's crust, data mining doesn't begin with a clear hypothesis of what insight it will find. Instead, it seeks out patterns and relationships that are yet to be mined and is, thus, well-suited for understanding large datasets with complex patterns. As noted by the authors of *Data Mining: Concepts and Techniques,* data mining developed as a result of advances in data collection and database management beginning in the early 1980s[14] and an urgent need to make sense of progressively larger and complicated datasets.[15]

Whereas data mining focuses on **analyzing input variables to predict a new output**, machine learning extends to **analyzing both input and output variables**. This includes supervised learning techniques that compare known combinations of input and output variables to discern patterns and make predictions, and reinforcement learning which randomly trials a massive number of input variables to produce a desired output. Another machine learning technique, called unsupervised learning, generates predictions based on the analysis of input variables with no known target output. This technique is often used in combination or in preparation for supervised learning under the name of *semi-*

[13] Remco Bouckaert, Eibe Frank, Mark Hall, Geoffrey Holmes, Bernhard Pfahringer, Peter Reutemann & Ian Witten, "WEKA—Experiences with a Java Open-Source Project," *Journal of Machine Learning Research,* Edition 11, https://www.cs.waikato.ac.nz/ml/publications/2010/bouckaert10a.pdf

[14] Data mining was originally known by other names including "database mining" and "information retrieval." The discipline became known as "knowledge discovery in databases" and "data mining" in the 1990s.

[15] Jiawei Han, Micheline Kamber & Jian Pei, "Data Mining: Concepts and Techniques (The Morgan Kaufmann Series in Data Management Systems)," *Morgan Kauffmann,* 3rd Edition, 2011.

supervised learning, and although it overlaps with data mining, unsupervised learning tends to deviate from standard data mining methods such as association and sequence analysis.

Technique	Input is Known	Output is Known	Methodology
Data Mining	✓		Analyzes inputs to generate an unknown output.
Supervised Learning	✓	✓	Analyzes combinations of known inputs and outputs to predict future outputs based on new input data.
Unsupervised Learning	✓		Analyzes inputs to generate an output—algorithms may differ from data mining.
Reinforcement Learning		✓	Randomly trials a high number of input variables to produce a desired output.

Table 1: Comparison of techniques based on the utility of input and output data/variables

To consolidate the difference between data mining and machine learning, let's consider an example of two teams of archaeologists. One team has little knowledge of their target excavation site and employs domain knowledge to optimize their excavation tools to find patterns and remove debris to reveal hidden artifacts. The team's goal is to manually excavate the area, find new valuable discoveries, and then pack up their equipment and move on. A day later, they fly to another exotic destination to start a new project with no relationship to the site they excavated the day before.

The second team is also in the business of excavating historical sites, but they pursue a different methodology. They refrain from excavating the main pit for several weeks. During this time, they visit other nearby archaeological sites and examine patterns regarding how each archaeological site is constructed. With exposure to each excavation site, they gain experience, thereby improving their ability to interpret patterns and reduce prediction error. When it comes time to excavate the final and most important pit, they execute their understanding and experience of the local terrain to interpret the target site and make predictions.

As is perhaps evident by now, the first team puts their faith in data mining whereas the second team relies on machine learning. While both teams make a living excavating historical sites to discover valuable insight, their goals and methodology are different. The machine learning team invests in self-learning to create a system that uses exposure to data to enhance its capacity to make predictions. The data mining team, meanwhile, concentrates on excavating the target area with a more direct and approximate approach that relies on human intuition rather than self-learning.

We will look more closely at self-learning specific to machine learning in the next chapter and how input and output variables are used to make predictions.

## 3

MACHINE LEARNING CATEGORIES

Machine learning incorporates several hundred statistical-based algorithms and choosing the right algorithm(s) for the job is a constant challenge of working in this field. Before examining specific algorithms, it's important to consolidate one's understanding of the three overarching categories of machine learning and their treatment of input and output variables.

Supervised Learning

Supervised learning imitates our own ability to extract patterns from known examples and use that extracted insight to engineer a repeatable outcome. This is how the car company Toyota designed its first car prototype. Rather than speculate or create a unique process for manufacturing cars, Toyota created its first vehicle prototype after taking apart a Chevrolet car in the corner of their family-run loom business. By observing the finished car (output) and then pulling apart its individual components (input), Toyota's engineers unlocked the design process kept secret by Chevrolet in America.

This process of understanding a known input-output combination is replicated in machine learning using supervised learning. The model analyzes and deciphers the relationship between input and output data to learn the underlying patterns. Input data is referred to as the independent variable (uppercase "X"), while the output data is called the dependent variable (lowercase "y"). An example of a dependent variable (y) might be the coordinates for a rectangle around a person in a digital photo (face recognition), the price of a house, or the class of an item (i.e. sports car, family car, sedan). Their independent variables—which supposedly impact the dependent variable—could be the pixel colors, the size and location of the house, and the specifications of the car respectively. After analyzing a sufficient number of examples, the machine creates a model: an algorithmic formula for producing an output based on patterns from previous input-output examples.

Using the model, the machine can then predict an output based exclusively on the input data. The market price of your used Lexus, for example, can be estimated using the labeled examples of other cars recently sold on a used car website.

	Input	Input	Input	Output
	Card Brand	Mileage (km)	Year of Make	Price (USD)
Car 1	Lexus	51715	2012	15985
Car 2	Lexus	7980	2013	19600
Car 3	Lexus	82497	2012	14095
Car 4	Lexus	85199	2011	12490
Car 5	Audi	62948	2008	13985

Table 2: Extract of a used car dataset

With access to the selling price of other similar cars, the model can work backward to determine the relationship between a car's value (output) and its attributes (input). The attributes of your own car can then be put into the model to generate a price prediction.

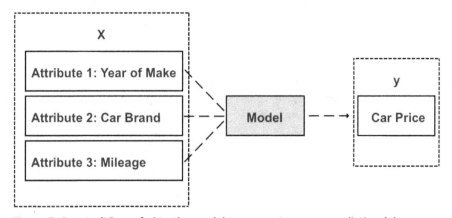

Figure 5: Inputs (X) are fed to the model to generate a new prediction (y)

While input data with an unknown output can be fed to the model to push out a prediction, unlabeled data cannot be used to build the model. When building a supervised learning model, each item (i.e. car, product, customer) must have labeled input and output values—known in data science as a "labeled dataset." Figure 6 is an example of an unlabeled dataset because the output value for the last row is unknown.

Input variables				Output
Land Size (ft)	Year Built	Distance to City (miles)	No. of Rooms	House Price (USD)
5000	1990	10	4	300000
6000	2005	5	5	450000
7500	1985	15	3	280000
5500	2010	3	6	500000
4800	2000	8	4	400000
6200	1995	12	5	

Labeled

Unlabeled

Figure 6: Labeled data vs. unlabeled data

Examples of common algorithms used in supervised learning include regression analysis (i.e. linear regression, logistic regression, non-linear regression), decision trees, *k*-nearest neighbors, neural networks, and support vector machines, each of which are examined in later chapters.

Unsupervised Learning

In the case of unsupervised learning, the output variables are unlabeled, and combinations of input and output variables aren't known. Unsupervised learning instead focuses on analyzing relationships between input variables and uncovering hidden patterns that can be extracted to create new labels regarding possible outputs.

If you group data points based on the purchasing behavior of SME (Small and Medium-sized Enterprises) and large enterprise customers, for example, you're likely to see two clusters of data points emerge. This is because SMEs and large enterprises tend to have different procurement needs. When it comes to purchasing cloud computing infrastructure, for example, essential cloud hosting products and a Content Delivery Network (CDN) should prove sufficient for most SME customers. Large enterprise customers, though, are likely to purchase a broader array of cloud products and complete solutions that include advanced security and networking products like WAF (Web Application Firewall), a dedicated private connection, and VPC (Virtual Private Cloud). By analyzing customer purchasing habits, unsupervised learning is capable of identifying these two groups of customers without specific labels that classify a given company as small/medium or large.

The advantage of unsupervised learning is that it enables you to discover patterns in the data that you were unaware of—such as the presence of two dominant customer types—and provides a springboard for conducting further analysis once new groups are identified. Unsupervised learning is especially compelling in the domain of fraud detection—where the most dangerous attacks are those yet to be classified. One interesting example is DataVisor; a company that has built its business model on unsupervised learning. Founded in 2013 in California, DataVisor protects customers from fraudulent online activities, including spam, fake reviews, fake app installs, and fraudulent transactions. Whereas traditional fraud protection services draw on supervised learning models and rule engines, DataVisor uses unsupervised learning to detect unclassified categories of attacks.

As DataVisor explains on their website, "to detect attacks, existing solutions rely on human experience to create rules or labeled training data to tune models. This means they are unable to detect new attacks that haven't already been identified by humans or labeled in training data." [16] Put another way, traditional solutions analyze chains of activity for a specific type of attack and then create rules to predict and detect repeat attacks. In this case, the dependent variable (output) is the event of an attack, and the independent variables (input) are the common predictor variables of an attack. Examples of independent variables could be:

a) A sudden large order from an unknown user. I.E., established customers might generally spend less than $100 per

---

[16] "Unsupervised Machine Learning Engine," *DataVisor*, accessed May 19, 2017, https://www.datavisor.com/unsupervised-machine-learning-engine

order, but a new user spends $8,000 on one order immediately upon registering an account.

b) A sudden surge of user ratings. I.E., As with most technology books sold on Amazon.com, the first edition of this book rarely receives more than one reader review per day. In general, approximately 1 in 200 Amazon readers leave a review and most books go weeks or months without a review. However, I notice other authors in this category (data science) attract 50-100 reviews in a single day! (Unsurprisingly, I also see Amazon remove these suspicious reviews weeks or months later.)

c) Identical or similar user reviews from different users. Following the same Amazon analogy, I sometimes see positive reader reviews of my book appear with other books (even with reference to my name as the author still included in the review!). Again, Amazon eventually removes these fake reviews and suspends these accounts for breaking their terms of service.

d) Suspicious shipping address. I.E., For small businesses that routinely ship products to local customers, an order from a distant location (where their products aren't advertised) can, in rare cases, be an indicator of fraudulent or malicious activity.

Standalone activities such as a sudden large order or a remote shipping address might not provide sufficient information to detect sophisticated cybercrime and are probably more likely to lead to a series of false-positive results. But a model that monitors combinations of independent variables, such as a large purchasing order from the other side of the globe or a landslide number of book reviews that reuse existing user content generally leads to a better prediction.

In supervised learning, the model deconstructs and classifies what these common variables are and designs a detection system to identify and prevent repeat offenses. Sophisticated cybercriminals, though, learn to evade these simple classification-based rule engines by modifying their tactics. Leading up to an attack, for example, the attackers often register and operate single or multiple accounts and incubate these accounts with activities that mimic legitimate users. They then utilize their established account history to evade detection systems, which closely monitor new users. As a result, solutions that use supervised learning often fail to detect sleeper cells until the damage has been inflicted and especially for new types of attacks.

DataVisor and other anti-fraud solution providers instead leverage unsupervised learning techniques to address these limitations. They analyze patterns across hundreds of millions of accounts and identify suspicious connections between users (input)—without knowing the actual category of future attacks (output). By grouping and identifying malicious actors whose actions deviate from standard user behavior, companies can take actions to prevent new types of attacks (whose outcomes are still unknown and unlabeled).

Examples of suspicious actions may include the four cases listed earlier or new instances of abnormal behavior such as a pool of newly registered users with the same profile picture. By identifying these subtle correlations across users, fraud detection companies like DataVisor can locate sleeper cells in their incubation stage. A swarm of fake Facebook accounts, for example, might be linked as friends and like the same pages but aren't linked with genuine users. As this type of fraudulent behavior relies on fabricated interconnections between accounts, unsupervised learning thereby helps to uncover collaborators and expose criminal rings.

The drawback, though, of using unsupervised learning is that because the dataset is unlabeled, there aren't any known output observations to check and validate the model, and predictions are therefore more subjective than those coming from supervised learning.

We will cover unsupervised learning later in this book specific to *k*-means clustering. Other examples of unsupervised learning algorithms include social network analysis and descending dimension algorithms.

Semi-supervised Learning

A hybrid form of unsupervised and supervised learning is also available in the form of semi-supervised learning, which is used for datasets that contain a mix of labeled and unlabeled cases. With the "more data the better" as a core motivator, the goal of semi-supervised learning is to leverage unlabeled cases to improve the reliability of the prediction model. One technique is to build the initial model using the labeled cases (supervised learning) and then use the same model to label the remaining cases (that are unlabeled) in the dataset.

The model can then be retrained using a larger dataset (with fewer or no unlabeled cases). Alternatively, the model could be iteratively re-trained using newly labeled cases that meet a set threshold of confidence and adding the new cases to the training data after they meet the set threshold. There is, however, no guarantee that a semi-supervised model will outperform a model trained with less data (based exclusively on the original labeled cases).

Reinforcement Learning

Reinforcement learning is the third and most advanced category of machine learning. Unlike supervised and unsupervised learning, reinforcement learning builds its prediction model by gaining feedback from random trial and error and leveraging insight from previous iterations.

The goal of reinforcement learning is to achieve a specific goal (output) by randomly trialing a vast number of possible input combinations and grading their performance.

Reinforcement learning can be complicated to understand and is probably best explained using a video game analogy. As a player progresses through the virtual space of a game, they learn the value of various actions under different conditions and grow more familiar with the field of play. Those learned values then inform and influence the player's subsequent behavior and their performance gradually improves based on learning and experience.

Reinforcement learning is similar, where algorithms are set to train the model based on continuous learning. A standard reinforcement learning model has measurable performance criteria where outputs are graded. In the case of self-driving vehicles, avoiding a crash earns a positive score, and in the case of chess, avoiding defeat likewise receives a positive assessment.

Q-learning

A specific algorithmic example of reinforcement learning is Q-learning. In Q-learning, you start with a set environment of *states,* represented as "S." In the game Pac-Man, states could be the challenges, obstacles or pathways that exist in the video game. There may exist a wall to the left, a ghost to the right, and a power pill above—each representing different states. The set of possible actions to respond to these states is referred to as "A." In Pac-Man, actions are limited to left, right, up, and down movements, as well as multiple combinations thereof. The third important symbol is "Q," which is the model's starting value and has an initial value of "0."

As Pac-Man explores the space inside the game, two main things happen:

1) Q drops as negative things occur after a given state/action.

2) Q increases as positive things occur after a given state/action.

In Q-learning, the machine learns to match the action for a given state that generates or preserves the highest level of Q. It learns initially through the process of random movements (actions) under different conditions (states). The model records its results (rewards and penalties) and how they impact its Q level and stores those values to inform and optimize its future actions.

While this sounds simple, implementation is computationally expensive and beyond the scope of an absolute beginner's introduction to machine learning. Reinforcement learning algorithms aren't covered in this book, but, I'll leave you with a link to a more comprehensive explanation of reinforcement learning and Q-learning using the Pac-Man case study.

https://inst.eecs.berkeley.edu/~cs188/sp12/projects/reinforcement/reinforcement.html

## 4

THE ML TOOLBOX

A handy way to learn a new skill is to visualize a toolbox of the essential tools and materials of that subject area. For instance, given the task of packing a dedicated toolbox to build a website, you would first need to add a selection of programming languages. This would include frontend languages such as HTML, CSS, and JavaScript, one or two backend programming languages based on personal preferences, and of course, a text editor. You might throw in a website builder such as WordPress and then pack another compartment with web hosting, DNS, and maybe a few domain names that you've purchased.

This is not an extensive inventory, but from this general list, you start to gain a better appreciation of what tools you need to master on the path to becoming a successful web developer.

Let's now unpack the basic toolbox for machine learning.

Compartment 1: Data

Stored in the first compartment of the toolbox is your data. Data constitutes the input needed to train your model and generate predictions. Data comes in many forms, including structured and unstructured data. As a beginner, it's best to start with (analyzing) structured data. This means that the data is defined, organized, and labeled in a table, as shown in Table 3. Images, videos, email messages, and audio recordings are examples of unstructured data as they don't fit into the organized structure of rows and columns.

Date	Bitcoin Price	No. of Days Transpired
19-05-2015	234.31	1
14-01-2016	431.76	240
09-07-2016	652.14	417
15-01-2017	817.26	607
24-05-2017	2358.96	736

Table 3: Bitcoin Prices from 2015-2017

Before we proceed, I first want to explain the anatomy of a tabular dataset. A tabular (table-based) dataset contains data organized in rows and columns. Contained in each column is a *feature*. A feature is also known as a *variable,* a *dimension* or an *attribute*— but they all mean the same thing. Each row represents a single observation of a given feature/variable. Rows are sometimes referred to as a *case* or *value*, but in this book, we use the term "row."

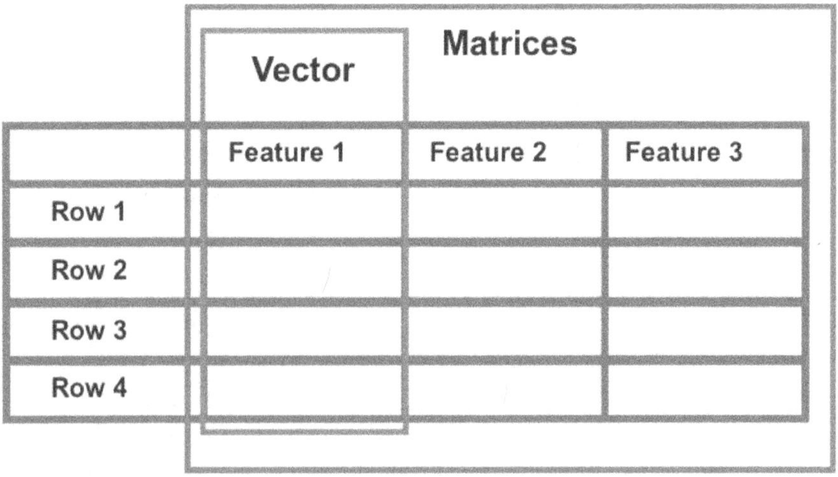

Figure 7: Example of a tabular dataset

Each column is known also as a *vector*. Vectors store your X and y values and multiple vectors (columns) are commonly referred to as *matrices*. In the case of supervised learning, y will already exist in your dataset and be used to identify patterns in relation to the independent variables (X). The y values are commonly expressed in the final vector, as shown in Figure 8.

	Vector	Matrices		
	Maker (X)	Year (X)	Model (X)	Price (y)
Row 1				
Row 2				
Row 3				
Row 4				

Figure 8: The y value is often but not always expressed in the far-right vector

Scatterplots, including 2-D, 3-D, and 4-D plots, are also packed into the first compartment of the toolbox with the data. A 2-D scatterplot consists of a vertical axis (known as the y-axis) and a horizontal axis (known as the x-axis) and provides the graphical canvas to plot variable combinations, known as data points. Each data point on the scatterplot represents an observation from the dataset with X values on the x-axis and y values on the y-axis.

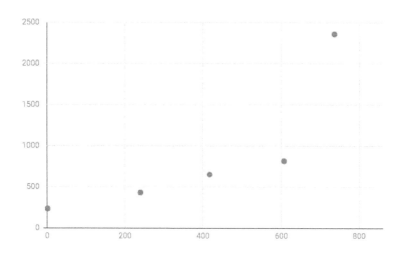

	Independent Variable (X)	Dependent Variable (y)
Row 1	1	243.31
Row 2	240	431.76
Row 3	417	653.14
Row 4	607	817.26
Row 5	736	2358.96

Figure 9: Example of a 2-D scatterplot. X represents days passed and y is Bitcoin price

Compartment 2: Infrastructure

The second compartment of the toolbox contains your machine learning infrastructure, which consists of platforms and tools for processing data. As a beginner to machine learning, you are likely to be using a web application (such as Jupyter Notebook) and a programming language like Python. There are then a series of machine learning libraries, including NumPy, Pandas, and Scikit-learn, which are compatible with Python. Machine learning libraries are a collection of pre-compiled programming routines frequently used in machine learning that enable you to manipulate data and execute algorithms with minimal use of code.

You will also need a machine to process your data, in the form of a physical computer or a virtual server. In addition, you may need specialized libraries for data visualization such as Seaborn and Matplotlib, or a standalone software program like Tableau, which supports a range of visualization techniques including charts, graphs, maps, and other visual options.

With your infrastructure sprayed across the table (hypothetically of course), you're now ready to build your first machine learning model. The first step is to crank up your computer. Standard desktop computers and laptops are both sufficient for working with smaller datasets that are stored in a central location, such as a CSV file. You then need to install a programming environment, such as Jupyter Notebook, and a programming language, which for most beginners is Python.

Python is the most widely used programming language for machine learning because:

a) It's easy to learn and operate.

b) It's compatible with a range of machine learning libraries.

c) It can be used for related tasks, including data collection (web scraping) and data piping (Hadoop and Spark).

Other go-to languages for machine learning include C and C++. If you're proficient with C and C++, then it makes sense to stick with what you know. C and C++ are the default programming languages for advanced machine learning because they can run directly on the GPU (Graphical Processing Unit). Python needs to be converted before it can run on the GPU, but we'll get to this and what a GPU is later in the chapter.

Next, Python users will need to import the following libraries: NumPy, Pandas, and Scikit-learn. NumPy is a free and open-source library that allows you to efficiently load and work with large datasets, including merging datasets and managing matrices.

Scikit-learn provides access to a range of popular shallow algorithms, including linear regression, clustering techniques, decision trees, and support vector machines. Shallow learning algorithms refer to learning algorithms that predict outcomes directly from the input features. Non-shallow algorithms or deep learning, meanwhile, produce an output based on preceding layers in the model (discussed in Chapter 13 in reference to artificial neural networks) rather than directly from the input features.[17]

Finally, Pandas enables your data to be represented as a virtual spreadsheet that you can control and manipulate using code. It shares many of the same features as Microsoft Excel in that it allows you to edit data and perform calculations. The name Pandas derives from the term "panel data," which refers to its ability to create a series of panels, similar to "sheets" in Excel. Pandas is also ideal for importing and extracting data from CSV files.

---

[17] Aside from artificial neural networks, most learning algorithms qualify as shallow.

```
In [1]:  1  # Import library
         2  import pandas as pd
         3
         4  # Read in data from CSV as a Pandas dataframe
         5  df = pd.read_csv('~/Downloads/Melbourne_housing_FULL.csv')
         6
         7  df.head()
```

	Suburb	Address	Rooms	Type	Price	Method	SellerG	Date	Distance	Postcode	...	Bathroom	Car	Landsize	BuildingArea	YearBuilt	Co
0	Abbotsford	68 Studley St	2	h	NaN	SS	Jellis	3/09/2016	2.5	3067.0	...	1.0	1.0	126.0	NaN	NaN	
1	Abbotsford	85 Turner St	2	h	1480000.0	S	Biggin	3/12/2016	2.5	3067.0	...	1.0	1.0	202.0	NaN	NaN	
2	Abbotsford	25 Bloomburg St	2	h	1035000.0	S	Biggin	4/02/2016	2.5	3067.0	...	1.0	0.0	156.0	79.0	1900.0	
3	Abbotsford	18/659 Victoria St	3	u	NaN	VB	Rounds	4/02/2016	2.5	3067.0	...	2.0	1.0	0.0	NaN	NaN	
4	Abbotsford	5 Charles St	3	h	1465000.0	SP	Biggin	4/03/2017	2.5	3067.0	...	2.0	0.0	134.0	150.0	1900.0	

5 rows × 21 columns

Figure 10: Previewing a table in Jupyter Notebook using Pandas

For those seeking alternative programming options for machine learning beyond Python, C, and C++, there is also R, MATLAB, and Octave.

R is a free and open-source programming language optimized for mathematical operations and useful for building matrices and performing statistical functions. Although more commonly used for data mining, R also supports machine learning.

The competitors to R are MATLAB and Octave. MATLAB is a commercial and proprietary programming language that is strong at solving algebraic equations and is a quick programming language to learn. MATLAB is widely used in the fields of electrical engineering, chemical engineering, civil engineering, and aeronautical engineering. Computer scientists and computer engineers, however, tend not to use MATLAB and especially in recent years. MATLAB, though, is still widely used in academia for machine learning. Thus, while you may see MATLAB featured in online courses for machine learning, and especially Coursera, this is not to say that it's as commonly used in industry. If, however, you're coming from an engineering background, MATLAB is certainly a logical choice.

Lastly, there is Octave, which is essentially a free version of MATLAB developed in response to MATLAB by the open-source community.

Compartment 3: Algorithms

Now that the development environment is set up and you've chosen your programming language and libraries, you can next import your data directly from a CSV file. You can find hundreds of interesting datasets in CSV format from kaggle.com. After registering as a Kaggle member, you can download a dataset of your choosing. Best of all, Kaggle datasets are free, and there's no cost to register as a user. The dataset will download directly to your computer as a CSV file, which means you can use Microsoft Excel to open and even perform basic algorithms such as linear regression on your dataset.

Next is the third and final compartment that stores the machine learning algorithms. Beginners typically start out using simple supervised learning algorithms such as linear regression, logistic regression, decision trees, and k-nearest neighbors. Beginners are also likely to apply unsupervised learning in the form of k-means clustering and descending dimension algorithms.

Visualization

No matter how impactful and insightful your data discoveries are, you need a way to communicate the results to relevant decision-makers. This is where data visualization comes in handy to highlight and communicate findings from the data to a general audience. The visual story conveyed through graphs, scatterplots, heatmaps, box plots, and the representation of numbers as shapes make for quick and easy storytelling.

In general, the less informed your audience is, the more important it is to visualize your findings. Conversely, if your audience is knowledgeable about the topic, additional details and technical terms can be used to supplement visual elements. To visualize your results, you can draw on a software program like Tableau or a Python library such as Seaborn, which are stored in the second compartment of the toolbox.

The Advanced Toolbox

We have so far examined the starter toolbox for a beginner, but what about an advanced user? What does their toolbox look like?

While it may take some time before you get to work with more advanced tools, it doesn't hurt to take a sneak peek.

The advanced toolbox comes with a broader spectrum of tools and, of course, data. One of the biggest differences between a beginner and an expert is the kind of data they manage and operate. Beginners work with small datasets that are easy to handle and downloaded directly to one's desktop as a simple CSV file. Advanced users, though, will be eager to tackle massive datasets, well in the vicinity of big data. This might mean that the data is stored across multiple locations, and its composition is streamed (imported and analyzed in real-time) rather than static, which makes the data itself a moving target.

Compartment 1: Big Data

Big data is used to describe a dataset that, due to its variety, volume, and velocity, defies conventional methods of processing and would be impossible for a human to process without the assistance of advanced technology. Big data doesn't have an exact definition in terms of size or a minimum threshold of rows and columns. At the moment, petabytes qualify as big data, but datasets are becoming increasingly bigger as we find new ways to collect and store data at a lower cost.

Big data is also less likely to fit into standard rows and columns and may contain numerous data types, such as structured data and a range of unstructured data, i.e. images, videos, email messages, and audio files.

Compartment 2: Infrastructure

Given that advanced learners are dealing with up to petabytes of data, robust infrastructure is required. Instead of relying on the CPU of a personal computer, the experts typically turn to distributed computing and a cloud provider such as Amazon Web Services (AWS) or Google Cloud Platform to run their data processing on a virtual graphics processing unit (GPU). As a specialized parallel computing chip, GPU instances are able to perform many more floating-point operations per second than a

CPU, allowing for much faster solutions with linear algebra and statistics than with a CPU.

GPU chips were originally added to PC motherboards and video consoles such as the PlayStation 2 and the Xbox for gaming purposes. They were developed to accelerate the rendering of images with millions of pixels whose frames needed to be continuously recalculated to display output in less than a second. By 2005, GPU chips were produced in such large quantities that prices dropped dramatically and they became almost a commodity. Although popular in the video game industry, their application in the space of machine learning wasn't fully understood or realized until quite recently. Kevin Kelly, in his novel *The Inevitable: Understanding the 12 Technological Forces That Will Shape Our Future*, explains that in 2009, Andrew Ng and a team at Stanford University made a discovery to link inexpensive GPU clusters to run neural networks consisting of hundreds of millions of connected nodes.

"Traditional processors required several weeks to calculate all the cascading possibilities in a neural net with one hundred million parameters. Ng found that a cluster of GPUs could accomplish the same thing in a day," explains Kelly.[18]

As mentioned, C and C++ are the preferred languages to directly edit and perform mathematical operations on the GPU. Python can also be used and converted into C in combination with a machine learning library such as TensorFlow from Google. Although it's possible to run TensorFlow on a CPU, you can gain up to about 1,000x in performance using the GPU. Unfortunately for Mac users, TensorFlow is only compatible with the Nvidia GPU card, which is no longer available with Mac OS X. Mac users can still run TensorFlow on their CPU but will need to run their workload on the cloud if they wish to use a GPU.

Amazon Web Services, Microsoft Azure, Alibaba Cloud, Google Cloud Platform, and other cloud providers offer pay-as-you-go GPU resources, which may also start off free using a free trial program. Google Cloud Platform is currently regarded as a leading choice for

---

[18] Kevin Kelly, "The Inevitable: Understanding the 12 Technological Forces That Will Shape Our Future," Penguin Books, 2016.

virtual GPU resources based on performance and pricing. Google also announced in 2016 that it would publicly release a Tensor Processing Unit designed specifically for running TensorFlow, which is already used internally at Google.

Compartment 3: Advanced Algorithms

To round out this chapter, let's take a look at the third compartment of the advanced toolbox containing machine learning algorithms. To analyze large datasets and respond to complicated prediction tasks, advanced practitioners work with a plethora of algorithms including Markov models, support vector machines, and Q-learning, as well as combinations of algorithms to create a unified model, known as ensemble modeling (explored further in Chapter 15). However, the algorithm family they're most likely to work with is artificial neural networks (introduced in Chapter 13), which comes with its own selection of advanced machine learning libraries.

While Scikit-learn offers a range of popular shallow algorithms, TensorFlow is the machine learning library of choice for deep learning/neural networks. It supports numerous advanced techniques including automatic calculus for back-propagation/gradient descent. The depth of resources, documentation, and jobs available with TensorFlow also make it an obvious framework to learn. Popular alternative libraries for neural networks include Torch, Caffe, and the fast-growing Keras.

Written in Python, Keras is an open-source deep learning library that runs on top of TensorFlow, Theano, and other frameworks, which allows users to perform fast experimentation in fewer lines of code. Similar to a WordPress website theme, Keras is minimal, modular, and quick to get up and running. It is, however, less flexible in comparison to TensorFlow and other libraries. Developers, therefore, will sometimes utilize Keras to validate their decision model before switching to TensorFlow to build a more customized model.

Caffe is also open-source and is typically used to develop deep learning architectures for image classification and image segmentation. Caffe is written in C++ but has a Python interface that supports GPU-based acceleration using the Nvidia cuDNN chip.

Released in 2002, Torch is also well established in the deep learning community and is used at Facebook, Google, Twitter, NYU, IDIAP, and Purdue University as well as other companies and research labs.[19] Based on the programming language Lua, Torch is open-source and offers a range of algorithms and functions used for deep learning.

Theano was another competitor to TensorFlow until recently, but as of late 2017, contributions to the framework have officially ceased.[20]

---

[19] "What is Torch?" *Torch*, accessed April 20, 2017, http://torch.ch
[20] Pascal Lamblin, "MILA and the future of Theano," *Google Groups Theano Users Forum*, https://groups.google.com/forum/#!topic/theano-users/7Poq8BZutbY

## 5

DATA SCRUBBING

Like most varieties of fruit, datasets need upfront cleaning and human manipulation before they're ready for consumption. The "clean-up" process applies to machine learning and many other fields of data science and is known in the industry as *data scrubbing*. This is the technical process of refining your dataset to make it more workable. This might involve modifying and removing incomplete, incorrectly formatted, irrelevant, or duplicated data. It might also entail converting text-based data to numeric values and the redesigning of features.

For data practitioners, data scrubbing typically demands the greatest application of time and effort.

Feature Selection

To generate the best results from your data, it's essential to identify which variables are most relevant to your hypothesis or objective. In practice, this means being selective in choosing the variables you include in your model. Moreover, preserving features that don't correlate strongly with the output value can manipulate and derail the model's accuracy. Let's consider the following data excerpt downloaded from kaggle.com documenting dying languages.

Name in English	Name in Spanish	Countries	Country Code	Num. of Speakers
South Italian	Napolitano -calabres	Italy	ITA	7500000
Sicilian	Siciliano	Italy	ITA	5000000
Low Saxon	Bajo Sajón	Germany, Denmark, Netherlands, Poland, Russian Federation	DEU, DNK, NLD, POL, RUS	4800000
Belarusian	Bielorruso	Belarus, Latvia, Lithuania, Poland, Russian Federation, Ukraine	BRB, LVA, LTU, POL, RUS, UKR	4000000
Lombard	Lombardo	Italy, Switzerland	ITA, CHE	3500000
Romani	Romaní	Albania, Germany, Austria, Belarus, Bosnia and Herzegovina, Bulgaria, Croatia, Estonia, Finland, France, Greece, Hungary, Italy, Latvia, Lithuania, The former Yugoslav Republic of Macedonia, Netherlands, Poland, Romania, United Kingdom of Great Britain and Northern Ireland, Russian Federation, Slovakia, Slovenia, Switzerland, Czech Republic, Turkey, Ukraine, Serbia, Montenegro	ALB, DEU, AUT, BRB, BIH, BGR, HRV, EST, FIN, FRA, GRC, HUN, ITA, LVA, LTU, MKD, NLD, POL, ROU, GBR, RUS, SVK, SVN, CHE, CZE, TUR, UKR, SRB, MNE	3500000
Yiddish	Yiddish	Israel	ISR	3000000
Gondi	Gondi	India	IND	2713790

Table 4: Endangered languages, database: https://www.kaggle.com/the-guardian/extinct-languages

Let's say our goal is to identify variables that contribute to a language becoming endangered. Based on the purpose of our analysis, it's unlikely that a language's "Name in Spanish" will lead to any relevant insight. We can therefore delete this vector (column) from the dataset. This helps to prevent over-complication and potential inaccuracies as well as improve the overall processing speed of the model.

Secondly, the dataset contains duplicated information in the form of separate vectors for "Countries" and "Country Code." Analyzing both of these vectors doesn't provide any additional insight; hence, we can choose to delete one and retain the other.

Another method to reduce the number of features is to roll multiple features into one, as shown in the following example.

	Protein Shake	Nike Sneakers	Adidas Boots	Fitbit	Powerade	Protein Bar	Fitness Watch	Vitamins
Buyer 1	1	1	0	1	0	5	1	0
Buyer 2	0	0	0	0	0	0	0	1
Buyer 3	3	0	1	0	5	0	0	0
Buyer 4	1	1	0	0	10	1	0	0

Table 5: Sample product inventory

Contained in Table 5 is a list of products sold on an e-commerce platform. The dataset comprises four buyers and eight products. This is not a large sample size of buyers and products—due in part to the spatial limitations of the book format. A real-life e-commerce platform would have many more columns to work with but let's go ahead with this simplified example.

To analyze the data more efficiently, we can reduce the number of columns by merging similar features into fewer columns. For instance, we can remove individual product names and replace the eight product items with fewer categories or subtypes. As all product items fall under the category of "fitness," we can sort by product subtype and compress the columns from eight to three. The three newly created product subtype columns are "Health Food," "Apparel," and "Digital."

	Health Food	Apparel	Digital
Buyer 1	6	1	2
Buyer 2	1	0	0
Buyer 3	8	1	0
Buyer 4	12	1	0

Table 6: Synthesized product inventory

This enables us to transform the dataset in a way that preserves and captures information using fewer variables. The downside to this transformation is that we have less information about the relationships between specific products. Rather than recommending products to users according to other individual products, recommendations will instead be based on associations between product subtypes or recommendations of the same product subtype.

Nonetheless, this approach still upholds a high level of data relevancy. Buyers will be recommended health food when they buy other health food or when they buy apparel (depending on the degree of correlation), and obviously not machine learning textbooks—unless it turns out that there is a strong correlation there! But alas, such a variable/category is outside the frame of this dataset.

Remember that data reduction is also a business decision and business owners in counsel with their data science team must consider the trade-off between convenience and the overall precision of the model.

Row Compression

In addition to feature selection, you may need to reduce the number of rows and thereby compress the total number of data points. This may involve merging two or more rows into one, as shown in the following dataset, with "Tiger" and "Lion" merged and renamed as "Carnivore."

Before

Animal	Meat Eater	Legs	Tail	Race Time
Tiger	Yes	4	Yes	2:01 mins
Lion	Yes	4	Yes	2:05 mins
Tortoise	No	4	No	55:02 mins

After

Animal	Meat Eater	Legs	Tail	Race Time
Carnivore	Yes	4	Yes	2:03 mins
Tortoise	No	4	No	55:02 mins

Table 7: Example of row merge

By merging these two rows (Tiger & Lion), the feature values for both rows must also be aggregated and recorded in a single row. In this case, it's possible to merge the two rows because they possess the same categorical values for all features except Race Time—which can be easily aggregated. The race time of the Tiger and the Lion can be added and divided by two.

Numeric values are normally easy to aggregate given they are not categorical. For instance, it would be impossible to aggregate an animal with four legs and an animal with two legs! We obviously can't merge these two animals and set "three" as the aggregate number of legs.

Row compression can also be challenging to implement in cases where numeric values aren't available. For example, the values "Japan" and "Argentina" are very difficult to merge. The values "Japan" and "South Korea" can be merged, as they can be categorized as countries from the same continent, "Asia" or "East Asia." However, if we add "Pakistan" and "Indonesia" to the same group, we may begin to see skewed results, as there are significant cultural, religious, economic, and other dissimilarities between these four countries.

In summary, non-numeric and categorical row values can be problematic to merge while preserving the true value of the original data. Also, row compression is usually less attainable than feature compression and especially for datasets with a high number of features.

One-hot Encoding

After finalizing the features and rows to be included in your model, you next want to look for text-based values that can be converted into numbers. Aside from set text-based values such as True/False (that automatically convert to "1" and "0" respectively), most algorithms are not compatible with non-numeric data.

One method to convert text-based values into numeric values is one-hot encoding, which transforms values into binary form, represented as "1" or "0"—"True" or "False." A "0," representing False, means that the value does not belong to a given feature, whereas a "1"—True or "hot"—confirms that the value does belong to that feature.

Below is another excerpt from the dying languages dataset which we can use to observe one-hot encoding.

Name in English	Speakers	Degree of Endangerment
South Italian	7500000	Vulnerable
Sicilian	5000000	Vulnerable
Low Saxon	4800000	Vulnerable
Belarusian	4000000	Vulnerable
Lombard	3500000	Definitely endangered
Romani	3500000	Definitely endangered
Yiddish	3000000	Definitely endangered
Gondi	2713790	Vulnerable
Picard	700000	Severely endangered

Table 8: Endangered languages

Before we begin, note that the values contained in the "No. of Speakers" column do not contain commas or spaces, e.g., 7,500,000 and 7 500 000. Although formatting makes large numbers easier for human interpretation, programming languages don't require such niceties. Formatting numbers can lead to an invalid syntax or trigger an unwanted result, depending on the programming language—so remember to keep numbers unformatted for programming purposes. Feel free, though, to add spacing or commas at the data visualization stage, as this will make it easier for your audience to interpret and especially when presenting large numbers.

On the right-hand side of the table is a vector categorizing the degree of endangerment of nine different languages. We can convert this column into numeric values by applying the one-hot encoding method, as demonstrated in the subsequent table.

Name in English	Speakers	Vulnerable	Definitely Endangered	Severely Endangered
South Italian	7500000	1	0	0
Sicilian	5000000	1	0	0
Low Saxon	4800000	1	0	0
Belarusian	4000000	1	0	0
Lombard	3500000	0	1	0
Romani	3500000	0	1	0
Yiddish	3000000	0	1	0
Gondi	2713790	1	0	0
Picard	700000	0	0	1

Table 9: Example of one-hot encoding

Using one-hot encoding, the dataset has expanded to five columns, and we have created three new features from the original feature (Degree of Endangerment). We have also set each column value to "1" or "0," depending on the value of the original feature. This now makes it possible for us to input the data into our model and choose from a broader spectrum of machine learning algorithms. The downside is that we have more dataset features, which may slightly extend processing time. This is usually manageable but can be problematic for datasets where the original features are split into a large number of new features.

One hack to minimize the total number of features is to restrict binary cases to a single column. As an example, a speed dating dataset on kaggle.com lists "Gender" in a single column using one-hot encoding. Rather than create discrete columns for both "Male" and "Female," they merged these two features into one. According to the dataset's key, females are denoted as "0" and males as "1." The creator of the dataset also used this technique for "Same Race" and "Match."

Subject Number ID	Gender	Same Race	Age	Match
1	0	0	27	0
1	0	0	22	0
1	0	1	22	1
1	0	0	23	1
1	0	0	24	1
1	0	0	25	0
1	0	0	30	0

Gender:	Same Race:	Match:
Female = 0	No = 0	No = 0
Male = 1	Yes = 1	Yes = 1

Table 10: Speed dating results, database: https://www.kaggle.com/annavictoria/speed-dating-experiment

Binning

Binning (also called bucketing) is another method of feature engineering but is used for converting continuous numeric values into multiple binary features called bins or buckets according to their range of values.

Whoa, hold on! Aren't numeric values a good thing? Yes, in most cases continuous numeric values are preferred as they are compatible with a broader selection of algorithms. Where numeric values are not ideal, is in situations where they list variations irrelevant to the goals of your analysis.

Let's take house price evaluation as an example. The exact measurements of a tennis court might not matter much when evaluating house property prices; the relevant information is whether the property has a tennis court. This logic probably also applies to the garage and the swimming pool, where the existence or non-existence of the variable is generally more influential than their specific measurements.

The solution here is to replace the numeric measurements of the tennis court with a True/False feature or a categorical value such as "small," "medium," and "large." Another alternative would be to apply one-hot encoding with "0" for homes that do not have a tennis court and "1" for homes that do have a tennis court.

Normalization

While machine learning algorithms can run without using the next two techniques, normalization and standardization help to improve model accuracy when used with the right algorithm. The former (normalization) rescales the range of values for a given feature into a set range with a prescribed minimum and maximum, such as [0, 1] or [−1, 1]. By containing the range of the feature, this technique helps to normalize the variance among the dataset's features which may otherwise be exaggerated by another factor. The variance of a feature measured in centimeters, for example, might distract the algorithm from another feature with a similar or higher degree of variance but that is measured in meters or another metric that downplays the actual variance of the feature.

Normalization, however, usually isn't recommended for rescaling features with an extreme range as the normalized range is too narrow to emphasize extremely high or low feature values.

Standardization

A better technique for emphasizing high or low feature values is standardization. This technique converts unit variance to a standard normal distribution with a mean of zero and a standard deviation (σ) of one.[21] This means that an extremely high or low value would be expressed as three or more standard deviations from the mean.

---

[21] Standard deviation is a measure of spread among data points. It measures variability by calculating the average squared distance of all data observations from the mean of the dataset.

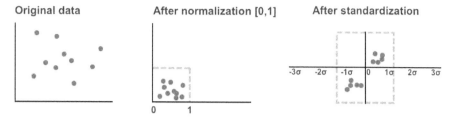

Figure 11: Examples of rescaled data using normalization and standardization

Standardization is generally more effective than normalization when the variability of the feature reflects a bell-curve shape of normal distribution and is often used in unsupervised learning. In other situations, normalization and standardization can be applied separately and compared for accuracy.

Standardization is usually recommended when preparing data for support vector machines (SVM), principal component analysis (PCA), and *k*-nearest neighbors (*k*-NN).

Missing Data

Dealing with missing data is never a desired situation. Imagine unpacking a jigsaw puzzle with five percent of the pieces missing. Missing values in your dataset can be equally frustrating and interfere with your analysis and the model's predictions. There are, however, strategies to minimize the negative impact of missing data.

One approach is to approximate missing values using the *mode* value. The mode represents the single most common variable value available in the dataset. This works best with categorical and binary variable types, such as one to five-star rating systems and positive/negative drug tests respectively.

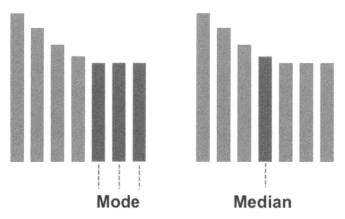

Mode   **Median**

Figure 12: A visual example of the mode and median respectively

The second approach is to approximate missing values using the *median* value, which adopts the value(s) located in the middle of the dataset. This works best with continuous variables, which have an infinite number of possible values, such as house prices.

As a last resort, rows with missing values can be removed altogether. The obvious downside to this approach is having less data to analyze and potentially less comprehensive insight.

## 6

SETTING UP YOUR DATA

After cleaning your dataset, the next job is to split the data into two segments for training and testing, also known as *split validation*. The ratio of the two splits is usually 70/30 or 80/20. This means, assuming that your variables are expressed horizontally and instances vertically (as shown in Figure 13), that your training data should account for 70 percent to 80 percent of the rows in your dataset, and the remaining 20 percent to 30 percent of rows are left for your test data.

		Variable 1	Variable 2	Variable 3
Training Data	Row 1			
	Row 2			
	Row 3			
	Row 4			
	Row 5			
	Row 6			
	Row 7			
Test Data	Row 8			
	Row 9			
	Row 10			

Figure 13: 70/30 partitioning of training and test data

While it's common to split the data 70/30 or 80/20, there is no set rule for preparing a training-test split. Given the growing size of modern datasets (with upwards of a million or more rows), it might be optimal to use a less even split such as 90/10 as this will give you more data to train your model while having enough data left over to test your model.

Before you split your data, it's essential that you randomize the row order. This helps to avoid bias in your model, as your original dataset might be arranged alphabetically or sequentially according to when the data was collected. If you don't randomize the data, you may accidentally omit significant variance from the training data that can cause unwanted surprises when you apply the training model to your test data. Fortunately, Scikit-learn provides a built-in command to shuffle and randomize your data with just one line of code as demonstrated in Chapter 17.

After randomizing the data, you can begin to design your model and apply it to the training data. The remaining 30 percent or so of data is put to the side and reserved for testing the accuracy of the model later; it's imperative not to test your model with the same data you used for training. In the case of supervised learning, the model is developed by feeding the machine the training data and analyzing relationships between the features (X) of the input data and the final output (y).

The next step is to measure how well the model performed. There is a range of performance metrics and choosing the right method depends on the application of the model. Area under the curve (AUC) – Receiver Operating Characteristic (ROC)[22], confusion matrix, recall, and accuracy are four examples of performance metrics used with classification tasks such as an email spam detection system. Meanwhile, mean absolute error and root mean square error (RMSE) are commonly used to assess models that provide a numeric output such as a predicted house value.

In this book, we use mean absolute error (MAE), which measures the average of the errors in a set of predictions on a numeric/continuous scale, i.e. how far is the regression hyperplane to a given data point. Using Scikit-learn, mean absolute error is

---

[22] The term owes its name to its origins in the field of radar engineering.

found by inputting the X values from the training data into the model and generating a prediction for each row in the dataset. Scikit-learn compares the predictions of the model to the correct output (y) and measures the model's accuracy. You'll know that the model is accurate when the error rate for the training and test dataset is low, which means the model has learned the dataset's underlying trends and patterns. If the average recorded MAE or RMSE is much higher using the test data than the training data, this is usually an indication of overfitting (discussed in Chapter 11) in the model. Once the model can adequately predict the values of the test data, it's ready to use in the wild.

If the model fails to predict values from the test data accurately, check that the training and test data were randomized. Next, you may need to modify the model's hyperparameters. Each algorithm has hyperparameters; these are your algorithm's learning settings (and not the settings of the actual model itself). In simple terms, hyperparameters control and impact how fast the model learns patterns and which patterns to identify and analyze. Discussion of algorithm hyperparameters and optimization is discussed in Chapter 11 and Chapter 18.

Cross Validation

While split validation can be effective for developing models using existing data, question marks naturally arise over whether the model can remain accurate when used on new data. If your existing dataset is too small to construct a precise model, or if the training/test partition of data is not appropriate, this may later lead to poor predictions with live data.

Fortunately, there is a valid workaround for this problem. Rather than split the data into two segments (one for training and one for testing), you can implement what's called *cross validation*. Cross validation maximizes the availability of training data by splitting data into various combinations and testing each specific combination.

Cross validation can be performed using one of two primary methods. The first method is *exhaustive cross validation*, which involves finding and testing all possible combinations to divide the original sample into a training set and a test set. The alternative and more common method is non-exhaustive cross validation, known as *k-fold validation*. The *k*-fold validation technique involves splitting data into *k* assigned buckets and reserving one of those buckets for testing the training model at each round.

To perform *k*-fold validation, data are randomly assigned to *k* number of equal-sized buckets. One bucket is reserved as the test bucket and is used to measure and evaluate the performance of the remaining (*k*-1) buckets.

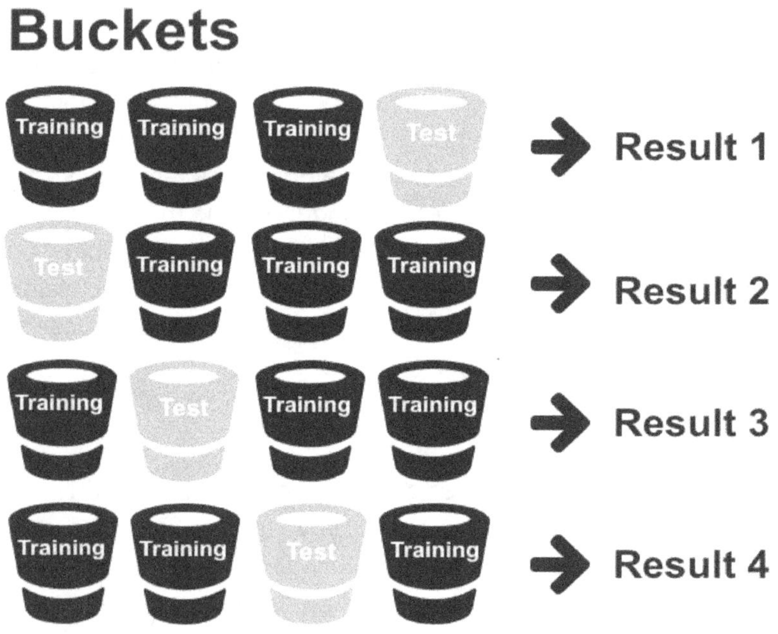

Buckets

Figure 14: k-fold validation

The cross validation technique is repeated *k* number of times ("folds"). At each fold, one bucket is reserved to test the training model generated by the other buckets. The process is repeated until all buckets have been utilized as both a training and test set. The results are then aggregated and combined to formulate a single model.

By using all available data for both training and testing and averaging the model's outputs, the *k*-fold validation technique minimizes the prediction error normally incurred by relying on a

200

fixed training-test split. This method, though, is slower because the training process is multiplied by the number of validation sets.

How Much Data Do I Need?

A common question for students starting out in machine learning is how much data do I need to train my model? In general, machine learning works best when your training dataset includes a full range of feature combinations.

What does a full range of feature combinations look like? Imagine you have a dataset about data scientists categorized into the following features:

- University degree (X)

- 5+ years of professional experience (X)

- Children (X)

- Salary (y)

To assess the relationship that the first three features (X) have to a data scientist's salary (y), we need a dataset that includes the y value for each combination of features. For instance, we need to know the salary for data scientists with a university degree and 5+ years of professional experience who don't have children, as well as data scientists with a university degree and 5+ years of professional experience that do have children.

The more available combinations in the dataset, the more effective the model is at capturing how each attribute affects y (the data scientist's salary). This ensures that when it comes to putting the model into practice on the test data or live data, it won't unravel at the sight of unseen combinations.

At an absolute minimum, a basic machine learning model should contain ten times as many data points as the total number of features. So, for a small dataset with 5 features, the training data should ideally have at least 50 rows. Datasets with a large number of features, though, require a higher number of data points as combinations grow exponentially with more variables.

Generally, the more relevant data you have available as training data, the more combinations you can incorporate into your prediction model, which can help to produce more accurate predictions. In some cases, it might not be possible or cost-effective to source data covering all possible combinations, and you may have to make do with what you have at your disposal. Conversely, there is a natural diminishing rate of return after an adequate volume of training data (that's widely representative of the problem) has been reached.

The last important consideration is matching your data to an algorithm. For datasets with less than 10,000 samples, clustering and dimensionality reduction algorithms can be highly effective, whereas regression analysis and classification algorithms are more suitable for datasets with less than 100,000 samples. Neural networks require even more samples to run effectively and are more cost-effective and time-efficient for working with massive quantities of data.

For more information, Scikit-learn has a cheat-sheet for matching algorithms to different datasets at http://scikit-learn.org/stable/tutorial/machine_learning_map/.

The following chapters examine specific algorithms commonly used in machine learning. Please note that I include some formulas out of necessity, and I have tried to keep them as simple as possible. Many of the machine learning techniques that are discussed in this book already have working implementations in your programming language of choice with no equation solving required.

You can also find video tutorials on how to code models in Python using algorithms mentioned in this book. You can find these free video tutorials a https://scatterplotpress. com/p/ml-code-exercises.

## 7

LINEAR REGRESSION

As the "Hello World" of supervised learning algorithms, regression analysis is a simple technique for predicting an unknown variable using the results you do know. The first regression technique we'll examine is linear regression, which generates a straight line to describe linear relationships. We'll start by examining the basic components of simple linear regression with one independent variable before discussing multiple regression with multiple independent variables.

Using the Seinfeld TV sitcom series as our data, let's start by plotting the two following variables, with season number as the x coordinate and the number of viewers per season (in millions) as the y coordinate.

Season (x)	Viewers (y)
1	19.22
2	18.07
3	17.67
4	20.52
5	29.59
6	31.27
7	33.19
8	32.24
9	38.11

Table 11: Seinfeld dataset

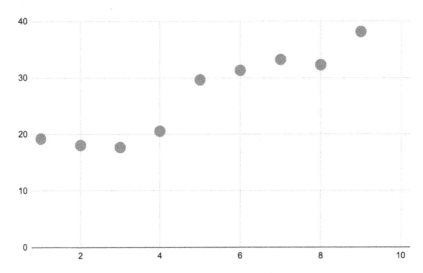

Figure 15: Seinfeld dataset plotted on a scatterplot

We can now see the dataset plotted on the scatterplot, with an upward trend in viewers starting at season 4 and peaking at season 9.

Let's next define the independent and dependent variables. For this example, we'll use the number of viewers per season as the dependent variable (what we want to predict) and the season number as the independent variable. Using simple linear regression, let's also insert a straight line to describe the upward linear trend of our small dataset.

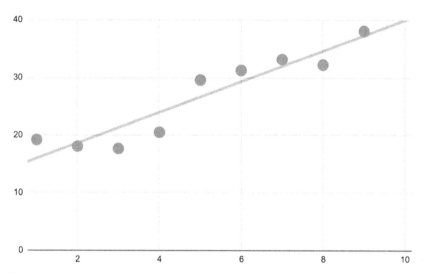

Figure 16: Linear regression hyperplane

As shown in Figure 16, this regression line neatly dissects the full company of data points. The technical term for the regression line is the *hyperplane*, and you'll see this term used throughout your study of machine learning. In a two-dimensional space, a hyperplane serves as a (flat) trendline, which is how Google Sheets titles linear regression in their scatterplot customization menu.

The goal of linear regression is to split the data in a way that minimizes the distance between the hyperplane and the observed values. This means that if you were to draw a vertical line from the hyperplane to each data point on the plot, the aggregate distance of each point would equate to the smallest possible distance to the hyperplane. The distance between the best-fit line and the observed values is called the residual or error and the closer those values are to the hyperplane, the more accurate the model's predictions.

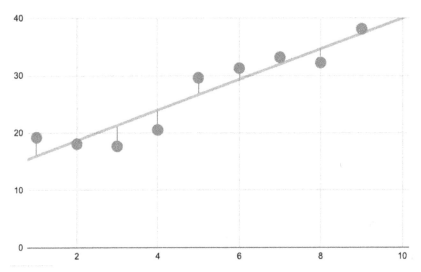

Figure 17: Error is the distance between the hyperplane and the observed value

The Slope

An important part of linear regression is the *slope*, which can be conveniently calculated by referencing the hyperplane. As one variable increases, the other variable will increase by the average value denoted by the hyperplane. The slope is therefore helpful for formulating predictions, such as predicting the number of season viewers for a potential tenth season of Seinfeld. Using the slope, we can input 10 as the x coordinate and find the corresponding y value, which in this case, is approximately 40 million viewers.

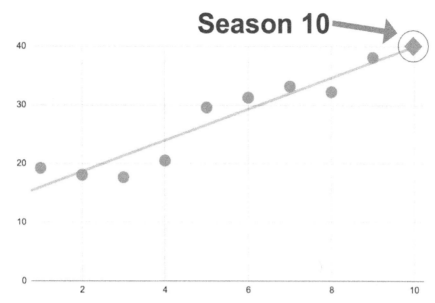

Figure 18: Using the slope/hyperplane to make a prediction

While linear regression isn't a fail-proof method for predicting trends, the trendline does offer a basic reference point for predicting unknown or future events.

Linear Regression Formula

The formula[23] for linear regression is $y = bx + a$.

"y" represents the dependent variable and "x" represents the independent variable.

"a" is the point where the hyperplane crosses the y-axis, known as the *y-intercept* or the value of y when $x = 0$.

"b" dictates the steepness of the slope and explains the relationship between x and y (what change in y is predicted for 1 unit change in x).

Calculation Example

---

[23] Although the formula is written differently in other disciplines, $y = bx + a$ is the preferred format used in statistics and machine learning. This formula could also be expressed using the notation of $y = \beta_0 + \beta_1 x_1 + e$, where β_0 is the intercept, β_1 is the slope, and e is the residual or error.)[23]

Although your programming language takes care of this automatically, it's interesting to know how simple linear regression works. We'll use the following dataset to break down the formula.

	(X)	(Y)	XY	X²
1	1	3	3	1
2	2	4	8	4
3	1	2	2	1
4	4	7	28	16
5	3	5	15	9
Σ (Total)	11	21	56	31

Table 12: Sample dataset
The final two columns of the table are not part of the original dataset and have been added for reference to complete the following formula.

$$a = \frac{(\Sigma y)(\Sigma x^2) - (\Sigma x)(\Sigma xy)}{n(\Sigma x^2) - (\Sigma x)^2}$$

$$b = \frac{n(\Sigma xy) - (\Sigma x)(\Sigma y)}{n(\Sigma x^2) - (\Sigma x)^2}$$

Where:

Σ = Total sum

Σx = Total sum of all x values $(1 + 2 + 1 + 4 + 3 = 11)$

Σy = Total sum of all y values $(3 + 4 + 2 + 7 + 5 = 21)$

Σxy = Total sum of x*y for each row $(3 + 8 + 2 + 28 + 15 = 56)$

Σx^2 = Total sum of x*x for each row $(1 + 4 + 1 + 16 + 9 = 31)$

n = Total number of rows. In the case of this example, n is equal to 5.

$$a = \frac{(\Sigma y)(\Sigma x^2) - (\Sigma x)(\Sigma xy)}{n(\Sigma x^2) - (\Sigma x)^2}$$

$$a = \frac{(21)(31) - (11)(56)}{5(31) - (11)^2}$$

$$b = \frac{n(\Sigma xy) - (\Sigma x)(\Sigma y)}{n(\Sigma x^2) - (\Sigma x)^2}$$

$$b = \frac{5(56) - (11)(21)}{5(31) - (11)^2}$$

a =

$((21 \times 31) - (11 \times 56)) / (5(31) - 11^2)$

$(651 - 616) / (155 - 121)$

$35 / 34 = 1.029$

b =

$(5(56) - (11 \times 21)) / (5(31) - 11^2)$

$(280 - 231) / (155 - 121)$

$49 / 34 = 1.441$

Insert the "a" and "b" values into the linear formula.

$y = bx + a$

$y = 1.441x + 1.029$

The linear formula $y = 1.441x + 1.029$ dictates how to draw the hyperplane.

Let's now test the linear regression model by looking up the coordinates for $x = 2$.

$y = 1.441(x) + 1.029$

$y = 1.441(2) + 1.029$

$y = 3.911$

In this case, the prediction is very close to the actual result of 4.0.

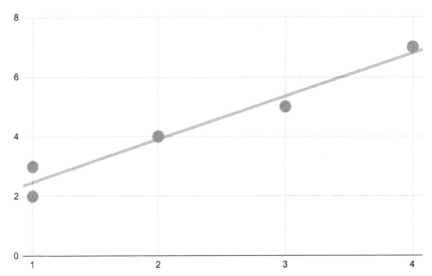

Figure 19: y = 1.441x + 1.029 plotted on the scatterplot

Multiple Linear Regression

Having summarized simple linear regression using a single independent variable, we can now look at multiple linear regression. This second technique is more applicable to machine learning given organizations use more than one independent variable to make decisions.

Multiple linear regression is simple linear regression but with more than one independent variable as the following formula shows.

$$y = a + b_1x_1 + b_2x_2 + b_3x_3 + ...$$

The y-intercept is still expressed as a, but now there are multiple independent variables (represented as x_1, x_2, x_3, etc.) each with their own respective coefficient (b_1, b_2, b_3, etc).

As with simple linear regression, various sums of X and y values (including squared values) from the training data are used to solve for a (y-intercept) and b (coefficient values).

Once a model has been built using the X and y values from the training data, the multiple linear regression formula can be used to make a prediction (y) using the X values from the test data (to assess accuracy).

Discrete Variables

While the output (dependent variable) of linear regression must be continuous in the form of a floating-point or integer (whole number) value, the input (independent variables) can be continuous or categorical. For categorical variables, i.e. sex, these variables must be expressed numerically using one-hot encoding (0 or 1) and not as a string of letters (male, female).

Variable Selection

Before finishing this chapter, it's important to address the dilemma of variable selection and choosing an appropriate number of independent variables. On the one hand, adding more variables helps to account for more potential factors that control patterns in the data. On the other hand, this rationale only holds if the variables are relevant and possess some correlation/linear relationship with the dependent variable.

The expansion of independent variables also creates more relationships to consider. In simple linear regression, we saw a one-to-one relationship between two variables, whereas in multiple linear regression there is a many-to-one relationship. In multiple linear regression, not only are the independent variables potentially related to the dependent variable, but they are also potentially related to each other.

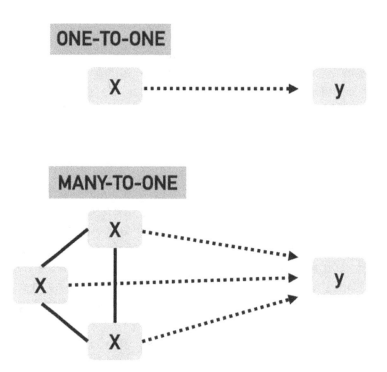

Figure 20: Simple linear regression (above) and multiple linear regression (below)

If a strong linear correlation exists between two independent variables, this can lead to a problem called multi-collinearity. When two independent variables are strongly correlated, they have a tendency to cancel each other out and provide the model with little to no unique information.

An example of two multi-collinear variables are liters of fuel consumed and liters of fuel in the tank to predict how far a jet plane will fly. Both independent variables are directly correlated, and in this case, negatively correlated; as one variable increases, the other variable decreases and vice versa. When both variables are used to predict the dependent variable of how far the jet will fly, one effectively cancels the other out. It's still worthwhile to include one of these variables in the model, but it would be redundant to include both variables.

To avoid multi-collinearity, we need to check the relationship between each combination of independent variables using a scatterplot, pairplot (a matrix of relationships between variables), or correlation score.

If we look at the pairplot in Figure 21, we can analyze the relationship between all three variables (total_bill, tip, and size). If we set tip as the dependent variable, then we need to assess whether the two independent variables (total_bill and size) are strongly correlated. Using our pairplot, we can see there are two scatterplots visualizing the relationship between total_bill and size (row 1 on the right, and row 3 on the left). These two plots are not identical (as the x-axis and y-axis are inverted), but you can refer to either one.

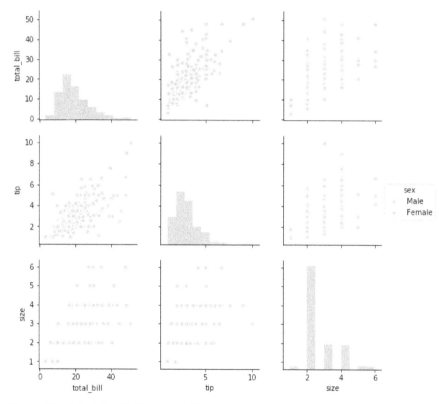

Figure 21: Pairplot with three variables

Judging by the upward linear trend, we can see that these two variables are partly correlated. However, if we were to insert a linear regression hyperplane, there would be significant residuals/errors on both sides of the hyperplane to confirm that these two variables aren't strongly or directly correlated and we can definitely include both these variables in our regression model.

The following heatmap, shown in Figure 22, also confirms a modest correlation score of 0.6 between total_bill and size.

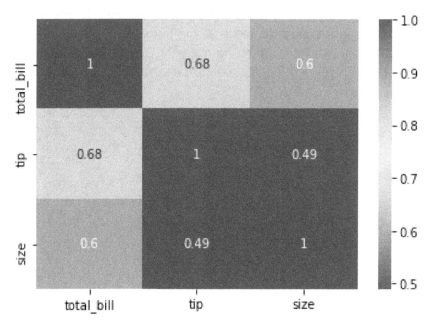

Figure 22: Heatmap with three variables

We can also use a pairplot, heatmap or correlation score to check if the independent variables are correlated to the dependent variable (and therefore relevant to the prediction outcome). In Figure 22, we can see that total_bill (0.68) and size (0.49) show some correlation with the dependent variable of tip. (Correlation is measured between -1 and 1, with a correlation of 1 describing a perfect positive relationship and a correlation of -1 indicating a perfect negative relationship. A coefficient of 0, meanwhile, denotes no relationship between two variables.)

In summary, the objective of multiple linear regression is for all the independent variables to be correlated with the dependent variable but not with each other.

CHAPTER QUIZ

Using **multiple linear regression,** your task is to create a model to predict the tip amount guests will leave the restaurant when paying for their meal. Note that this is a snippet of the actual dataset and the full dataset has 244 rows (diners).

	total_bill	tip	sex	smoker	day	time	size
0	16.99	1.01	Female	No	Sun	Dinner	2
1	10.34	1.66	Male	No	Sun	Dinner	3
2	21.01	3.50	Male	No	Sun	Dinner	3
3	23.68	3.31	Male	No	Sun	Dinner	2
4	24.59	3.61	Female	No	Sun	Dinner	4
5	25.29	4.71	Male	No	Sun	Dinner	4
6	8.77	2.00	Male	No	Sun	Dinner	2
7	26.88	3.12	Male	No	Sun	Dinner	4
8	15.04	1.96	Male	No	Sun	Dinner	2
9	14.78	3.23	Male	No	Sun	Dinner	2

1) **The dependent variable for this model should be which variable?**
   A) size
   B) total_bill and tip
   C) total_bill
   D) tip

2) **From looking only at the data preview above, which variable(s) appear to have a linear relationship with tip?**
   A) smoker
   B) total_bill and size
   C) time
   D) sex

3) **It's important for the independent variables to be strongly correlated with the dependent variable and one or more of the other independent variables. True or False?**

ANSWERS

1) D, tip

2) B, total_bill and size

(When there is an increase in both of these variables, we see a general increase in the tip for most rows. Other variables might be correlated to tip, but it's not clear to judge using only these 10 rows.)

3) False

(Ideally, the independent variables should not be strongly correlated with each other.)

LOGISTIC REGRESSION

As demonstrated in the previous chapter, linear regression is useful for quantifying relationships between variables to predict a continuous outcome. Total bill and size (number of guests) are both examples of continuous variables.

However, what if we want to predict a categorical variable such as "new customer" or "returning customer"? Unlike linear regression, the dependent variable (y) is no longer a continuous variable (such as total tip) but rather a discrete categorical variable.

Rather than quantify the linear relationship between variables, we need to use a classification technique such as logistic regression.

Logistic regression is still a supervised learning technique but produces a qualitative prediction rather than a quantitative prediction. This algorithm is often used to predict two discrete classes, e.g., *pregnant* or *not pregnant*. Given its strength in binary classification, logistic regression is used in many fields including fraud detection, disease diagnosis, emergency detection, loan default detection, or to identify spam email through the process of discerning specific classes, e.g., non-spam and spam.

Using the sigmoid function, logistic regression finds the probability of independent variables (X) producing a discrete dependent variable (y) such as "spam" or "non-spam."

$$y = \frac{1}{1+e^{-x}}$$

Where:

x = the independent variable you wish to transform

e = Euler's constant, 2.718

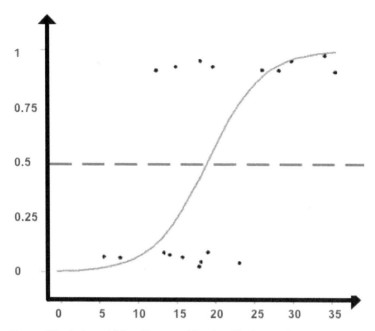

Figure 23: A sigmoid function used to classify data points

The sigmoid function produces an S-shaped curve that can convert any number and map it into a numerical value between 0 and 1 but without ever reaching those exact limits. Applying this formula, the sigmoid function converts independent variables into an expression of probability between 0 and 1 in relation to the dependent variable. In a binary case, a value of 0 represents no chance of occurring, and 1 represents a certain chance of occurring. The degree of probability for values located between 0 and 1 can be found according to how close they rest to 0 (impossible) or 1 (certain possibility).

Based on the found probabilities of the independent variables, logistic regression assigns each data point to a discrete class. In the case of binary classification (shown in Figure 22), the cut-off line to classify data points is 0.5. Data points that record a value above 0.5 are classified as Class A, and data points below 0.5 are classified as Class B. Data points that record a result of precisely 0.5 are unclassifiable but such instances are rare due to the mathematical component of the sigmoid function.

Following the logistic transformation using the Sigmoid function, the data points are assigned to one of two classes as presented in Figure 24.

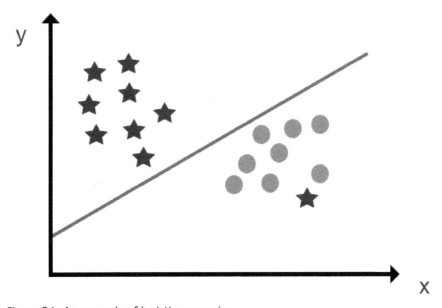

Figure 24: An example of logistic regression

Similar to linear regression, the independent variables, used as input to predict the dependent variable, can be categorical or continuous as long as they are expressed as numbers and not as strings of letters. In the case of discrete categorical variables, this involves using one-hot encoding to create a new set of variables to represent the original variable numerically.

Although logistic regression shares a visual resemblance to linear regression, the logistic hyperplane represents a classification/decision boundary rather than a prediction trendline. Thus, instead of using the hyperplane to make numeric predictions, the hyperplane is used to divide the dataset into classes.

The other distinction between logistic and linear regression is that the dependent variable (y) isn't placed along the y-axis in logistic regression. Instead, independent variables can be plotted along both axes, and the class (output) of the dependent variable is determined by the position of the data point in relation to the decision boundary. Data points on one side of the decision boundary are classified as Class A, and data points on the opposing side of the decision boundary are Class B.

For classification scenarios with more than two possible discrete outcomes, multinomial logistic regression can be used as shown in Figure 25.

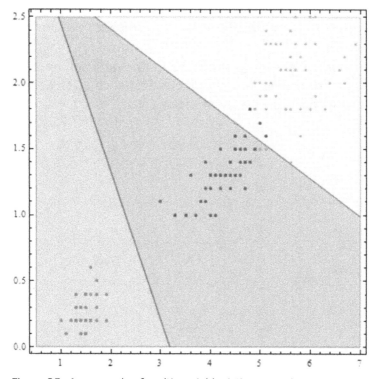

Figure 25: An example of multinomial logistic regression

As a similar classification method, multinomial logistic regression solves multiclass problems with more than two possible discrete outcomes. Multinomial logistic regression can also be applied to ordinal cases where there are a set number of discrete outcomes, e.g., pre-undergraduate, undergraduate, and postgraduate. Keep in mind, though, that logistic regression's core strength lies in binary prediction, and other classification algorithms including decision trees or support vector machines may be a better option for solving multiclass problems.

221

Two tips to remember when using logistic regression are that the dataset should be free of missing values and that all independent variables are independent and not strongly correlated with each other. There should also be sufficient data for each output variable to ensure high accuracy. A good starting point would be approximately 30-50 data points for each output, i.e., 60-100 total data points for binary logistic regression. In general, logistic regression normally doesn't work so well with large datasets, and especially messy data containing outliers, complex relationships, and missing values.

If you would like to learn more about the mathematical foundation of logistic regression, you can check out *Statistics 101: Logistic Regression* series on YouTube by Brandon Foltz.[24]

---

[24] Brandon Foltz, "Logistic Regression," *YouTube*,
https://www.youtube.com/channel/UCFrjdcImgcQVyFbK04MBEhA

CHAPTER QUIZ

Using **logistic regression**, your task is to classify penguins into different classes based on the following dataset. Please note that this dataset has 344 rows and the following screenshot is a snippet of the full dataset.

	species	island	bill_length_mm	bill_depth_mm	flipper_length_mm	body_mass_g	sex
0	Adelie	Torgersen	39.1	18.7	181.0	3750.0	MALE
1	Adelie	Torgersen	39.5	17.4	186.0	3800.0	FEMALE
2	Adelie	Torgersen	40.3	18.0	195.0	3250.0	FEMALE
3	Adelie	Torgersen	NaN	NaN	NaN	NaN	NaN
4	Adelie	Torgersen	36.7	19.3	193.0	3450.0	FEMALE
5	Adelie	Torgersen	39.3	20.6	190.0	3650.0	MALE
6	Adelie	Torgersen	38.9	17.8	181.0	3625.0	FEMALE
7	Adelie	Torgersen	39.2	19.6	195.0	4675.0	MALE
8	Adelie	Torgersen	34.1	18.1	193.0	3475.0	NaN
9	Adelie	Torgersen	42.0	20.2	190.0	4250.0	NaN

1) **Which three variables (in their current form) could we use as the dependent variable to <u>classify</u> penguins?**

2) **Which row(s) contains missing values?**

3) **Which variable in the dataset preview is a binary variable?**

ANSWERS

1) species, island, or sex

2) Row 3, 8, and 9

(NaN = missing value)

3) sex

(Species and island might also be binary but we can't judge from the dataset screenshot alone.)

k-NEAREST NEIGHBORS

Another popular classification technique in machine learning is *k*-nearest neighbors (*k*-NN). As a supervised learning algorithm, *k*-NN classifies new data points based on their position to nearby data points.

In many ways, *k*-NN is similar to a voting system or a popularity contest. Imagine you're the new kid at school and you need to know how to dress in order to fit in with the rest of the class. On your first day at school, you see six of the nine students sitting closest to you with their sleeves rolled-up. Based on numerical supremacy and close proximity, the following day you also make the decision to roll up your sleeves.

Let's now look at another example. In Figure 26, the data points have been classified into two classes, and a new data point, whose class is unknown, is added to the plot. Using *k*-NN, we can predict the category of the new data point based on its position to the existing data points.

First, though, we need to set "*k*" to determine how many data points we want to use to classify the new data point. If we set *k* to 3, *k*-NN analyzes the new data point's position with respect to the three nearest data points (neighbors). The outcome of selecting the three closest neighbors returns two Class B data points and one Class A data point. Defined by *k* (3), the model's prediction for determining the category of the new data point is Class B as it returns two out of the three nearest neighbors.

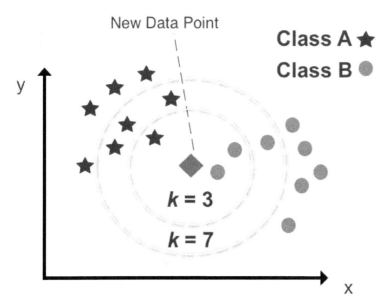

Figure 26: Using k-NN clustering to predict the class of a new data point

The chosen number of neighbors identified, defined by k, is crucial in determining the results. In Figure 26, you can see that the outcome of classification changes by altering k from "3" to "7." It's therefore useful to test numerous k combinations to find the best fit and avoid setting k too low or too high. Setting k too low will increase bias and lead to misclassification and setting k too high will make it computationally expensive. Setting k to an uneven number will also help to eliminate the possibility of a statistical stalemate and an invalid result. Five is the default number of neighbors for this algorithm using Scikit-learn.

Given that the scale of the individual variables has a major impact on the output of k-NN, the dataset usually needs to be scaled to standardize variance as discussed in Chapter 5. This transformation will help to avoid one or more variables with a high range unfairly pulling the focus of the k-NN model.

In regards to what type of data to use with k-NN, this algorithm works best with continuous variables. It is still possible to use binary categorical variables represented as 0 and 1, but the results are more likely to be informed by the binary splits relative to the dispersion across other variables as visualized in Figure 27.

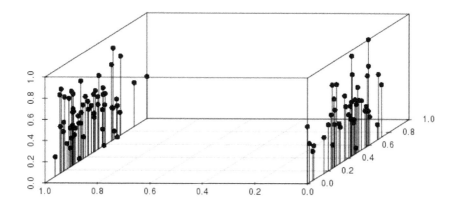

Figure 27: One binary variable and two continuous variables

Above, we can see that the horizontal x-axis is binary (0 or 1), which splits the data into two distinct sides. Moreover, if we switch one of the existing continuous variables to a binary variable (as shown in Figure 28), we can see that the distance between variables is influenced even more greatly by the outcome of the binary variables.

If you wish to examine binary variables as part of *k*-NN analysis, it's therefore best to only include critical binary variables in your prediction model.

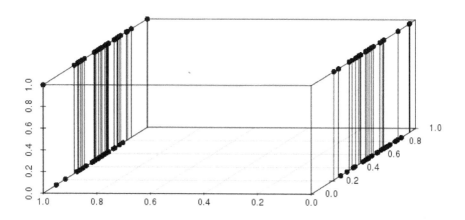

Figure 28: Two binary variables and one continuous variable

While k-NN is generally accurate and easy to comprehend, storing an entire dataset and calculating the distance between each new data point and all existing data points puts a heavy burden on computing resources. This means that the number of data points in the dataset is proportional to the time it takes to execute a single prediction, which can lead to slower processing times. For this reason, k-NN is generally not recommended for analyzing large datasets.

Another downside is that it can be challenging to apply k-NN to high-dimensional data with a high number of features. Measuring multiple distances between data points in a high-dimensional space is also taxing on computing resources and it becomes more difficult to perform accurate classification.

CHAPTER QUIZ

Your task is to classify penguins into different species using the **k-nearest neighbors** algorithm, with k set to 5 (neighbors).

	species	bill_length_mm	bill_depth_mm	flipper_length_mm	body_mass_g	sex
0	Adelie	39.1	18.7	181.0	3750.0	MALE
1	Adelie	39.5	17.4	186.0	3800.0	FEMALE
2	Adelie	40.3	18.0	195.0	3250.0	FEMALE
3	Adelie	NaN	NaN	NaN	NaN	NaN
4	Adelie	36.7	19.3	193.0	3450.0	FEMALE
5	Adelie	39.3	20.6	190.0	3650.0	MALE
6	Adelie	38.9	17.8	181.0	3625.0	FEMALE
7	Adelie	39.2	19.6	195.0	4675.0	MALE
8	Adelie	34.1	18.1	193.0	3475.0	NaN
9	Adelie	42.0	20.2	190.0	4250.0	NaN

1) **Which of the following variables should we consider removing from our k-NN model (if not strictly relevant)?**
   A. sex
   B. species
   C. body_mass_g
   D. bill_depth_mm

2) **If we want to reduce the processing time of our model, which of the following methods is recommended?**
   A. Increase k from 5 to 10
   B. Reduce k from 5 to 3
   C. Re-run the model and hope for a faster result
   D. Increase the size of the training data

3) **To include the variable 'sex' in our model, which data scrubbing technique would we need to use?**

ANSWERS

1) A, sex

(Binary variables should only be used when critical to the model's accuracy.)

2) B, Reduce k from 5 to 3

3) One-hot encoding (to convert the variable into a numerical identifier of 0 or 1)

k-MEANS CLUSTERING

The next method of analysis involves grouping or clustering data points that share similar attributes using unsupervised learning. An online business, for example, wants to examine a segment of customers that purchase at the same time of the year and discern what factors influence their purchasing behavior. By understanding a given cluster of customers, they can then form decisions regarding which products to recommend to customer groups using promotions and personalized offers. Outside of market research, clustering can also be applied to other scenarios, including pattern recognition, fraud detection, and image processing.

One of the most popular clustering techniques is *k*-means clustering. As an unsupervised learning algorithm, *k*-means clustering attempts to divide data into *k* number of discrete groups and is highly effective at uncovering new patterns. Examples of potential groupings include animal species, customers with similar features, and housing market segmentation.

Original Data

Clustered Data

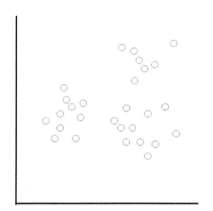 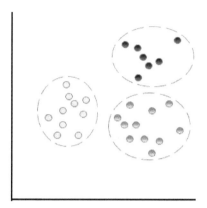

Figure 29: Comparison of original data and clustered data using k-means

The *k*-means clustering algorithm works by first splitting data into *k* number of clusters, with *k* representing the number of clusters you wish to create. If you choose to split your dataset into three clusters, for example, then *k* should be set to 3. In Figure 29, we can see that the original data has been transformed into three clusters (*k* = 3). If we were to set *k* to 4, an additional cluster would be derived from the dataset to produce four clusters.

How does *k*-means clustering separate the data points? The first step is to examine the unclustered data and manually select a centroid for each cluster. That centroid then forms the epicenter of an individual cluster.

Centroids can be chosen at random, which means you can nominate any data point on the scatterplot to act as a centroid. However, you can save time by selecting centroids dispersed across the scatterplot and not directly adjacent to each other. In other words, start by guessing where you think the centroids for each cluster might be positioned. The remaining data points on the scatterplot are then assigned to the nearest centroid by measuring the Euclidean distance.

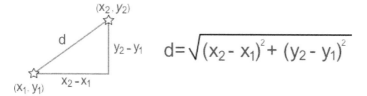

$$d = \sqrt{(x_2 - x_1)^2 + (y_2 - y_1)^2}$$

Figure 30: Calculating Euclidean distance

Each data point can be assigned to only one cluster, and each cluster is discrete. This means that there's no overlap between clusters and no case of nesting a cluster inside another cluster. Also, all data points, including anomalies, are assigned to a centroid irrespective of how they impact the final shape of the cluster. However, due to the statistical force that pulls nearby data points to a central point, clusters will typically form an elliptical or spherical shape.

After all data points have been allocated to a centroid, the next step is to aggregate the mean value of the data points in each cluster, which can be found by calculating the average x and y values of the data points contained in each cluster.

Next, take the mean value of the data points in each cluster and plug in those x and y values to update your centroid coordinates. This will most likely result in one or more changes to the location of your centroid(s). The total number of clusters, however, remains the same as you are not creating new clusters but rather updating their position on the scatterplot. Like musical chairs, the remaining data points rush to the closest centroid to form *k* number of clusters.

Should any data point on the scatterplot switch clusters with the changing of centroids, the previous step is repeated. This means, again, calculating the average mean value of the cluster and updating the x and y values of each centroid to reflect the average coordinates of the data points in that cluster.

Once you reach a stage where the data points no longer switch clusters after an update in centroid coordinates, the algorithm is complete, and you have your final set of clusters.

The following diagrams break down the full algorithmic process.

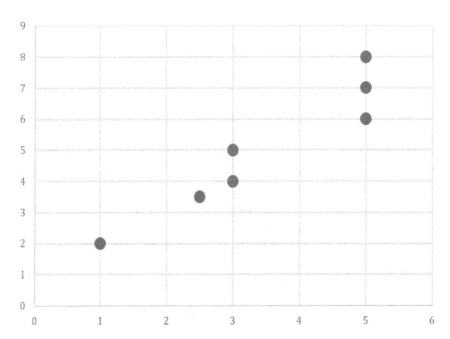

Figure 31: Sample data points are plotted on a scatterplot

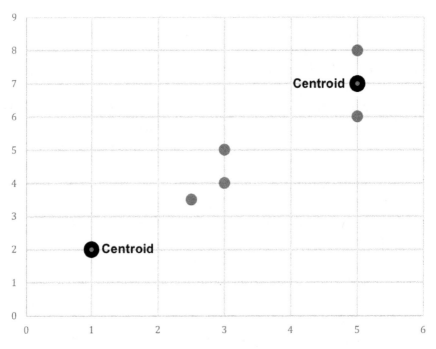

Figure 32: Two existing data points are nominated as the centroids

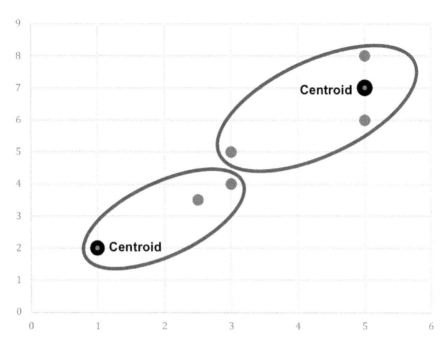

Figure 33: Two clusters are formed after calculating the Euclidean distance of the remaining data points to the centroids.

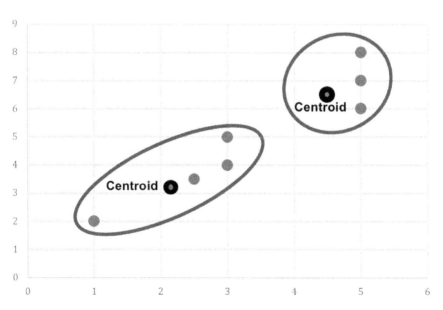

Figure 34: The centroid coordinates for each cluster are updated to reflect the cluster's mean value. The two previous centroids stay in their original position and two new centroids are added to the scatterplot. Lastly, as one data point has

switched from the right cluster to the left cluster, the centroids of both clusters need to be updated one last time.

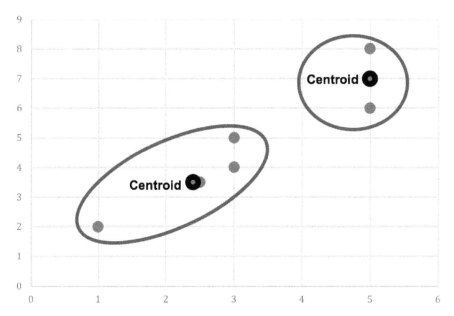

Figure 35: Two final clusters are produced based on the updated centroids for each cluster

For this example, it took two iterations to successfully create our two clusters. However, k-means clustering is not always able to reliably identify a final combination of clusters. In such cases, you will need to switch tactics and utilize another algorithm to formulate your classification model.

Also, be aware that you may need to rescale the input features using standardization before running the k-means algorithm. This will help to preserve the true shape of the clusters and avoid exaggerated variance from affecting the final output (i.e. over-stretched clusters).

Setting *k*

When setting "k" for k-means clustering, it's important to find the right number of clusters. In general, as k increases, clusters become smaller and variance falls. However, the downside is that neighboring clusters become less distinct from one another as k increases. If you set k to the same number of data points in your dataset, each data point automatically becomes a standalone cluster. Conversely, if you set k to 1, then all data points will be deemed as homogenous and fall inside one large cluster. Needless to say, setting k to either extreme does not provide any worthwhile insight.

In order to optimize k, you may wish to use a scree plot for guidance. A scree plot charts the degree of scattering (variance) inside a cluster as the total number of clusters increases. Scree plots are famous for their iconic "elbow," which reflects several pronounced kinks in the plot's curve. A scree plot compares the Sum of Squared Error (SSE) for each variation of total clusters. SSE is measured as the sum of the squared distance between the centroid and the other neighbors inside the cluster. In a nutshell, SSE drops as more clusters are produced.

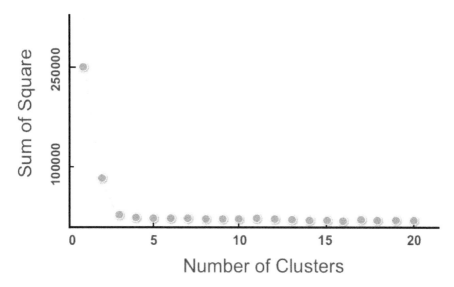

Figure 36: A scree plot

This asks the question of what's an optimal number of clusters? In general, you should opt for a cluster solution where SSE subsides dramatically to the left on the scree plot but before it reaches a point of negligible change with cluster variations to its right. For instance, in Figure 36, there is little change in SSE for four or more clusters. This would result in clusters that would be small and difficult to distinguish.

In this scree plot, two or three clusters appear to be an ideal solution. There exists a significant kink to the left of these two cluster variations due to a pronounced drop-off in SSE. Meanwhile, there is still some change in SSE with the solution to their right. This will ensure that these two cluster solutions are distinct and have an impact on data classification.

Another useful technique to decide the number of cluster solutions is to divide the total number of data points (n) by two and to find the square root.

$$\sqrt{\frac{n}{2}}$$

If we have 200 data points, for example, the recommended number of clusters is 10, whereas if we have 18 data points, the suggested number of clusters is 3.

A more simple and non-mathematical approach to setting k is to apply domain knowledge. I might want to set k to 2, for example, if I am analyzing data about visitors to the website of a major IT provider. Why two clusters? Because I already know there is a significant discrepancy in spending behavior between returning visitors and new visitors. First-time visitors rarely purchase enterprise-level IT products and services, as these customers usually go through a lengthy research and vetting process before procurement can be approved.

Based on this knowledge, I can use k-means clustering to create two clusters and test my hypothesis. After producing two clusters, I may then choose to examine one of the two clusters further, by either applying another technique or again using k-means clustering. For instance, I might want to split the returning users into two clusters (using k-means clustering) to test my hypothesis that mobile users and desktop users produce two disparate groups of data points. Again, by applying domain knowledge, I know it's uncommon for large enterprises to make big-ticket purchases on a mobile device and I can test this assumption using *k*-means clustering.

If, though, I am analyzing a product page for a low-cost item, such as a $4.99 domain name, new visitors and returning visitors are less likely to produce two distinct clusters. As the item price is low, new users are less likely to deliberate before purchasing. Instead, I might choose to set *k* to 3 based on my three primary lead generators: organic traffic, paid traffic, and email marketing. These three lead sources are likely to produce three discrete clusters based on the fact that:

a) **Organic traffic** generally consists of both new and returning customers with the intention to purchase from my website (through pre-selection, e.g., word of mouth, previous customer experience).

b) **Paid traffic** targets new customers who typically arrive on the site with a lower level of trust than organic traffic, including potential customers who click on the paid advertisement by mistake.

c) **Email marketing** reaches existing customers who already have experience purchasing from the website and have established and verified user accounts.

This is an example of domain knowledge based on my occupation but understand that the effectiveness of "domain knowledge" diminishes dramatically past a low number of *k* clusters. In other words, domain knowledge might be sufficient for determining two to four clusters but less valuable when choosing between a higher number of clusters, such as 20 or 21 clusters.

CHAPTER QUIZ

Your task is to group the flights dataset (which tracks flights from 1949 to 1960) into discrete clusters using **k-means clustering**. The full dataset has 145 rows.

	year	month	passengers
0	1949	January	112
1	1949	February	118
2	1949	March	132
3	1949	April	129
4	1949	May	121
5	1949	June	135
6	1949	July	148
7	1949	August	148
8	1949	September	136
9	1949	October	119

1) **Using *k*-means clustering to analyze all variables, what may be a good initial number of *k* clusters (based on domain knowledge)?**
   A. $k = 2$
   B. $k = 100$
   C. $k = 12$

2) **What mathematical technique might we use to find the appropriate number of clusters?**
   A. Big elbow method
   B. Mean absolute error
   C. Scree plot

3) **Which variable requires data scrubbing in order to perform *k*-means clustering?**

ANSWERS

1) 12

(Given there are 12 months in a year, there may be some reoccurring patterns in regard to the number of passengers flying each month.)

2) C, Scree plot

3) month

(This variable needs to be converted into a numerical identifier in order to measure its distance to other variables.)

## 11

BIAS & VARIANCE

Algorithm selection is an essential step in understanding patterns in your data but designing a generalized model that accurately predicts new data points can be a challenging task. The fact that most algorithms have many different hyperparameters also leads to a vast number of potential outcomes.

As a quick recap, hyperparameters are lines of code that act as the algorithm's settings, similar to the controls on the dashboard of an airplane or knobs used to tune radio frequency.

```
model = ensemble.GradientBoostingRegressor(
    n_estimators=150,
    learning_rate=0.1,
    max_depth=4,
    min_samples_split=4,
    min_samples_leaf=4,
    max_features=0.5,
    loss='huber'
)
```

Figure 37: Example of hyperparameters in Python for the algorithm gradient boosting

Underfitting and Overfitting

A constant challenge in machine learning is navigating *underfitting* and *overfitting*, which describe how closely your model follows the actual patterns of the data. To comprehend underfitting and overfitting, you must first understand *bias* and *variance*.

Bias refers to the gap between the value predicted by your model and the actual value of the data. In the case of high bias, your predictions are likely to be skewed in a particular direction away from the true values. Variance describes how scattered your predicted values are in relation to each other. Bias and variance can be better understood by viewing the following visual representation.

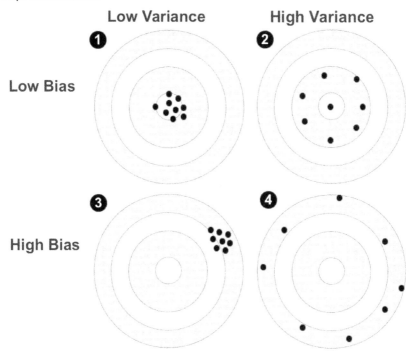

Figure 38: Shooting targets used to represent bias and variance

Shooting targets, as seen in Figure 38, are not a visualization technique used in machine learning but can be used here to explain bias and variance.[25]

Imagine that the center of the target, or the bull's-eye, perfectly predicts the correct value of your data. The dots marked on the target represent an individual prediction of your model based on the training or test data provided. In certain cases, the dots will

---

[25] Prratek Ramchandani, "Random Forests and the Bias-Variance Tradeoff," *Towards Data Science*, https://towardsdatascience.com/random-forests-and-the-bias-variance-tradeoff-3b77fee339b4

be densely positioned close to the bull's-eye, ensuring that predictions made by the model are close to the actual values and patterns found in the data. In other cases, the model's predictions will lie more scattered across the target. The more the predictions deviate from the bull's-eye, the higher the bias and the less reliable your model is at making accurate predictions.

In the first target, we can see an example of low bias and low variance. The bias is low because the model's predictions are closely aligned to the center, and there is low variance because the predictions are positioned densely in one general location.

The second target (located on the right of the first row) shows a case of low bias and high variance. Although the predictions are not as close to the bull's-eye as the previous example, they are still near to the center, and the bias is therefore relatively low. However, there is a high variance this time because the predictions are spread out from each other.

The third target (located on the left of the second row) represents high bias and low variance and the fourth target (located on the right of the second row) shows high bias and high variance.

Ideally, you want a situation where there's both low variance and low bias. In reality, however, there's a trade-off between optimal bias and optimal variance. Bias and variance both contribute to error but it's the prediction error that you want to minimize, not the bias or variance specifically.

Like learning to ride a bicycle for the first time, finding an optimal balance is one of the more challenging aspects of machine learning. Peddling algorithms through the data is the easy part; the hard part is navigating bias and variance while maintaining a state of balance in your model.

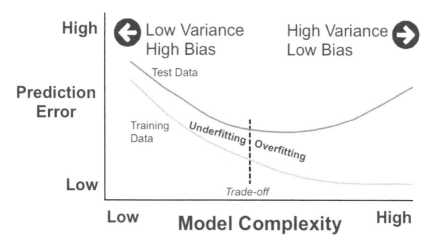

Figure 39: Model complexity based on the prediction error

Let's explore this problem further using a visual example. In Figure 39, we can see two curves. The upper curve represents the test data, and the lower curve depicts the training data. From the left, both curves begin at a point of high prediction error due to low variance and high bias. As they move toward the right, they change to the opposite: high variance and low bias. This leads to low prediction error in the case of the training data and high prediction error in the case of the test data. In the middle of the plot is an optimal balance of prediction error between the training and test data. This midground is a typical illustration of the bias-variance trade-off.

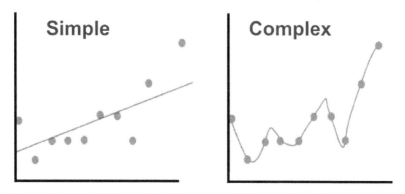

Figure 40: Underfitting on the left and overfitting on the right

245

Mismanaging the bias-variance trade-off can lead to poor results. As seen in Figure 40, this can result in the model being overly simple and inflexible (underfitting) or overly complex and flexible (overfitting).

Underfitting (low variance, high bias) on the left and overfitting (high variance, low bias) on the right are shown in these two scatterplots. A natural temptation is to add complexity to the model (as shown on the right) to improve accuracy, but this can, in turn, lead to overfitting. An overfitted model yields accurate predictions using the training data but is less precise at making predictions using the test data. Overfitting can also occur if the training and test data aren't randomized before they are split and patterns in the data aren't distributed evenly across the two segments of data.

Underfitting is when your model is overly simple, and again, has not scratched the surface of the underlying patterns in the data. This can lead to inaccurate predictions for both the training data and test data. Common causes of underfitting include insufficient training data to adequately cover all possible combinations, and situations where the training and test data weren't properly randomized.

To mitigate underfitting and overfitting, you may need to modify the model's hyperparameters to ensure that they fit the patterns of both the training and test data and not just one split of the data. A suitable fit should acknowledge significant trends in the data and play down or even omit minor variations. This might mean re-randomizing your training and test data, adding new data points to better detect underlying patterns or switching algorithms to manage the issue of the bias-variance trade-off. Linear regression, for example, is one learning algorithm that rarely encounters overfitting (but may be susceptible to underfitting).

Switching from linear regression to non-linear regression can also reduce bias by increasing variance. Alternatively, increasing "k" in k-NN minimizes variance (by averaging together more neighbors). A third example could be reducing variance by switching from a single decision tree (which is prone to overfitting) to random forests with many decision trees.

An advanced strategy to combat overfitting is to introduce *regularization*, which reduces the risk of overfitting by constraining the model to make it simpler. In effect, this add-on hyperparameter artificially amplifies bias error by penalizing an increase in a model's complexity and provides a warning alert to keep high variance in check while other hyperparameters are being tested and optimized.

Setting the regularization hyperparameter to a high value will avoid overfitting the model to the training data but may lead to some underfitting. In linear regression, this would constitute a relatively flat slope (close to zero) for the hyperplane or an overly wide margin in the case of support vector machines.

Lastly, one other technique to improve model accuracy is to perform cross validation, as covered earlier in Chapter 6, to minimize pattern discrepancies between the training data and the test data.

## 12

SUPPORT VECTOR MACHINES

Developed inside the computer science community in the 1990s, support vector machines (SVM) was initially designed for predicting numeric and categorical outcomes as a double-barrel prediction technique. Today, though, SVM is mostly used as a classification technique for predicting categorical outcomes.

As a classification technique, SVM is similar to logistic regression, in that it's used to filter data into a binary or multiclass target variable. But, as seen in Figure 41, SVM sets a different emphasis on the location of the classification boundary line.

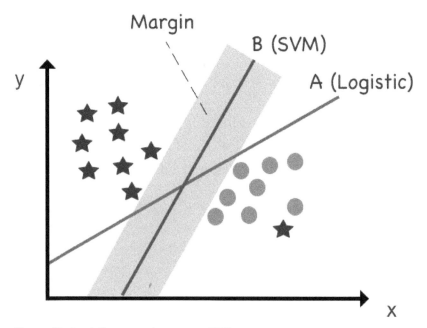

Figure 41: Logistic regression versus SVM

The scatterplot in Figure 41 consists of 17 data points that are linearly separable. We can see that the logistic decision boundary (A) splits the data points into two classes in a way that minimizes the distance between all data points and the decision boundary. The second line, the SVM boundary (B), also separates the two classes but it does so from a position of maximum distance between itself and the two classes of data points.

You'll also notice a gray zone that denotes *margin*, which is the distance between the decision boundary and the nearest data point, multiplied by two. The margin is a key part of SVM and is important because it offers additional support to cope with new data points that may infringe on the decision boundary (as is the case with logistic regression). To illustrate this scenario, let's consider the same scatterplot with the inclusion of a new data point.

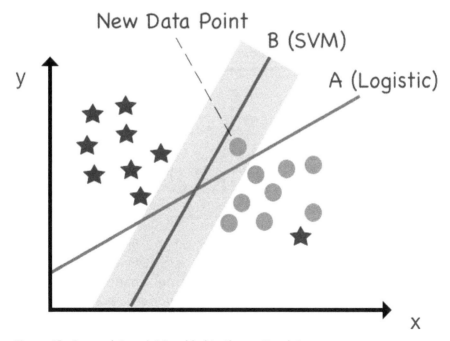

Figure 42: A new data point is added to the scatterplot

The new data point is a circle, but it's located incorrectly on the left side of the logistic (A) decision boundary (designated for stars). The new data point, though, remains correctly located on the right side of the SVM (B) decision boundary (designated for circles) courtesy of ample "support" supplied by the margin.

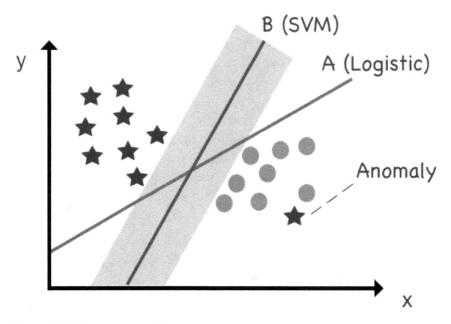

Figure 43: Mitigating anomalies

SVM is also useful for untangling complex relationships and mitigating outliers and anomalies. A limitation of standard logistic regression is that it goes out of its way to fit outliers and anomalies (as seen in the scatterplot with the star in the bottom right corner in Figure 43). SVM, however, is less sensitive to such data points and actually minimizes their impact on the final location of the boundary line. In Figure 43, we can see that Line B (SVM) is less sensitive to the anomalous star on the right-hand side. SVM can thus be used as a method for managing variant data.

The SVM boundary can also be modified to ignore misclassified cases in the training data using a hyperparameter called C. In machine learning, you typically want to generalize patterns rather than precisely decode the training data (which is bound to contain some degree of noise[26]) as incurring some mistakes in training the

---

[26] Random and/or useless information that obscures the key meaning of the data.

model may lead to a model that generalizes better on real data. There is therefore a trade-off in SVM between a **wide margin/more mistakes** and a **narrow margin/fewer mistakes**. The higher goal of your model is to strike a balance between "not too strict" and "not too loose", and, by modifying the C hyperparameter, you can regulate to what extent the misclassified cases (on the wrong side of the margin) are ignored.

Adding flexibility to the model using the hyperparameter C introduces what's called a "soft margin," which ignores a determined portion of cases that cross over the soft margin— leading to greater generalization in the model. The margin is made wider or softer when C is set to a low value. A C value of '0,' meanwhile, enforces no penalty on misclassified cases. Conversely, a large C value[27] makes the cost of misclassification high, thereby narrowing the width of the margin (hard margin) to avoid misclassification. This may force the model to overfit the training data and thereby misclassify new data points.

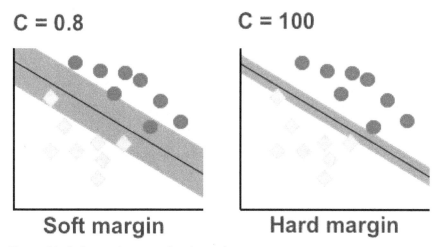

Figure 44: Soft margin versus hard margin

---

[27] In Scikit-learn, the default for the C hyperparameter is 1.0 and the strength of the regularization (the penalty for overfitting) is inversely proportional to C. This means any value below 1.0 effectively adds regularization to the model, and the penalty is squared L2 (L2 is calculated as the square root of the sum of the squared vector values).

251

You can combat overfitting—where the model performs well on the training data but not on new data—by reducing C as this adds regularization to the model. Finding an optimal C value is generally chosen experimentally based on trial and error, which can be automated using a technique called grid search (discussed in Chapter 18).

While the examples discussed so far have comprised two features plotted on a two-dimensional scatterplot, SVM's real strength lies with high-dimensional data and handling multiple features. SVM has numerous advanced variations available to classify high-dimensional data using what's called the Kernel Trick. This is an advanced solution to map data from a low-dimensional to a high-dimensional space when a dataset cannot be separated using a linear decision boundary in its original space. Transitioning from a two-dimensional to a three-dimensional space, for example, allows us to use a linear plane to split the data within a 3-D area. In other words, the kernel trick lets us classify data points with non-linear characteristics using linear classification in a higher dimension.

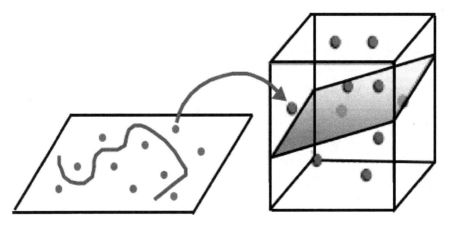

Figure 45: In this example, the decision boundary provides a non-linear separator between the data in a 2-D space but transforms into a linear separator between data points when projected into a 3-D space

A factor to be mindful of when using SVM is that it can be sensitive to feature scales and you may need to rescale the data prior to training.[28] Using standardization, you can convert the range of each feature to a standard normal distribution with a mean of zero. Standardization is implemented in Scikit-learn using StandardScaler. Documentation for StandardScaler can be found at http://bit.ly/378pf9Q.

Lastly, the processing time to train a model relative to logistic regression and other classification algorithms can be a drawback to using SVM. In particular, SVM is not recommended for datasets with a low feature-to-row ratio (low number of features relative to rows) due to speed and performance constraints. SVM does, though, excel at untangling outliers from complex small and medium-sized datasets and managing high-dimensional data.

---

[28] It's generally good practice to train the model twice—with and without standardization—and compare the performance of the two models.

CHAPTER QUIZ

Using an **SVM classifier**, your task is to classify which island a penguin has come from after arriving on your own island. To predict the island, you can use any or all of the variables from the penguin dataset.

	species	island	bill_length_mm	bill_depth_mm	flipper_length_mm	body_mass_g	sex
0	Adelie	Torgersen	39.1	18.7	181.0	3750.0	MALE
1	Adelie	Torgersen	39.5	17.4	186.0	3800.0	FEMALE
2	Adelie	Torgersen	40.3	18.0	195.0	3250.0	FEMALE
3	Adelie	Torgersen	NaN	NaN	NaN	NaN	NaN
4	Adelie	Torgersen	36.7	19.3	193.0	3450.0	FEMALE
5	Adelie	Torgersen	39.3	20.6	190.0	3650.0	MALE
6	Adelie	Torgersen	38.9	17.8	181.0	3625.0	FEMALE
7	Adelie	Torgersen	39.2	19.6	195.0	4675.0	MALE
8	Adelie	Torgersen	34.1	18.1	193.0	3475.0	NaN
9	Adelie	Torgersen	42.0	20.2	190.0	4250.0	NaN

1) Which variable is the dependent variable for this model?

A. island
B. species
C. sex

2) Which variable(s) could we use as the independent variable(s)?

A. island
B. All of the variables
C. All of the variables except island

3) Which two data scrubbing techniques are often used with this algorithm?

ANSWERS

1) A, island

2) C, All of the variables except island

3) Regularization and standardization

## 13

ARTIFICIAL NEURAL NETWORKS

This penultimate chapter on machine learning algorithms brings us to artificial neural networks (ANN) and the gateway to reinforcement learning. Artificial neural networks, also known as *neural networks*, is a popular machine learning technique for analyzing data through a network of decision layers. The naming of this technique was inspired by the algorithm's structural resemblance to the human brain. While this doesn't mean artificial neural networks are a virtual reproduction of the brain's decision-making process, there do exist some general similarities.

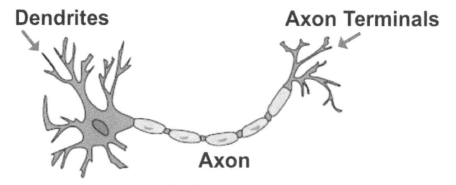

Figure 46: Anatomy of a human brain neuron

The brain, for example, contains interconnected neurons with dendrites that receive inputs. From these inputs, the neuron produces an electric signal output from the axon and emits these signals through axon terminals to other neurons. Similarly, artificial neural networks consist of interconnected decision functions, known as *nodes,* which interact with each other through axon-like *edges.*

The nodes of a neural network are separated into layers and generally start with a wide base. This first layer consists of raw input data (such as numeric values, text, image pixels or sound) divided into nodes. Each input node then sends information to the next layer of nodes via the network's edges.

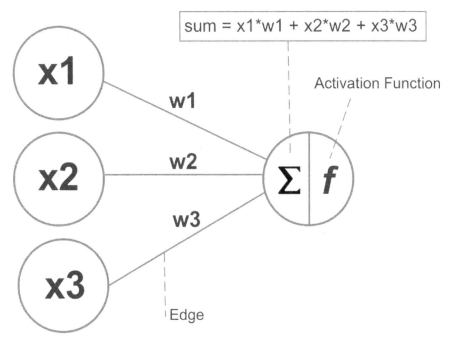

Figure 47: The nodes, edges/weights, and sum/activation function of a basic neural network

Each edge in the network has a numeric weight that can be altered based on experience. If the sum of the connected edges satisfies a set threshold, known as the *activation function*, this activates a neuron at the next layer. If the sum of the connected edges does not meet the set threshold, the activation function fails, which results in an *all or nothing* arrangement. Moreover, the weights assigned to each edge are unique, which means the nodes fire differently, preventing them from producing the same solution.

Using supervised learning, the model's predicted output is compared to the actual output (that's known to be correct), and the difference between these two results is measured as the *cost* or *cost value*. The purpose of training is to reduce the cost value until the model's prediction closely matches the correct output. This is achieved by incrementally tweaking the network's weights until the lowest possible cost value is obtained. This particular process of training the neural network is called *back-propagation*. Rather than navigate from left to right like how data is fed into the network, back-propagation rolls in reverse from the output layer on the right to the input layer on the left.

The Black-box Dilemma

One of the downsides of a network-based model is the black-box dilemma. Although the network can approximate accurate outputs, tracing its decision structure reveals limited to no insight about how specific variables influence its decision. For instance, if we use a neural network to predict the outcome of a Kickstarter campaign (an online funding platform for creative projects), the network can analyze numerous independent variables including campaign category, currency, deadline, and minimum pledge amount, etc. However, the model is unable to specify the relationship of these independent variables to the dependent variable of the campaign reaching its funding target. Algorithms such as decision trees and linear regression, meanwhile, are transparent as they show the variables' relationships to a given output. Moreover, it's possible for two neural networks with different topologies and weights to produce the same output, which makes it even more challenging to trace the impact of specific variables on the final output.

This raises the question of when should you use a neural network (given it's a black-box technique)? To answer this question, neural networks generally fit prediction tasks with a large number of input features and complex patterns, and especially problems that are difficult for computers to decipher but simple and almost trivial for humans. One example is the CAPTCHA (Completely Automated Public Turing test to tell Computers and Humans Apart) challenge-response test on websites to determine whether a user is human. Another example is identifying if a pedestrian is preparing to step into the path of an oncoming vehicle. In both examples, obtaining a fast and accurate prediction is more important than decoding the specific variables and their relationship to the final output.

Building a Neural Network

A typical neural network can be divided into input, hidden, and output layers. Data is first received by the input layer, where features are detected. The hidden layer(s) then analyze and process the input features, and the final result is shown as the output layer.

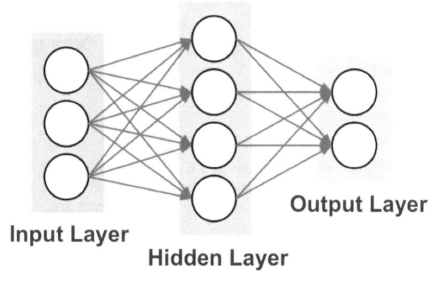

Figure 48: The three general layers of a neural network

The middle layers are considered hidden because, like human vision, they covertly process objects between the input and output layers. When faced with four lines connected in the shape of a square, our eyes instantly recognize those four lines as a square. We don't notice the mental processing that is involved in registering the four polylines (input) as a square (output).

Neural networks work in a similar way as they break data into layers and process the hidden layers to produce a final output. As more hidden layers are added to the network, the model's capacity to analyze complex patterns also improves. This is why models with a deep number of layers are often referred to as *deep learning*[29] to distinguish their deeper and superior processing abilities.

While there are many techniques to assemble the nodes of a neural network, the simplest method is the feed-forward network where signals flow only in one direction and there's no loop in the network. The most basic form of a feed-forward neural network is the *perceptron*, which was devised in the 1950s by Professor Frank Rosenblatt.

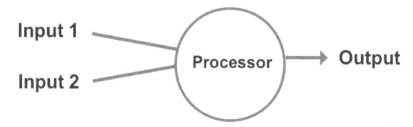

Figure 49: Visual representation of a perceptron neural network

The perceptron was designed as a decision function for receiving inputs to produce a binary output. Its structure consists of one or more inputs, a processor, and a single output. Inputs are fed into the processor (neuron), processed, and an output is then generated.

A perceptron supports one of two potential outputs, "0" or "1." An output of "1" triggers the activation function, while "0" does not. When working with a larger neural network with additional layers, the "1" output can be configured to pass the output to the next layer. Conversely, "0" is configured to be ignored and is not passed to the next layer for processing.

As a supervised learning technique, the perceptron builds a prediction model based on these five steps:

1) Inputs are fed into the processor.

---

[29] Geoffrey Hinton et al. published a paper in 2006 on recognizing handwritten digits using a deep neural network which they named *deep learning*.

2) The perceptron applies weights to estimate the value of those inputs.
3) The perceptron computes the error between the estimate and the actual value.
4) The perceptron adjusts its weights according to the error.
5) These four steps are repeated until you are satisfied with the model's accuracy. The training model can then be applied to the test data.

To illustrate this process, let's say we have a perceptron consisting of two inputs:

Input 1: $x1 = 24$
Input 2: $x2 = 16$

We then add a random weight to these two inputs, and they are sent to the neuron for processing.

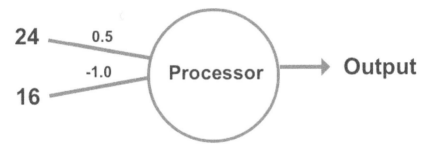

Figure 50: Weights are added to the perceptron

Weights
Input 1: 0.5
Input 2: -1

Next, we multiply each weight by its input:
Input 1: $24 * 0.5 = 12$
Input 2: $16 * -1 = -16$

Although the perceptron produces a binary output (0 or 1), there are many ways to configure the activation function. For this example, we will set the activation function to ≥ 0. This means that if the sum is a positive number or equal to zero, then the output is 1. Meanwhile, if the sum is a negative number, the output is 0.

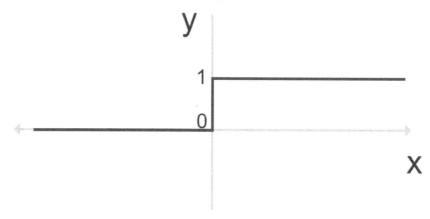

Figure 51: Activation function where the output (y) is 0 when x is negative, and the output (y) is 1 when x is positive

Thus:
Input 1: 24 * 0.5 = 12
Input 2: 16 * -1.0 = -16
Sum (Σ): 12 + -16 = -4

As a numeric value less than zero, the result produces "0" and does not trigger the perceptron's activation function. Given this error, the perceptron needs to adjust its weights in response.

Updated weights:
Input 1: 24 * 0.5 = 12
Input 2: 16 * -0.5 = -8
Sum (Σ): 12 + -8 = 4

As a positive outcome, the perceptron now produces "1" which triggers the activation function, and if in a larger network, this would trigger the next layer of analysis.

In this example, the activation function was ≥ 0. We could, though, modify the activation threshold to follow a different rule, such as:

x > 3, y = 1
x ≤ 3, y = 0

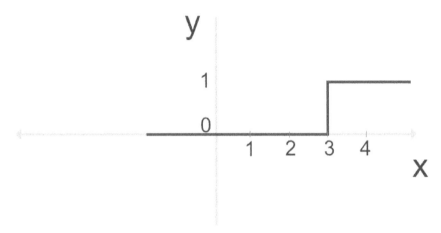

Figure 52: Activation function where the output (y) is 0 when x is equal to or less than 3, and the output (y) is 1 when x is greater than 3

A weakness of a perceptron is that because the output is binary (0 or 1), small changes in the weights or bias in any single perceptron within a larger neural network can induce polarizing results. This can lead to dramatic changes within the network and flip the final output, which makes it difficult to train a model that is accurate with new data.

An alternative to the perceptron is the *sigmoid neuron*. A sigmoid neuron is similar to a perceptron, but the presence of a sigmoid function rather than a binary filter now accepts any value between 0 and 1. This enables more flexibility to absorb small changes in edge weights without triggering inverse results—as the output is no longer binary. In other words, the output won't flip due to a minor change to an edge weight or input value.

While more flexible than a perceptron, a sigmoid neuron is unable to generate negative values. Hence, a third option is the *hyperbolic tangent function*.

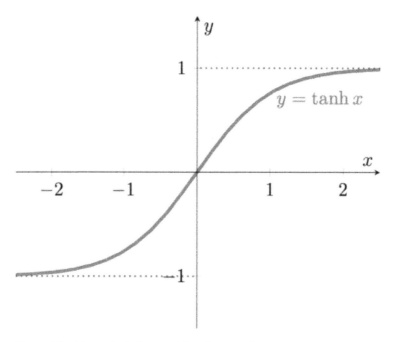

Figure 53: A hyperbolic tangent function graph

We have so far discussed basic neural networks; to develop a more advanced neural network, we can link sigmoid neurons and other classifiers to create a network with a higher number of layers or combine multiple perceptrons to form a multilayer perceptron.

Multilayer Perceptrons

The multilayer perceptron (MLP), as with other ANN techniques, is an algorithm for predicting a categorical (classification) or continuous (regression) target variable. Multilayer perceptrons are powerful because they aggregate multiple models into a unified prediction model, as demonstrated by the classification model shown in Figure 54.

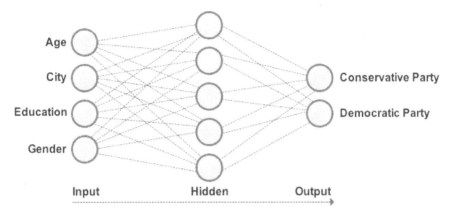

Figure 54: A multilayer perceptron used to classify a social media user's political preference

In this example, the MLP model is divided into three layers. The input layer consists of four nodes representing an input feature used to predict a social media user's political preference: Age, City, Education, and Gender. A function is then applied to each input variable to create a new layer of nodes called the middle or hidden layer. Each node in the hidden layer represents a function, such as a sigmoid function, but with its own unique weights/hyperparameters. This means that each input variable, in effect, is exposed to five different functions. Simultaneously, the hidden layer nodes are exposed to all four features.

The final output layer for this model consists of two discrete outcomes: Conservative Party or Democratic Party, which classifies the sample user's likely political preference. Note that the number of nodes at each layer will vary according to the number of input features and the target variable(s).

In general, multilayer perceptrons are ideal for interpreting large and complex datasets with no time or computational restraints. Less compute-intensive algorithms, such as decision trees and logistic regression, for example, are more efficient for working with smaller datasets. Given their high number of hyperparameters, multilayer perceptrons also demand more time and effort to tune than other algorithms. In regards to processing time, a multilayer perceptron takes longer to run than most shallow learning techniques including logistic regression but is generally faster than SVM.

Deep Learning

For analyzing less complex patterns, a basic multilayer perceptron or an alternative classification algorithm such as logistic regression and *k*-nearest neighbors can be put into practice. However, as patterns in the data become more complicated—especially in the form of a model with a high number of inputs such as image pixels—a shallow model is no longer reliable or capable of sophisticated analysis because the model becomes exponentially complicated as the number of inputs increases. A neural network, with a deep number of layers, though, can be used to interpret a high number of input features and break down complex patterns into simpler patterns, as shown in Figure 55.

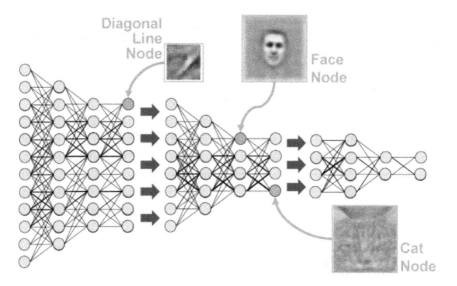

Figure 55: Facial recognition using deep learning. Source: kdnuggets.com

This deep neural network uses edges to detect different physical features to recognize faces, such as a diagonal line. Like building blocks, the network combines the node results to classify the input as, say, a human's face or a cat's face and then advances further

266

to recognize individual characteristics. This is known as *deep learning*. What makes deep learning "deep" is the stacking of at least 5-10 node layers.

Object recognition, as used by self-driving cars to recognize objects such as pedestrians and other vehicles, uses upward of 150 layers and is a popular application of deep learning. Other applications of deep learning include time series analysis to analyze data trends measured over set time periods or intervals, speech recognition, and text processing tasks including sentiment analysis, topic segmentation, and named entity recognition. More usage scenarios and commonly paired deep learning techniques are listed in Table 13.

	Recurrent Network	Recursive Neural Tensor Network	Deep Belief Network	Convolution Network	MLP
Text Processing	✔	✔		✔	
Image Recognition			✔	✔	
Object Recognition		✔		✔	
Speech Recognition	✔				
Time Series Analysis	✔				
Classification			✔	✔	✔

Table 13: Common usage scenarios and paired deep learning techniques

As can be seen from this table, multilayer perceptrons (MLP) have largely been superseded by new deep learning techniques such as convolution networks, recurrent networks, deep belief networks, and recursive neural tensor networks (RNTN). These more advanced versions of a neural network can be used effectively across a number of practical applications that are in vogue today. While convolution networks are arguably the most popular and powerful of deep learning techniques, new methods and variations are continuously evolving.

CHAPTER QUIZ

Using a **multilayer perceptron**, your job is to create a model to classify the sex (male or female) of penguins that have been affected and rescued during a natural disaster. However, you can only use the physical attributes of penguins to train your model. Please note that this dataset has 344 rows.

	species	island	bill_length_mm	bill_depth_mm	flipper_length_mm	body_mass_g	sex
0	Adelie	Torgersen	39.1	18.7	181.0	3750.0	MALE
1	Adelie	Torgersen	39.5	17.4	186.0	3800.0	FEMALE
2	Adelie	Torgersen	40.3	18.0	195.0	3250.0	FEMALE
3	Adelie	Torgersen	NaN	NaN	NaN	NaN	NaN
4	Adelie	Torgersen	36.7	19.3	193.0	3450.0	FEMALE
5	Adelie	Torgersen	39.3	20.6	190.0	3650.0	MALE
6	Adelie	Torgersen	38.9	17.8	181.0	3625.0	FEMALE
7	Adelie	Torgersen	39.2	19.6	195.0	4675.0	MALE
8	Adelie	Torgersen	34.1	18.1	193.0	3475.0	NaN
9	Adelie	Torgersen	42.0	20.2	190.0	4250.0	NaN

1) **How many output nodes does the multilayer perceptron need to predict the dependent variable of sex?**

2) **Which of the seven variables could we use as independent variables based on only the penguin's physical attributes?**

3) **What is a more transparent classification algorithm that we could use in place of a multilayer perceptron?**
A. Simple linear regression
B. Logistic regression
C. *k*-means clustering
D. Multiple linear regression

ANSWERS

1) 2 nodes (male and female)

2) bill_length_mm, bill_depth_mm, flipper_length_mm, body_mass_g

3) B, Logistic regression

## 14

DECISION TREES

The idea that artificial neural networks can be used to solve a wider spectrum of learning tasks than other techniques has led some pundits to hail ANN as the ultimate machine learning algorithm. While there is a strong case for this argument, this isn't to say that ANN fits the bill as a silver bullet algorithm. In certain cases, neural networks fall short, and decision trees are held up as a popular counterargument.

The huge amount of input data and computational resources required to train a neural network is the first downside of any attempt to solve all machine learning problems using this technique. Neural network-based applications like Google's image recognition engine rely on millions of tagged examples to recognize classes of simple objects (i.e. dogs) and not every organization has the resources available to feed and power a model of that size. The other major downside of neural networks is the black-box dilemma, which conceals the model's decision structure. Decision trees, on the other hand, are transparent and easy to interpret. They work with less data and consume less computational resources. These benefits make decision trees a popular alternative to a neural network for less complex use cases.

Decision trees are used primarily for solving classification problems but can also be used as a regression model to predict numeric outcomes. Classification trees predict categorical outcomes using numeric and categorical variables as input, whereas regression trees predict numeric outcomes using numeric and categorical variables as input. Decision trees can be applied to a wide range of use cases; from picking a scholarship recipient, to predicting e-commerce sales, and selecting the right job applicant.

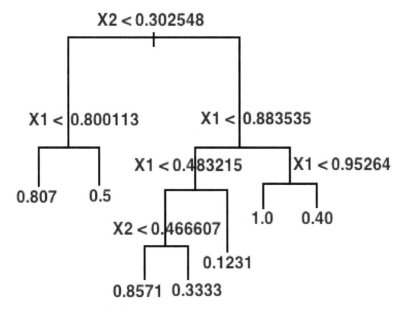

Figure 56: Example of a regression tree

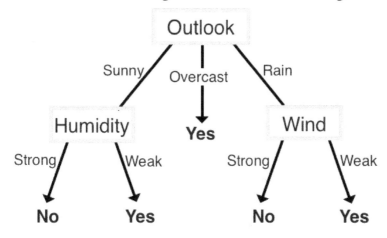

Figure 57: Example of a classification tree

Part of the appeal of decision trees is they can be displayed graphically and they are easy to explain to non-experts. When a customer queries why they weren't selected for a home loan, for example, you can share the decision tree to show the decision-making process, which isn't possible using a black-box technique.

Building a Decision Tree

Decision trees start with a root node that acts as a starting point and is followed by splits that produce branches, also known as *edges*. The branches then link to leaves, also known as *nodes*, which form decision points. This process is repeated using the data points collected in each new leaf. A final categorization is produced when a leaf no longer generates any new branches and results in what's called a terminal node.

Beginning first at the root node, decision trees analyze data by splitting data into subsets, with a node for each value of the variable (i.e. sunny, overcast, rainy). The aim is to keep the tree as small as possible. This is achieved by selecting a variable that optimally splits the data into homogenous groups, such that it minimizes the level of data entropy at the next branch.

Entropy is a mathematical concept that explains the measure of variance in the data among different classes. In simple terms, we want the data at each layer to be more homogenous than the previous partition. We therefore want to pick a "greedy" algorithm that can reduce entropy at each layer of the tree. An example of a greedy algorithm is the Iterative Dichotomizer (ID3), invented by J.R. Quinlan. This is one of three decision tree implementations developed by Quinlan, hence the "3." At each layer, ID3 identifies a variable (converted into a binary question) that produces the least entropy at the next layer.

To understand how this works, let's consider the following example.

Employees	Exceeded KPIs	Leadership Capability	Aged < 30	Outcome
6	6	2	3	Promoted
4	0	2	4	Not promoted

Table 14: Employee characteristics

In this table we have ten employees, three input variables (Exceeded KPIs, Leadership Capability, Aged < 30), and one output variable (Outcome). Our aim is to classify whether an employee will be promoted/not promoted based on the assessment of the three input variables.

Let's first split the data by variable 1 (Exceeded Key Performance Indicators):

- Six promoted employees who exceeded their KPIs (Yes).

- Four employees who did not exceed their KPIs and who were not promoted (No).

This variable produces two homogenous groups at the next layer.

Exceeded KPIs?

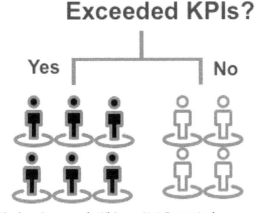

Black = Promoted, White = Not Promoted

Now let's try variable 2 (Leadership Capability), which produces:

- Two promoted employees with leadership capabilities (Yes).
- Four promoted employees with no leadership capabilities (No).
- Two employees with leadership capabilities who were not promoted (Yes).
- Two employees with no leadership capabilities who were not promoted (No).

This variable produces two groups of mixed data points.

Leadership Capability?

Black = Promoted, White = Not Promoted

Lastly, we have variable 3 (Aged Under 30), which produces:

- Three promoted employees aged under thirty (Yes).
- Three promoted employees aged over thirty (No).
- Four employees aged under thirty who were not promoted (Yes).

This variable produces one homogenous group and one mixed group of data points.

Aged < 30?

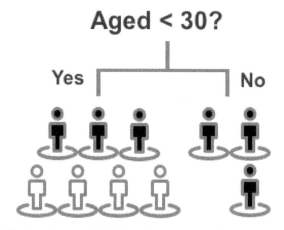

Black = Promoted, White = Not Promoted

Of these three variables, variable 1 (Exceeded KPIs) produces the best split with two perfectly homogenous groups. Variable 3 produces the second-best outcome, as one leaf is homogenous. Variable 2 produces two leaves that are heterogeneous. Variable 1 would therefore be selected as the first binary question to split this dataset.

Whether it's ID3 or another algorithm, this process of splitting data into sub-partitions, known as *recursive partitioning*, is repeated until a stopping criterion is met. A stopping point can be based on a range of criteria, such as:

- When all leaves contain less than 3-5 items.
- When a branch produces a result that places all items in one binary leaf.

Calculating Entropy

In this next section, we will review the mathematical calculations for finding the variables that produce the lowest entropy.

As mentioned, building a decision tree starts with setting a variable as the root node, with each outcome for that variable assigned a branch to a new decision node, i.e. "Yes" and "No." A second variable is then chosen to split the variables further to create new branches and decision nodes.

As we want the nodes to collect as many instances of the same class as possible, we need to select each variable strategically based on entropy, also called *information value*. Measured in units called bits (using a base 2 logarithm expression), entropy is calculated based on the composition of data points found in each node.

Using the following logarithm formula, we will calculate the entropy for each potential variable split expressed in bits between 0 and 1.

$(-p_1 \log p_1 - p_2 \log p_2)$ / log2

Please note the logarithm formula can be quickly calculated online using Google Calculator.

Exceeded KPIs?

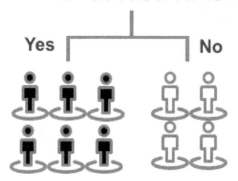

Yes: $p_1[6,6]$ and $p_2[0,6]$
No: $p_1[0,4]$ and $p_2[4,4]$

Step 1: Find entropy of each node
$(-p_1 \log p_1 - p_2 \log p_2) / \log 2$
Yes: $(-6/6 * \log 6/6 - 0/6 * \log 0/6) / \log 2 = 0$
No: $(-0/4 * \log 0/4 - 4/4 * \log 4/4) / \log 2 = 0$

Step 2: Multiply entropy of the two nodes in accordance to the total number of data points (10)
$(6/10) \times 0 + (4/10) \times 0 = 0$

Leadership Capability?

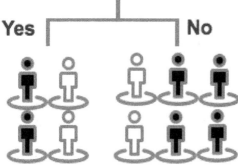

Yes: $p_1[2,4]$ and $p_2[2,4]$
No: $p_1[4,6]$ and $p_2[2,6]$

Step 1: Find entropy of each node
Yes: (-2/4*log2/4 - 2/4*log2/4) / log2 = 1
No: (-4/6*log4/6 - 2/6*log2/6) / log2 = 0.91829583405

Step 2: Multiply entropy of the two nodes by total number of data points
(4/10) x 1 + (6/10) x 0.918
0.4 + 0.5508 = 0.9508

Aged < 30?

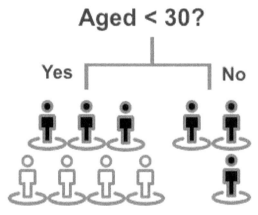

Yes: $p_1[3,7]$ and $p_2[4,7]$
No: $p_1[3,3]$ and $p_2[0,3]$

Step 1: Find entropy of each node
Yes: (-3/7*log3/7 - 4/7*log4/7) / log2 = 0.98522813603
No: (-3/3*log3/3 - 0/3*log0/3) / log2 = 0

Step 2: Multiply entropy of the two nodes by total number of data points
(7/10) x 0.985 + (3/10) x 0
0.6895 + 0 = 0.6895

Results

Exceeded KPIs = 0 bits

Leadership Capability = 0.9508 bits

Aged < 30 = 0.6895 bits

Based on our calculations, the variable **Exceeded KPIs** generates a perfect classification, which means we don't need to develop the tree any further after examining this variable. The next best candidate was the variable **Aged < 30** at 0.6895 bits. **Leadership Capability** had the highest entropy with 0.9508 bits, which equates to a high level of disorder and almost no information gain. In fact, we can calculate the entropy of the data prior to any potential split to question the need for analyzing this variable.

Promoted 6/10, Not Promoted 4/10

(-6/10*log6/10 - 4/10*log4/10) / log2 = 0.971

0.971 - 0.9508 = 0.0202

Thus, subtracting the original entropy of the dataset by the variable of **Leadership Capability** leads to a marginal 0.0202 bits in overall information gain.

Overfitting

A notable caveat of decision trees is their susceptibility to overfit the model to the training data. Based on the patterns extracted from the training data, a decision tree is precise at analyzing and decoding the first round of data. However, the same decision tree may then fail to classify the test data, as there could be rules that it's yet to encounter or because the training/test data split was not representative of the full dataset. Also, because decision trees are formed by repeatedly splitting data points into partitions, a slight change to how the data is split at the top or middle of the tree could dramatically alter the final prediction and produce a different tree altogether. The offender, in this case, is our greedy algorithm.

Starting with the first split of the data, the greedy algorithm picks a variable that best partitions the data into homogenous groups.

Like a kid seated in front of a box of cupcakes, the greedy algorithm is oblivious to the future repercussions of its short-term actions. The variable used to first split the data does not guarantee the most accurate model at the end of production. Instead, a less effective split at the top of the tree might produce a more accurate model. Thus, although decision trees are highly visual and excel at classifying a single set of data, they are inflexible and vulnerable to overfitting, especially for datasets with high pattern variance.

Bagging

Rather than aiming for the most efficient split at each round of recursive partitioning, an alternative technique is to construct multiple trees and combine their predictions. A popular example of this technique is *bagging,* which involves growing multiple decision trees using a randomized selection of input data for each tree and combining the results by averaging the output (for regression) or voting (for classification).

A key characteristic of bagging is *bootstrap sampling*. For multiple decision trees to generate unique insight, there needs to be an element of variation and randomness across each model. There's little sense in compiling five or ten identical models. Bootstrap sampling overcomes this problem by extracting a random variation of the data at each round, and in the case of bagging, different variations of the training data are run through each tree. While this doesn't eliminate the problem of overfitting, the dominant patterns in the dataset will appear in a higher number of trees and emerge in the final class or prediction. As a result, bagging is an effective algorithm for dealing with outliers and lowering the degree of variance typically found with a single decision tree.

Random Forests

A closely related technique to bagging is *random forests*. While both techniques grow multiple trees and utilize bootstrap sampling to randomize the data, random forests artificially limit the choice of variables by capping the number of variables considered for each split. In other words, the algorithm is not allowed to consider all *n* variables at each partition.

In the case of bagging, the trees often look similar because they use the same variable early in their decision structure in a bid to reduce entropy. This means the trees' predictions are highly correlated and closer to a single decision tree in regards to overall variance. Random forests sidestep this problem by forcing each split to consider a limited subset of variables, which gives other variables a greater chance of selection, and by averaging unique and uncorrelated trees, the final decision structure is less variable and often more reliable. As the model is trained using a subset of variables fewer than those actually available, random forests are considered a weakly-supervised learning technique.

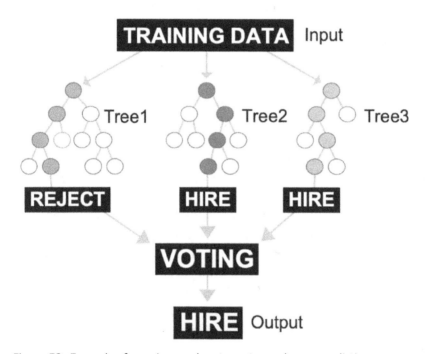

Figure 58: Example of growing random trees to produce a prediction

In general, random forests favor a high number of trees (i.e. 100+) to smooth out the potential impact of outliers, but there is a diminishing rate of effectiveness as more trees are added. At a certain level, new trees may not add any significant improvement to the model other than to extend the model's processing time. While it will depend on your dataset, 100-150 decision trees is a recommended starting point. Author and data expert Scott Hartshorn advises focusing on optimizing other hyperparameters before adding more trees to the initial model, as this will reduce processing time in the short-term and increasing the number of trees later should provide at least some added benefit.[30]

While random forests are versatile and work well at interpreting complex data patterns, other techniques including gradient boosting tend to return superior prediction accuracy. Random forests, though, are fast to train and work well for obtaining a quick benchmark model.

Boosting

Boosting is another family of algorithms that centers on aggregating a large pool of decision trees. The emphasis of boosting algorithms is on combining "weak" models into one "strong" model. The term "weak" means the initial model is a poor predictor and perhaps marginally better than a random guess. A "strong" model, meanwhile, is considered a reliable predictor of the true target output.

The concept of developing strong learners from weak learners is achieved by adding weights to trees based on misclassified cases in the previous tree. This is similar to a school teacher improving his or her class' performance by offering extra tutoring to students that performed badly on a recent test.

One of the more popular boosting algorithms is *gradient boosting*. Rather than selecting combinations of variables at random, gradient boosting selects variables that improve prediction accuracy with each new tree. The decision trees are therefore grown sequentially, as each tree is created using information derived from the previous tree, rather than independently. Mistakes incurred in the training data are recorded and then applied to the next round of training data.

At each iteration, weights are added to the training data based on the results of the previous iteration. A higher weighting is applied to instances that were incorrectly predicted from the training data,

---

[30] Scott Hartshorn, "Machine Learning With Random Forests And Decision Trees: A Visual Guide For Beginners," *Scott Hartshorn*, 2016.

and instances that were correctly predicted receive less attention. Earlier iterations that don't perform well and that perhaps misclassified data can subsequently be improved upon in further iterations. This process is repeated until there's a low level of error. The final result is then obtained from a weighted average of the total predictions derived from each decision tree.

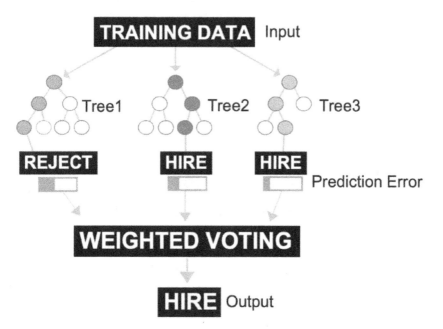

Figure 59: Example of reducing prediction error across multiple trees to produce a prediction

Boosting also mitigates the issue of overfitting and it does so using fewer trees than random forests. While adding more trees to a random forest usually helps to offset overfitting, the same process can cause overfitting in the case of boosting and caution should be taken as new trees are added.

The tendency of boosting algorithms towards overfitting can be explained by their highly-tuned focus on learning and reiterating from earlier mistakes. Although this typically translates to more accurate predictions—superior to that of most algorithms—it can lead to mixed results in the case of data stretched by a high number of outliers. In general, machine learning models should not fit too close to outlier cases, but this can be difficult for boosting algorithms to obey as they are constantly reacting to errors observed and isolated during production. For complex datasets with a large number of outliers, random forests may be a preferred alternative approach to boosting.

The other main downside of boosting is the slow processing speed that comes with training a sequential decision model. As trees are trained sequentially, each tree must wait for the previous tree, thereby limiting the production scalability of the model and especially as more trees are added. A random forest, meanwhile, is trained in parallel, making it faster to train.

The final downside, which applies to boosting as well as random forests and bagging, is the loss of visual simplicity and ease of interpretation that comes with using a single decision tree. When you have hundreds of decision trees it becomes more difficult to visualize and interpret the overall decision structure.

If, however, you have the time and resources to train a boosting model and a dataset with consistent patterns, the final model *can be* extremely worthwhile. Once deployed, predictions from the trained decision model can be generated quickly and accurately using this algorithm, and outside of deep learning, boosting is one of the most popular algorithms in machine learning today.

CHAPTER QUIZ

Your task is to predict the body mass (body_mass_g) of penguins using the penguin dataset and the **random forests regression** algorithm.

	species	bill_length_mm	bill_depth_mm	flipper_length_mm	body_mass_g	sex
0	Adelie	39.1	18.7	181.0	3750.0	MALE
1	Adelie	39.5	17.4	186.0	3800.0	FEMALE
2	Adelie	40.3	18.0	195.0	3250.0	FEMALE
3	Adelie	NaN	NaN	NaN	NaN	NaN
4	Adelie	36.7	19.3	193.0	3450.0	FEMALE
5	Adelie	39.3	20.6	190.0	3650.0	MALE
6	Adelie	38.9	17.8	181.0	3625.0	FEMALE
7	Adelie	39.2	19.6	195.0	4675.0	MALE
8	Adelie	34.1	18.1	193.0	3475.0	NaN
9	Adelie	42.0	20.2	190.0	4250.0	NaN

1) Which variables could we use as independent variables to train our model?

2) To train a quick benchmark model, gradient boosting is faster to train than random forests. True or False?

3) Which tree-based technique can be easily visualized?

A. Decision trees

B. Gradient boosting

C. Random forests

ANSWERS

1) All variables except for body_mass_g

(Tree-based techniques work well with both discrete and continuous variables as input variables.)

2) False

(Gradient boosting runs sequentially, making it slower to train. A random forest is trained simultaneously, making it faster to train.)

3) A, Decision trees

## 15

ENSEMBLE MODELING

When making important decisions, we generally prefer to collate multiple opinions as opposed to listening to a single perspective or the first person to voice their opinion. Similarly, it's important to consider and trial more than one algorithm to find the best model for your data. In advanced machine learning, it can even be advantageous to combine algorithms or models using a method called *ensemble modeling*, which amalgamates outputs to build a unified prediction model. By combining the output of different models (instead of relying on a single estimate), ensemble modeling helps to build a consensus on the meaning of the data. Aggregated estimates are also generally more accurate than any one technique. It's vital, though, for the ensemble models to display some degree of variation to avoid mishandling the same errors.

In the case of classification, multiple models are consolidated into a single prediction using a voting system[31] based on frequency, or numeric averaging in the case of regression problems.[32,33] Ensemble models can also be divided into sequential or parallel and homogenous or heterogeneous.

Let's start by looking at sequential and parallel models. In the case of the former, the model's prediction error is reduced by adding weights to classifiers that previously misclassified data. Gradient boosting and AdaBoost (designed for classification problems) are both examples of sequential models. Conversely, parallel

---

[31] The class that receives the most votes is taken as the final output.

[32] Generally, the more votes or numeric outputs that are taken into consideration the more accurate the final prediction.

[33] The aim of approaching regression problems is to produce a numeric prediction, such as the price of a house, rather than to predict a discrete class (classification).

ensemble models work concurrently and reduce error by averaging. Random forests are an example of this technique.

Ensemble models can be generated using a single technique with numerous variations, known as a homogeneous ensemble, or through different techniques, known as a heterogeneous ensemble. An example of a homogeneous ensemble model would be multiple decision trees working together to form a single prediction (i.e. bagging). Meanwhile, an example of a heterogeneous ensemble would be the usage of k-means clustering or a neural network in collaboration with a decision tree algorithm.

Naturally, it's important to select techniques that complement each other. Neural networks, for instance, require complete data for analysis, whereas decision trees are competent at handling missing values.[34] Together, these two techniques provide added benefit over a homogeneous model. The neural network accurately predicts the majority of instances where a value is provided, and the decision tree ensures that there are no "null" results that would otherwise materialize from missing values using a neural network.

While the performance of an ensemble model outperforms a single algorithm in the majority of cases,[35] the degree of model complexity and sophistication can pose a potential drawback. An ensemble model triggers the same trade-off in benefits as a single decision tree and a collection of trees, where the transparency and ease of interpretation of, say decision trees, is sacrificed for the accuracy of a more complex algorithm such as random forests, bagging or boosting. The performance of the model will win out in most cases, but interpretability is an important factor to consider when choosing the right algorithm(s) for your data.

In terms of selecting a suitable ensemble modeling technique, there are four main methods: bagging, boosting, a bucket of models, and stacking.

As a heterogeneous ensemble technique, a **bucket of models** trains multiple different algorithmic models using the same

---

[34] Decision trees can treat missing values as another variable. For instance, when assessing the weather outlook, the data points can be classified as *sunny, overcast, rainy* or *missing*.
[35] Ian H. Witten, Eibe Frank, Mark A. Hall, "Data Mining: Practical Machine Learning Tools and Techniques," *Morgan Kaufmann*, Third Edition, 2011.

training data and then picks the one that performed most accurately on the test data.

Bagging, as we know, is an example of parallel model averaging using a homogenous ensemble, which draws upon randomly drawn data and combines predictions to design a unified model.

Boosting is a popular alternative technique that is still a homogenous ensemble but addresses error and data misclassified by the previous iteration to produce a sequential model. Gradient boosting and AdaBoost are both examples of boosting algorithms.

Stacking runs multiple models simultaneously on the data and combines those results to produce a final model. Unlike boosting and bagging, stacking usually combines outputs from different algorithms (heterogenous) rather than altering the hyperparameters of the same algorithm (homogenous).

Also, rather than assigning equal trust to each model using averaging or voting, stacking attempts to identify and add emphasis to well-performing models. This is achieved by smoothing out the error rate of models at the base level (known as level-0) using a weighting system, before pushing those outputs to the level-1 model where they are combined and consolidated into a final prediction.

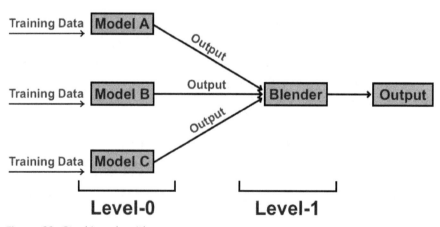

Figure 60: Stacking algorithm

While this technique is sometimes used in industry, the gains of using a stacking technique are marginal in line with the level of the complexity, and organizations usually opt for the ease and efficiency of boosting or bagging. Stacking, though, is a go-to technique for machine learning competitions like the Kaggle Challenges and the Netflix Prize.

The Netflix competition, held between 2006 and 2009, offered a prize for a machine learning model that could significantly improve Netflix's content recommender system. One of the winning techniques, from the team *BellKor's Pragmatic Chaos*, adopted a form of linear stacking that blended predictions from hundreds of different models using different algorithms.

## 16

DEVELOPMENT ENVIRONMENT

After examining the statistical underpinnings of numerous algorithms, it's time to turn our attention to the coding component of machine learning and installing a development environment.

Although there are various options in regard to programming languages (as outlined in Chapter 4), Python has been chosen for this three-part exercise as it's easy to learn and widely used in industry and online learning courses.

As for our development environment, we will be installing Jupyter Notebook, which is an open-source web application that allows for the editing and sharing of code notebooks. As discussed in book 1 (Python for Absolute Beginners), Jupyter Notebook can be installed using the Anaconda Distribution or Python's package manager, pip. As an experienced Python user, you may wish to install Jupyter Notebook via pip, and there are instructions available on the Jupyter Notebook website (http://jupyter.org/install.html) outlining this option. For beginners, I recommend choosing the Anaconda Distribution option, which offers an easy click-and-drag setup (https://www.anaconda.com/products/individual/).

This installation option will direct you to the Anaconda website. From there, you can select an Anaconda installer for Windows, macOS, or Linux. Again, you can find instructions available on the Anaconda website as per your choice of operating system.

After installing Anaconda to your machine, you'll have access to a range of data science applications including rstudio, Jupyter Notebook, and graphviz for data visualization. For this exercise, select Jupyter Notebook by clicking on "Launch" inside the Jupyter Notebook tab.

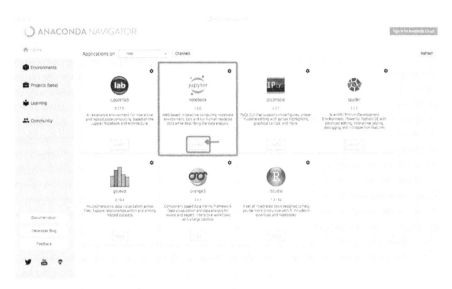

Figure 61: The Anaconda Navigator portal

To initiate Jupyter Notebook, run the following command from the Terminal (for Mac/Linux) or Command Prompt (for Windows):

```
jupyter notebook
```

Terminal/Command Prompt then generates a URL for you to copy and paste into your web browser. Example: http://localhost:8888/ Copy and paste the generated URL into your web browser to load Jupyter Notebook. Once you have Jupyter Notebook open in your browser, click on "New" in the top right-hand corner of the web application to create a new notebook project, and then select "Python 3." You're now ready to begin coding. Next, we'll explore the basics of working in Jupyter Notebook.

Figure 62: Screenshot of a new notebook

Import Libraries

The first step of any machine learning project in Python is installing the necessary code libraries. These libraries will differ from project to project based on the composition of your data and what you wish to achieve, i.e., data visualization, ensemble modeling, deep learning, etc.

```
In [1]:    1  # Import library
           2  import pandas as pd
           3
```

Figure 63: Import Pandas

In the code snippet above is the example code to import Pandas, which is a popular Python library used in machine learning.

Import Dataset and Preview

We can now use Pandas to import our dataset. I've selected a free and publicly available dataset from kaggle.com which contains data on house, unit, and townhouse prices in Melbourne, Australia. This dataset comprises data scraped from publicly available listings posted weekly on www.domain.com.au. The full dataset contains 34,857 property listings and 21 variables including address, suburb, land size, number of rooms, price, longitude, latitude, postcode, etc.

The Melbourne_housing_FULL dataset can be downloaded from this link: https://www.kaggle.com/anthonypino/melbourne-housing-market/.

After registering a free account and logging into kaggle.com, download the dataset as a zip file. Next, unzip the downloaded file and import it into Jupyter Notebook. To import the dataset, you can use `pd.read_csv` to load the data into a Pandas dataframe (tabular dataset).

```
df = pd.read_csv('~/Downloads/Melbourne_housing_FULL.csv')
```

This command directly imports the dataset into Jupyter Notebook. However, please note that the file path depends on the saved location of your dataset and your computer's operating system. For example, if you saved the CSV file to your (Mac) desktop, you would need to import the .csv file using the following command:

```
df = pd.read_csv('~/Desktop/Melbourne_housing_FULL.csv')
```

In my case, I imported the dataset from my Downloads folder. As you move forward in machine learning and data science, it's important that you save datasets and projects in standalone and named folders for organized access. If you opt to save the .csv in the same folder as your Jupyter Notebook, you won't need to append a directory name or ~/.

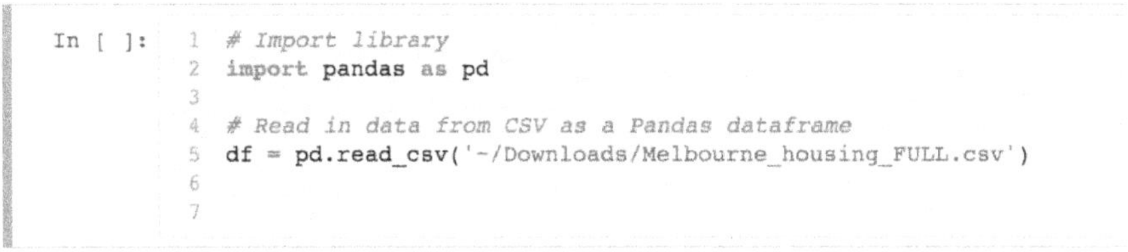

```
In [ ]:   1  # Import library
          2  import pandas as pd
          3
          4  # Read in data from CSV as a Pandas dataframe
          5  df = pd.read_csv('~/Downloads/Melbourne_housing_FULL.csv')
          6
          7
```

Figure 64: Import dataset as a dataframe

If saved to Desktop on Windows, you would import the .csv file using a structure similar to this example:

293

```
df = pd.read_csv('C:\\Users\\John\\Desktop\\Melbourne_housing_FULL.csv')
```

Next, use the `head()` command to preview the dataframe.

```
df.head()
```

Right-click and select "Run" or navigate from the Jupyter Notebook menu: Cell > Run All

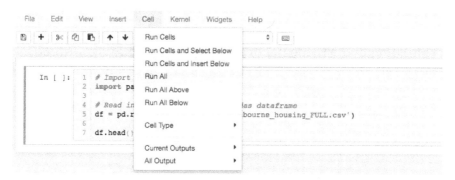

Figure 65: "Run All" from the navigation menu

This populates the dataset as a Pandas dataframe within Jupyter Notebook as shown in Figure 65.

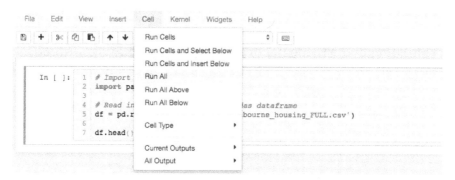

Figure 65: Previewing a dataframe in Jupyter Notebook

The default number of rows displayed using the `head()` command is five. To set an alternative number of rows to display, enter the desired number directly inside the parentheses as shown below in Figure 67.

```
df.head(10)
```

In [2]:
```
1  # Import library
2  import pandas as pd
3
4  # Read in data from CSV as a Pandas dataframe
5  df = pd.read_csv('~/Downloads/Melbourne_housing_FULL.csv')
6
7  df.head(10)
```

Out[2]:

	Suburb	Address	Rooms	Type	Price	Method	SellerG	Date	Distance	Postcode	...	Bathroom	Car	Landsize
0	Abbotsford	68 Studley St	2	h	NaN	SS	Jellis	3/09/2016	2.5	3067.0	...	1.0	1.0	126.0
1	Abbotsford	85 Turner St	2	h	1480000.0	S	Biggin	3/12/2016	2.5	3067.0	...	1.0	1.0	202.0
2	Abbotsford	25 Bloomburg St	2	h	1035000.0	S	Biggin	4/02/2016	2.5	3067.0	...	1.0	0.0	156.0
3	Abbotsford	18/659 Victoria St	3	u	NaN	VB	Rounds	4/02/2016	2.5	3067.0	...	2.0	1.0	0.0
4	Abbotsford	5 Charles St	3	h	1465000.0	SP	Biggin	4/03/2017	2.5	3067.0	...	2.0	0.0	134.0
5	Abbotsford	40 Federation La	3	h	850000.0	PI	Biggin	4/03/2017	2.5	3067.0	...	2.0	1.0	94.0
6	Abbotsford	55a Park St	4	h	1600000.0	VB	Nelson	4/06/2016	2.5	3067.0	...	1.0	2.0	120.0
7	Abbotsford	16 Maugie St	4	h	NaN	SN	Nelson	6/08/2016	2.5	3067.0	...	2.0	2.0	400.0
8	Abbotsford	53 Turner St	2	h	NaN	S	Biggin	6/08/2016	2.5	3067.0	...	1.0	2.0	201.0
9	Abbotsford	99 Turner St	2	h	NaN	S	Collins	6/08/2016	2.5	3067.0	...	2.0	1.0	202.0

10 rows × 21 columns

Figure 67: Previewing a dataframe with 10 rows

This now previews a dataframe with ten rows. You'll also notice that the total number of rows and columns (10 rows x 21 columns) is listed below the dataframe on the left-hand side.

Find Row Item

While the `head` command is useful for gaining a general idea of the shape of your dataframe, it's difficult to find specific information from datasets with hundreds or thousands of rows. In machine learning, you often need to locate a specific row by matching a row number with its row information. For example, if our machine learning model finds that row 100 is the most suitable house to recommend to a potential buyer, we next need to see which house that is in the dataframe.

This can be achieved by using the `iloc[]` command as shown here:

```
In [3]:    1  # Import library
           2  import pandas as pd
           3
           4  # Read in data from CSV as a Pandas dataframe
           5  df = pd.read_csv('~/Downloads/Melbourne_housing_FULL.csv')
           6
           7  df.iloc[100]
           8
```

```
Out[3]: Suburb                        Airport West
        Address                       180 Parer Rd
        Rooms                                    3
        Type                                     h
        Price                               830000
        Method                                   S
        SellerG                              Barry
        Date                            16/04/2016
        Distance                              13.5
        Postcode                              3042
        Bedroom2                                 3
        Bathroom                                 1
        Car                                      2
        Landsize                               971
        BuildingArea                           113
        YearBuilt                             1960
        CouncilArea      Moonee Valley City Council
        Lattitude                         -37.7186
        Longtitude                         144.876
        Regionname            Western Metropolitan
        Propertycount                         3464
        Name: 100, dtype: object
```

Figure 68: Finding a row using .iloc[ ]

In this example, `df.iloc[100]` is used to find the row indexed at position 100 in the dataframe, which is a property located in Airport West. Be careful to note that the first row in a Python dataframe is indexed as 0. Thus, the Airport West property is technically the 101st property contained in the dataframe.

Print Columns

The final code snippet I'd like to introduce to you is columns, which is a convenient method to print the dataset's column titles. This will prove useful later when configuring which features to select, modify or remove from the model.

```
df.columns
```

```
In [4]:    1  # Import library
           2  import pandas as pd
           3
           4  # Read in data from CSV as a Pandas dataframe
           5  df = pd.read_csv('~/Downloads/Melbourne_housing_FULL.csv')
           6
           7  df.columns
           8

Out[4]:  Index(['Suburb', 'Address', 'Rooms', 'Type', 'Price', 'Method', 'SellerG',
                'Date', 'Distance', 'Postcode', 'Bedroom2', 'Bathroom', 'Car',
                'Landsize', 'BuildingArea', 'YearBuilt', 'CouncilArea', 'Lattitude',
                'Longtitude', 'Regionname', 'Propertycount'],
               dtype='object')
```

Figure 69: Print columns

Again, "Run" the code to view the outcome, which in this case is the 21 column titles and their data type (dtype), which is 'object.' You may notice that some of the column titles are misspelled. We'll discuss this issue in the next chapter.

## 17

BUILDING A MODEL IN PYTHON

We're now ready to design a full machine learning model building on the code introduced in the previous chapter.

For this exercise, we will design a house price valuation system using gradient boosting following these six steps:

1) Import libraries

2) Import dataset

3) Scrub dataset

4) Split data into training and test data

5) Select an algorithm and configure its hyperparameters

6) Evaluate the results

1) Import Libraries

To build our model, we first need to import Pandas and a number of functions from Scikit-learn, including gradient boosting (ensemble) and mean absolute error to evaluate performance.

Import each of the following libraries by entering these exact commands in Jupyter Notebook:

```
#Import libraries
import pandas as pd
from sklearn.model_selection import train_test_split
from sklearn import ensemble
from sklearn.metrics import mean_absolute_error
```

Don't worry if you don't recognize each of the Scikit-learn libraries displayed in the code as they will be covered in later steps.

2) Import Dataset

Use the `pd.read_csv` command to load the Melbourne Housing Market dataset (as we did in the previous chapter) into a Pandas dataframe.

```
df = pd.read_csv('~/Downloads/Melbourne_housing_FULL.csv')
```

Please also note that the property values in this dataset are expressed in Australian Dollars—$1 AUD is approximately $0.77 USD (as of 2017).

Feature	Data Type	Continuous/Discrete
Suburb	String	Discrete
Address	String	Discrete
Rooms	Integer	Continuous
Type	String	Discrete
Price	Integer	Continuous
Method	String	Discrete
SellerG (seller's name)	String	Discrete
Date	TimeDate	Discrete
Distance	Floating-point	Continuous
Postcode	Integer	Discrete
Bedroom2	Integer	Continuous
Bathroom	Integer	Continuous
Car	Integer	Continuous
Landsize	Integer	Continuous
BuildingArea	Integer	Continuous
YearBuilt	TimeDate	Discrete
CouncilArea	String	Discrete
Lattitude	String	Discrete
Longtitude	String	Discrete
Regionname	String	Discrete
Propertycount (in that suburb)	Integer	Continuous

Table 15: Melbourne housing dataset variables

3) Scrub Dataset

This next stage involves scrubbing the dataset. Remember, scrubbing is the process of refining your dataset such as modifying or removing incomplete, irrelevant or duplicated data. It may also entail converting text-based data to numeric values and the redesigning of features.

It's worthwhile to note that some aspects of data scrubbing may take place prior to importing the dataset into the development environment. For instance, the creator of the Melbourne Housing Market dataset misspelled "Longitude" and "Latitude" in the head columns. As we will not be examining these two variables in our model, there's no need to make any changes. If, however, we did choose to include these two variables in our model, it would be prudent to amend this error in the source file.

From a programming perspective, spelling mistakes contained in the column titles don't pose a problem as long as we apply the same spelling to perform our code commands. However, this misnaming of columns could lead to human errors, especially if you are sharing your code with other team members. To avoid confusion, it's best to fix spelling mistakes and other simple errors in the source file before importing the dataset into Jupyter Notebook or another development environment. You can do this by opening the CSV file in Microsoft Excel (or equivalent program), editing the dataset, and then resaving it again as a CSV file.

While simple errors can be corrected in the source file, major structural changes to the dataset such as removing variables or missing values are best performed in the development environment for added flexibility and to preserve the original dataset for future use. Manipulating the composition of the dataset in the development environment is less permanent and is generally easier and quicker to implement than doing so in the source file.

Scrubbing Process

Let's remove columns we don't wish to include in the model using the delete command and entering the vector (column) titles we wish to remove.

```
# The misspellings of "longitude" and "latitude" are preserved here
del df['Address']
del df['Method']
del df['SellerG']
del df['Date']
```

```
del df['Postcode']
del df['Lattitude']
del df['Longtitude']
del df['Regionname']
del df['Propertycount']
```

The Address, Regionname, Postcode, Latitude, and Longitude columns were removed as property location is contained in other columns (Suburb and CouncilArea). My assumption is that Suburb and CouncilArea have more sway in buyers' minds than Postcode, Latitude, and Longitude—although Address deserves an honorable mention.

Method, SellerG, Propertycount, and Date were also removed because they were deemed to have less relevance in comparison to other variables. This is not to say that these variables don't impact property prices; rather the other eleven independent variables are sufficient for building our initial model. We can decide to add any one of these variables into the model later, and you may choose to include them in your own model.

The remaining eleven independent variables from the dataset are Suburb, Rooms, Type, Distance, Bedroom2, Bathroom, Car, Landsize, BuildingArea, YearBuilt, and CouncilArea. The twelfth variable is the dependent variable which is Price. As mentioned, decision tree-based models (including gradient boosting and random forests) are adept at managing large and high-dimensional datasets with a high number of input variables.

The next step for scrubbing the dataset is to remove missing values. While there's a number of methods to manage missing values (e.g., populating empty cells with the dataset's mean value, median value or deleting missing values altogether), for this exercise, we want to keep the dataset as simple as possible, and we'll not be examining rows with missing values. The obvious downside is that we have a reduced amount of data to analyze.

As a beginner, it makes sense to master complete datasets before adding an extra dimension of complexity in attempting to deal with missing values. Unfortunately, in the case of our sample dataset, we do have a lot of missing values! Nonetheless, there are still ample rows available to proceed with building our model after removing those that contain missing values.

The following Pandas command can be used to remove rows with missing values. For more information about the dropna method and its parameters, please see Table 16 or the Pandas documentation.[36]

```
df.dropna(axis = 0, how = 'any', subset = None, inplace = True)
```

Parameter	Argument	Explanation	Default
axis	0	Drops rows with missing values	✓
	1	Drops columns with missing values	
how	any	Drops rows or columns with any missing values	✓
	all	Drops rows or columns with all values missing	
subset	variable	Define which columns to search for missing values, i.e. 'genre'	
	None	Select "None" if you do not wish to set a subset.	
inplace	True	If True, do operation inplace (update rather than replace)	
	False		✓

Table 16: Dropna parameters

Keep in mind too that it's important to drop rows with missing values after applying the delete command to remove columns (as shown in the previous step). This way, there's a better chance of preserving more rows from the original dataset. Imagine dropping a whole row because it was missing the value for a variable that would later be deleted such as a missing post code!

Next, let's convert columns that contain non-numeric data to numeric values using one-hot encoding. With Pandas, one-hot encoding can be performed using the pd.get_dummies method.

```
df = pd.get_dummies(df, columns = ['Suburb', 'CouncilArea', 'Type'])
```

---

[36]   "Dropna,"   Pandas,   https://pandas.pydata.org/pandas-docs/stable/generated/pandas.DataFrame.dropna.html

This code command converts column values for Suburb, CouncilArea, and Type into numeric values through the application of one-hot encoding.

Lastly, assign the dependent and independent variables with Price as y and X as the remaining 11 variables (with Price dropped from the dataframe using the `drop` method).

```
X = df.drop('Price',axis=1)
y = df['Price']
```

4) Split the Dataset

We are now at the stage of splitting the data into training and test segments. For this exercise, we'll proceed with a standard 70/30 split by calling the Scikit-learn command below with a `test_size` of "0.3" and shuffling the dataset.

```
X_train, X_test, y_train, y_test = train_test_split(X, y, test_size =
0.3, shuffle = True)
```

5) Select Algorithm and Configure Hyperparameters

Next we need to assign our chosen algorithm (gradient boosting regressor) as a new variable (model) and configure its hyperparameters as demonstrated below.

```
model = ensemble.GradientBoostingRegressor(
    n_estimators = 150,
    learning_rate = 0.1,
    max_depth = 30,
    min_samples_split = 10,
    min_samples_leaf = 6,
    max_features = 0.6,
    loss = 'huber'
)
```

The first line is the algorithm itself (gradient boosting) and comprises just one line of code. The code below dictates the hyperparameters that accompany this algorithm.

n_estimators states the number of decision trees. Recall that a high number of trees generally improves accuracy (up to a certain point) but will inevitably extend the model's processing time. I have selected 150 decision trees as an initial starting point.

learning_rate controls the rate at which additional decision trees influence the overall prediction. This effectively shrinks the contribution of each tree by the set `learning_rate`. Inserting a low rate here, such as 0.1, should help to improve accuracy.

max_depth defines the maximum number of layers (depth) for each decision tree. If "None" is selected, then nodes expand until all leaves are pure or until all leaves contain less than `min_samples_leaf`. Here, I have chosen a high maximum number of layers (30), which will have a dramatic effect on the final output, as we'll soon see.

min_samples_split defines the minimum number of samples required to execute a new binary split. For example, `min_samples_split = 10` means there must be ten available samples in order to create a new branch.

min_samples_leaf represents the minimum number of samples that must appear in each child node (leaf) before a new branch can be implemented. This helps to mitigate the impact of outliers and anomalies in the form of a low number of samples found in one leaf as a result of a binary split. For example, `min_samples_leaf = 4` requires there to be at least four available samples within each leaf for a new branch to be created.

max_features is the total number of features presented to the model when determining the best split. As mentioned in Chapter 14, random forests and gradient boosting restrict the number of features fed to each individual tree to create multiple results that can be voted upon later.

If an integer (whole number), the model will consider `max_features` at each split (branch). If the value is a float (e.g., 0.6), then `max_features` is the percentage of total features randomly selected. Although it sets a maximum number of features to consider in identifying the best split, total features may exceed the set limit if no split can initially be made.

loss calculates the model's error rate. For this exercise, we are using `huber` which protects against outliers and anomalies. Alternative error rate options include `ls` (least squares regression), `lad` (least absolute deviations), and `quantile` (quantile regression). Huber is actually a combination of least squares regression and least absolute deviations.

To learn more about gradient boosting hyperparameters, please refer to the Scikit-learn documentation for this algorithm.[37]

After setting the model's hyperparameters, we'll use the `fit()` function from Scikit-learn to link the training data to the learning algorithm stored in the variable `model` to train the prediction model.

```
model.fit(X_train, y_train)
```

6) Evaluate the Results

After the model has been trained, we can use the `predict()` function from Scikit-learn to run the model on the `X_train` data and evaluate its performance against the actual `y_train` data. As mentioned earlier, for this exercise we are using mean absolute error to evaluate the accuracy of the model.

```
mae_train = mean_absolute_error(y_train, model.predict(X_train))
print ("Training Set Mean Absolute Error: %.2f" % mae_train)
```

Here, we input our y_train values, which represent the correct results from the training dataset. The `predict()` function is called on the `X_train` set and generates predictions. The `mean_absolute_error` function then compares the difference between the actual values and the model's predictions. The second line of the code then prints the results to two decimal places alongside the string (text) "Training Set Mean Absolute Error:". The same process is also repeated using the test data.

```
mae_test = mean_absolute_error(y_test, model.predict(X_test))
```

---

[37] "Gradient Boosting Regressor," *Scikit-learn*, http://scikit-learn.org/stable/modules/generated/sklearn.ensemble.GradientBoostingRegressor.html

```
print ("Test Set Mean Absolute Error: %.2f" % mae_test)
```

Let's now run the entire model by right-clicking and selecting "Run" or navigating from the Jupyter Notebook menu: Cell > Run All.

Wait 30 seconds or longer for the computer to process the training model. The results, as shown below, will then appear at the bottom of the notebook.

```
Training Set Mean Absolute Error: 27256.70
Test Set Mean Absolute Error: 166103.04
```

For this model, our training set's mean absolute error is $27,256.70, and the test set's mean absolute error is $166,103.04. This means that on average, the training set miscalculated the actual property value by $27,256.70. The test set, meanwhile, miscalculated the property value by $166,103.04 on average.

This means that our training model was accurate at predicting the actual value of properties contained in the training data. While $27,256.70 may seem like a lot of money, this average error value is low given the maximum range of our dataset is $8 million. As many of the properties in the dataset are in excess of seven figures ($1,000,000+), $27,256.70 constitutes a reasonably low error rate.

How did the model fare with the test data? The test data provided less accurate predictions with an average error rate of $166,103.04. A high discrepancy between the training and test data is usually an indicator of overfitting in the model. As our model is tailored to patterns in the training data, it stumbled when making predictions using the test data, which probably contains new patterns that the model hasn't seen. The test data, of course, is likely to carry slightly different patterns and new potential outliers and anomalies.

However, in this case, the difference between the training and test data is exacerbated because we configured our model to overfit the training data. An example of this issue was setting max_depth to "30." Although placing a high maximum depth improves the chances of the model finding patterns in the training data, it does tend to lead to overfitting.

Lastly, please take into account that because the training and test data are shuffled randomly, and data is fed to decision trees at random, the predicted results will differ slightly when replicating this model on your own machine.

A video version of this chapter is available as a mini course at scatterplotpress.com/p/house-prediction-model**. The mini course is free and lets you follow along step-by-step through the workflow described in this chapter.**

## 18

MODEL OPTIMIZATION

In the previous chapter we built our first supervised learning model. We now want to improve its prediction accuracy with future data and reduce the effects of overfitting. A good starting point is to modify the model's hyperparameters. Holding the other hyperparameters constant, let's begin by adjusting the maximum depth from "30" to "5." The model now generates the following results:

```
Training Set Mean Absolute Error: 134918.47
```

Although the mean absolute error of the training set is now higher, this helps to reduce the issue of overfitting and should improve the model's performance. Another step to optimize the model is to add more trees. If we set `n_estimators` to 250, we now see these results from the model:

```
Training Set Mean Absolute Error: 124703.6
Test Set Mean Absolute Error: 159532.18
```

This second optimization reduces the training set's absolute error rate by approximately $10,000 and there is a smaller gap between the training and test results for mean absolute error compared to the first iteration of the model.[38]

---

[38] In machine learning, the test data is used exclusively to assess model performance rather than optimize the model. As the test data cannot be used to build and optimize the model, data scientists commonly use a third independent dataset called the *validation set*. After building an initial model with the training set, the validation set can be fed into the prediction model and used as feedback to optimize the model's hyperparameters. The test set is then used to assess the prediction error of the final model.

Together, these two optimizations underline the importance of understanding the impact of individual hyperparameters. If you decide to replicate this supervised machine learning model at home, I recommend that you test modifying each of the hyperparameters individually and analyze their impact on mean absolute error using the training data. In addition, you'll notice changes in the machine's processing time based on the chosen hyperparameters. Changing the maximum number of branch layers (`max_depth`), for example, from "30" to "5" will dramatically reduce total processing time. Processing speed and resources will become an important consideration when you move on to working with larger datasets.

Another important optimization technique is feature selection. Earlier, we removed nine features from the dataset but now might be a good time to reconsider those features and test whether they have an impact on the model's prediction accuracy. "SellerG" would be an interesting feature to add to the model because the real estate company selling the property might have some impact on the final selling price.

Alternatively, dropping features from the current model may reduce processing time without having a significant impact on accuracy—or may even improve accuracy. When selecting features, it's best to isolate feature modifications and analyze the results, rather than applying various changes at once.

While manual trial and error can be a useful technique to understand the impact of variable selection and hyperparameters, there are also automated techniques for model optimization, such as *grid search*. Grid search allows you to list a range of configurations you wish to test for each hyperparameter and methodically test each of those possible hyperparameters. An automated voting process then takes place to determine the optimal model. As the model must examine each possible combination of hyperparameters, grid search does take a long time to run![39] It sometimes helps to run a relatively coarse grid search using consecutive powers of 10 (i.e. 0.01, 0.1, 1, 10) and then run a finer grid search around the best value identified.[40] Example

---

[39] Most readers of this book report waiting up to 30 minutes for the model to run.
[40] Aurélien Géron, "Hands-On Machine Learning with Scikit-Learn and TensorFlow: Concepts,

code for grid search using Scikit-learn is included at the end of this chapter.

Another way of optimizing algorithm hyperparameters is the randomized search method using Scikit-learn's RandomizedSearchCV. This method trials far more hyperparameters per round than grid search (which only changes one single hyperparameter per round) as it uses a random value for each hyperparameter at each round. Randomized search also makes it simple to specify the number of trial rounds and control computing resources. Grid search, meanwhile, runs based on the full number of hyperparameter combinations, which isn't obvious from looking at the code and might take more time than expected.

Finally, if you wish to use a different supervised machine learning algorithm and not gradient boosting, the majority of the code used in this exercise can be reused. For instance, the same code can be used to import a new dataset, preview the dataframe, remove features (columns), remove rows, split and shuffle the dataset, and evaluate mean absolute error. The official website http://scikit-learn.org is also a great resource to learn more about other algorithms as well as gradient boosting used in this exercise.

To learn how to input and test an individual house valuation using the model we have built in these two chapters, please see this more advanced tutorial available at **scatterplotpress.com/p/house-prediction-model**. In addition, if you have trouble implementing the model using the code found in this book, please contact the author by email for assistance (**oliver.theobald@scatterplotpress.com**).

Tools, and Techniques to Build Intelligent Systems," *O'Reilly Media*, 2017.

Code for the Optimized Model

```python
# Import libraries
import pandas as pd
from sklearn.model_selection import train_test_split
from sklearn import ensemble
from sklearn.metrics import mean_absolute_error

# Read in data from CSV
df = pd.read_csv('~/Downloads/Melbourne_housing_FULL.csv')

# Delete unneeded columns
del df['Address']
del df['Method']
del df['SellerG']
del df['Date']
del df['Postcode']
del df['Lattitude']
del df['Longtitude']
del df['Regionname']
del df['Propertycount']

# Remove rows with missing values
df.dropna(axis = 0, how = 'any', subset = None, inplace = True)

# Convert non-numeric data using one-hot encoding
df = pd.get_dummies(df, columns = ['Suburb', 'CouncilArea', 'Type'])

# Assign X and y variables
X = df.drop('Price',axis=1)
y = df['Price']
# Split data into test/train set (70/30 split) and shuffle
X_train, X_test, y_train, y_test = train_test_split(X, y, test_size =
0.3, shuffle = True)

# Set up algorithm
model = ensemble.GradientBoostingRegressor(
    n_estimators = 250,
    learning_rate = 0.1,
    max_depth = 5,
    min_samples_split = 10,
    min_samples_leaf = 6,
    max_features = 0.6,
```

```
    loss = 'huber'
)

# Run model on training data
model.fit(X_train, y_train)

# Check model accuracy (up to two decimal places)
mae_train = mean_absolute_error(y_train, model.predict(X_train))
print ("Training Set Mean Absolute Error: %.2f" % mae_train)

mae_test = mean_absolute_error(y_test, model.predict(X_test))
print ("Test Set Mean Absolute Error: %.2f" % mae_test)
```

Code for the Grid Search Model

```python
# Import libraries, including GridSearchCV
import pandas as pd
from sklearn.model_selection import train_test_split
from sklearn import ensemble
from sklearn.metrics import mean_absolute_error
from sklearn.model_selection import GridSearchCV

# Read in data from CSV
df = pd.read_csv('~/Downloads/Melbourne_housing_FULL.csv')

# Delete unneeded columns
del df['Address']
del df['Method']
del df['SellerG']
del df['Date']
del df['Postcode']
del df['Lattitude']
del df['Longtitude']
del df['Regionname']
del df['Propertycount']

# Remove rows with missing values
df.dropna(axis = 0, how = 'any', subset = None, inplace = True)

# Convert non-numeric data using one-hot encoding
df = pd.get_dummies(df, columns = ['Suburb', 'CouncilArea', 'Type'])

# Assign X and y variables
X = df.drop('Price',axis=1)
y = df['Price']

# Split data into test/train set (70/30 split) and shuffle
X_train, X_test, y_train, y_test = train_test_split(X, y, test_size = 0.3, shuffle = True)

# Input algorithm
model = ensemble.GradientBoostingRegressor()

# Set the configurations that you wish to test. To minimize processing
time, limit num. of variables or experiment on each hyperparameter
separately.
```

```python
hyperparameters = {
    'n_estimators': [200, 300],
    'max_depth': [8, 6],
    'min_samples_split': [8, 10],
    'min_samples_leaf': [5, 6],
    'learning_rate': [0.01, 0.02],
    'max_features': [0.8, 0.9],
    'loss': ['ls', 'lad', 'huber']
}


# Define grid search. Run with four CPUs in parallel if applicable.
grid = GridSearchCV(model, hyperparameters, n_jobs = 4)

# Run grid search on training data
grid.fit(X_train, y_train)

# Return optimal hyperparameters
grid.best_params_

# Check model accuracy using optimal hyperparameters
mae_train = mean_absolute_error(y_train, grid.predict(X_train))
print ("Training Set Mean Absolute Error: %.2f" % mae_train)

mae_test = mean_absolute_error(y_test, grid.predict(X_test))
print ("Test Set Mean Absolute Error: %.2f" % mae_test)
```

NEXT STEPS

6 Video Tutorials

To take the next step in machine learning, I have prepared the following six video tutorials, which provide a gentle introduction to coding your own prediction models in Python using free online datasets. After completing these exercises, you will be well on your way to designing your own prediction models and tackling more advanced resources.

- Linear regression
- Logistic regression
- Support vector machines
- k-nearest neighbors
- k-means clustering
- Decision trees

You can find these six free video tutorials at

scatterplotpress.com/p/ml-code-exercises

Building a House Prediction Model in Python

Also, remember that there is a free bonus chapter available online where you'll learn the code and steps to generate an individual house valuation using the model we built in Chapter 17 in video format.

You can view this free video tutorial at

scatterplotpress.com/p/house-prediction-model

Other Resources

To further your study of machine learning, I strongly recommend enrolling in the free Andrew Ng Machine Learning course on Coursera and also check out OCDevel's podcast series: *Machine Learning Guide*, which is the best put-together audio resource available for beginners.

Also, if you enjoyed the pace of this introduction to machine learning, you may also like to read the next two books in the series, **Machine Learning with Python for Beginners** and **Machine Learning: Make Your Own Recommender System**. These two books build on the knowledge you've gained here and aim to extend your knowledge of machine learning with practical coding exercises in Python.

THANK YOU

Thank you for purchasing this book. You now have a baseline understanding of the key concepts in AI and machine learning and are ready to tackle this challenging subject in earnest. You can find further free learning materials and videos at **scatterplotpress.com**.

If you have any direct feedback, both positive and negative, or suggestions to improve this book, please feel free to send me an email at oliver.theobald@scatterplotpress.com. This feedback is highly valued, and I look forward to hearing from you.

Finally, I would like to express my gratitude to my colleagues Jeremy Pedersen and Rui Xiong for their assistance in kindly sharing practical tips and sections of code used in this book as well as my two editors Chris Dino (Red to Black Editing) and again Jeremy Pedersen.

FURTHER RESOURCES

This section lists relevant learning materials for readers who wish to progress further in the field of machine learning. Please note that certain details listed in this section, including prices, may be subject to change in the future.

| Machine Learning |

Machine Learning
Format: Free Coursera course
Presenter: Andrew Ng
Suggested Audience: Beginners (especially those with a preference for MATLAB)

A free and expert introduction from Adjunct Professor Andrew Ng, one of the most influential figures in this field. This course is a virtual rite of passage for anyone interested in machine learning.

Project 3: Reinforcement Learning
Format: Online blog tutorial
Author: EECS Berkeley
Suggested Audience: Upper-intermediate to advanced

A practical demonstration of reinforcement learning, and Q-learning specifically, explained through the game Pac-Man.

| Basic Algorithms |

Machine Learning With Random Forests And Decision Trees: A Visual Guide For Beginners
Format: E-book
Author: Scott Hartshorn
Suggested Audience: Established beginners

A short, affordable ($3.20 USD), and engaging read on decision trees and random forests with detailed visual examples, useful practical tips, and clear instructions.

Linear Regression And Correlation: A Beginner's Guide

Format: E-book

Author: Scott Hartshorn

Suggested Audience: All

A well-explained and affordable ($3.20 USD) introduction to linear regression as well as correlation.

| The Future of AI |

The Inevitable: Understanding the 12 Technological Forces That Will Shape Our Future

Format: E-Book, Book, Audiobook

Author: Kevin Kelly

Suggested Audience: All (with an interest in the future)

A well-researched look into the future with a major focus on AI and machine learning by The New York Times Best Seller, Kevin Kelly. It provides a guide to twelve technological imperatives that will shape the next thirty years.

Homo Deus: A Brief History of Tomorrow

Format: E-Book, Book, Audiobook

Author: Yuval Noah Harari

Suggested Audience: All (with an interest in the future)

As a follow-up title to the success of *Sapiens: A Brief History of Mankind,* Yuval Noah Harari examines the possibilities of the future with notable sections of the book examining machine consciousness, applications in AI, and the immense power of data and algorithms.

| Programming |

Learning Python, 5th Edition
Format: E-Book, Book
Author: Mark Lutz
Suggested Audience: All (with an interest in learning Python)
A comprehensive introduction to Python published by O'Reilly Media.

Hands-On Machine Learning with Scikit-Learn and TensorFlow: Concepts, Tools, and Techniques to Build Intelligent Systems
Format: E-Book, Book
Author: Aurélien Géron
Suggested Audience: All (with an interest in programming in Python, Scikit-Learn, and TensorFlow)
As a popular O'Reilly Media book written by machine learning consultant Aurélien Géron, this is an excellent advanced resource for anyone with a solid foundation in machine learning and computer programming.

| Recommender Systems |

The Netflix Prize and Production Machine Learning Systems: An Insider Look
Format: Blog
Author: Mathworks
Suggested Audience: All
A very interesting blog post demonstrating how Netflix applies machine learning to formulate movie recommendations.

Recommender Systems
Format: Coursera course

Presenter: The University of Minnesota

Cost: Free 7-day trial or included with $49 USD Coursera subscription

Suggested Audience: All

Taught by the University of Minnesota, this Coursera specialization covers fundamental recommender system techniques including content-based and collaborative filtering as well as non-personalized and project-association recommender systems.

.

| Deep Learning |

Deep Learning Simplified

Format: Blog

Channel: DeepLearning.TV

Suggested Audience: All

A short video series to get you up to speed with deep learning. Available for free on YouTube.

Deep Learning Specialization: Master Deep Learning, and Break into AI

Format: Coursera course

Presenter: deeplearning.ai and NVIDIA

Cost: Free 7-day trial or included with $49 USD Coursera subscription

Suggested Audience: Intermediate to advanced (with experience in Python)

A robust curriculum for those wishing to learn how to build neural networks in Python and TensorFlow, as well as career advice, and how deep learning theory applies to industry.

Deep Learning Nanodegree

Format: Udacity course

Presenter: Udacity

Cost: $599 USD

Suggested Audience: Upper beginner to advanced, with basic experience in Python

A comprehensive and practical introduction to convolutional neural networks, recurrent neural networks, and deep reinforcement learning taught online over a four-month period. Practical components include building a dog breed classifier, generating TV scripts, generating faces, and teaching a quadcopter how to fly.

OTHER BOOKS BY THE AUTHOR

ChatGPT Prompt Engineering Book
Maximize your results with ChatGPT using a series of proven text prompt strategies.

Machine Learning with Python for Beginners
Progress your career in machine learning by learning how to code in Python and build your own prediction models to solve real-life problems.

Machine Learning: Make Your Own Recommender System
Learn how to make your own recommender system in an afternoon using Python.

Data Analytics for Absolute Beginners
Make better decisions using every variable with this deconstructed introduction to data analytics.

Generative AI Art for Beginners
Master the use of text prompts to generate stunning AI art in seconds.

Statistics for Absolute Beginners
Master the fundamentals of inferential and descriptive statistics with a mix of practical demonstrations, visual examples, historical origins, and plain English explanations.